Prisoners of War

Prisoners of War

A Reference Handbook

Arnold Krammer

Contemporary Military, Strategic, and Security Issues

PRAEGER SECURITY INTERNATIONAL
Westport, Connecticut • London

Library of Congress Cataloging-in-Publication Data

Krammer, Arnold, 1941–
    Prisoners of war : a reference handbook / Arnold Krammer.
        p. cm. – (Contemporary military, strategic, and security issues, ISSN 1932-295X)
    Includes bibliographical references and index.
    ISBN 978-0-275-99300-9 (alk. paper)
1. Prisoners of war–History.   2. Prisoners of war–Legal status, laws, etc.–History.
I. Title.
    UB800.K73   2008
    355.1′296–dc22   2007038895

British Library Cataloguing in Publication Data is available.

Library of Congress Catalog Card Number: 2007038895
ISBN-13: 978-0-275-99300-9
ISSN: 1932-295X

First published in 2008

Praeger Security International, 88 Post Road West, Westport, CT 06881
An imprint of Greenwood Publishing Group, Inc.
www.praeger.com

Printed in the United States of America

The paper used in this book complies with the
Permanent Paper Standard issued by the National
Information Standards Organization (Z39.48–1984).

10 9 8 7 6 5 4 3 2 1

Every reasonable effort has been made to trace the owners of copyright materials in this
book, but in some instances this has proven impossible. The author and publisher will
be glad to receive information leading to more complete acknowledgments in subsequent
printings of the book and in the meantime extend their apologies for any omissions.

This book is dedicated to

Avery Lorraine

with the hope that she will grow up in a more peaceful world.

Contents

A photo essay follows page 80.

Acknowledgments

Because the story of prisoners of war throughout history varies so widely, I had the pleasure of drawing on the knowledge of numerous experts. I am particularly indebted to the doyen of POW studies, Prof. Robert C. Doyle, from Franciscan University of Steubenville, Ohio; and Robert D. Billinger, Jr., at Wingate University, North Carolina. My colleagues, Profs. Olga Dror, Chester Dunning, Joseph Dawson III, and Charles Grear, from my institution, Texas A&M University, have been particularly helpful, as were Amos Simpson and Vaughan Baker Simpson, both distinguished historians and both longtime department chairs at the University of Louisiana at Lafayette.

Leslie McDonald, a product of the prestigious Bush School of Government and Public Service was my source for the legalities and intricacies of Europe's many conventions in The Hague and Geneva. Thanks to Marko Schubert at Friedrich Schiller University, Jena, Germany, as well as to Dr. Alicja Siniarska of Jagiellonian University in Krakow, Poland. Ms. Tracey Hayes, at the University of Tennessee (Knoxville), was my computer guru. The book also benefited greatly from ongoing contributions by Tamara Haygood, Ph.D., M.D., who is writing her own book on the medical treatment experienced by POWs. Two particularly useful sources of information can be found in the German POW collections at the Aliceville (Alabama), Museum and Cultural Arts Center, directed by Ms. Ann Kirksey, (1-888/751-2340), and at the Camp Ruston (Louisiana) Special Collection at the Prescott Memorial Library at Louisiana Tech University, directed by Archivist Peggy Carter and Librarian Specialist Tanya Arant (318/257-2935).

I had the help of the finest researchers in the business: Roger Horky, Amanda M. Henarie, Ralph Morales, Chris Thomas, and Damon Bach.

Ms. Joyce Smith spent endless hours photographing a large collection of POW items from which the illustrations in this book are drawn.

I am deeply grateful to them all.

My greatest debt, of course, goes to my family: my wife Jan; Adam, Douglas, and Kristy, for their patience and support. The future is now in the hands of the newest member of the Krammer clan: Avery Lorraine.

CHAPTER 1

War Prisoners through the Ages

The history of the prisoner of war is as old as the history of warfare and certainly as brutal. Each side in any conflict expects to win, of course, and demonizes the other. In nearly every conflict one side will win, whether by strength or guile, except in the highly unlikely cases of a draw, in which case the sides will doubt-less try again. Such a rare example occurred during World War I when 200,000 exhausted Italians and Austrians rushed at each other twelve times at the bat-tles of the sixty-mile-long Isonzo River between June 1915 and November 1917. The outcome was questionable and the casualties to both sides were horrendous: one-half of the entire Italian war losses—some 300,000 of a total of 600,000—were suffered at the Isonzo. The other side, Austria, lost *only* 200,000 men during those same three years of stupidity. Aside from rare battles like the Isonzo dur-ing World War I when there were no winners, the normal outcome of history's countless wars and armed struggles see one side triumph over the other. History worships the winner—the warrior, the hero, the knight—but the loser is seldom considered. The losers, for the purpose of this study, are the prisoners of war (POWs), that is, captured members of an opposing army, in or out of uniform, who were armed with anything from knives and lances to modern machine guns.

The important distinction between war prisoners and, say, the civilian inhab-itants of a town in the path of a rampaging army is that the civilians have few, if any, weapons. Or many options, for that matter. In a military standoff, the civilian inhabitants never stand much of a chance. Most aren't fighting an enemy as much as defending themselves and have no stake or interest in the war around them except to be left alone to raise their families and tend to their crops and livestock and pursue their livelihood. Local inhabitants have been routinely killed and their land appropriated as far back as the biblical battle of Canaan and this has con-tinued into more modern times with General Sherman's Civil War march across Georgia, or the destruction of Dresden, Hamburg, Coventry, and Hiroshima. The causes of the conflicts may vary from religion to politics, vengeance, or greed, but a basic assumption is that civilians may be captured or even killed but they cannot be considered war prisoners.

Military men, on the other hand, have been armed with the most destructive weapons of the eras and have the advantage of being able to initiate a fight or, if attacked, to defend themselves. Violence among soldiers is expected. It is the currency of their profession. However, civilians are vulnerable and their helpless persecution cannot be compared with the situation in which a disarmed enemy soldier may find himself. In the direct eloquence of Winston Churchill, "A prisoner of war is a man who tries to kill you and fails, and then asks you not to kill him."[1]

This is not to say that once captured either group has a particular advantage. Real POWs, that is, disarmed soldiers in the hands of their enemies, have not been historically much better off than the helpless civilians both sides often slaughtered. From the dawn of civilization to nearly modern times, the victors of most conflicts killed their war prisoners as a matter of policy. Indeed, more than tradition, this policy was often a matter of necessity. In an era when armies lived off the land, it was difficult enough to feed one's own soldiers. To feed captives was considered foolish. Imagine the end of any battle in history: the scene is a picture of destruction, awash in testosterone, with the cries of the wounded mingled with the dying noises of battle. Terrified prisoners are surrounded by wildly angry soldiers who may have witnessed the deaths of their friends and comrades and probably killed their share of the enemy. The lives and safety of war captives are very much in question.

But it was not an easy thing to surrender, to be taken prisoner. The moment when the enemy soldier raises his hands is the moment when time stands still. His life hangs in the balance. In the midst of the bloody Battle of the Somme in 1916, a line of Germans emerged from their trench with their hands up. According to a British eyewitness, "They were holding up photographs of their families and watches and other valuables in an attempt to gain mercy but as the Germans came up the steps, a soldier, not from our battalion, shot each one in the stomach with a burst from his Lewis gun." On another occasion, on a cavalry charge in September 1914, Sergeant James Taylor of the British 9th Lancers remembers a scene of, "horses neighing and a lot of yelling and shouting. I remember seeing Corporal Bolte run his lance through a dismounted German who had his hands up and thinking that this was rather a bad thing to do."

It makes little difference as to when the war takes place or in what part of the world. "During the Second World War, Brigadier Fitzroy Maclean, head of the British military mission to Yugoslavia, asked a Russian officer how they dealt with prisoners. 'If they surrender in large groups,' replied the Russian, 'we send them back to base; but if there are only a few of them, we don't bother.'" Also during World War II, in December 1941, "a German sailor threw a hand grenade at Lieutenant Colonel J.F. Durnford-Slater, missed and raised his hands. A sergeant advanced on the sailor, rifle at the hip. 'Nein, nein,' cried the sailor. 'Ja, ja!' replied Sergeant Mills, and shot him. 'Yeah, well, Mills, you shouldn't have done that,' said Durnford-Slater."[2]

According to the former German officer, Ernst Jünger, wounded and decorated countless times in front-line action during World War One, neither side should have any expectations to surrender without cost.

> The defending force, after driving their bullets into the attacking one at five paces' distance, must take the consequences. A man cannot change his feelings again during the last rush with a veil of blood before his eyes. He does not want to take prisoners but to kill. He has no scruples left; only the spell of primeval instinct remains. It is not till blood has flowed that the mist gives way to his soul.[3]

One of the factors that influenced the fate of surrendering soldiers, regardless of the war, was the prisoners' military specialty. The survival of ordinary soldiers often depended on such fleeting things as the enemy's state of mind, whether the prisoner is a burden, or if a close friend of the enemy soldier has been recently killed, but certain specialists are singled out to be killed upon surrender. Longbow men, crossbow men, and those handling burning pitch or burning oil stood little chance. In more modern times, snipers are universally feared and hated, hidden as they are and killing from a distance. Every army kills enemy snipers without further consideration—something every sniper knows. Another prisoner who surrenders at his peril is the man with the flamethrower. Because of the horror of being burned alive by a stream of liquid napalm, the soldier assigned to carry the flamethrower is usually burned alive by the enemy. Enemy pilots and aircrews are particularly despised since their bombers shatter the lives and cities of unknown civilians from the safe distance of 30,000 feet. American crews who parachuted from their crippled planes into enemy territory, whether into Nazi Germany, Japan, North Korea, North Vietnam, Panama, Afghanistan, or Iraq, were subject to the anger and hysteria of armed civilians. In many cases, the aircrews had to be rescued by enemy government officials who recognized the intelligence value of the captives. Many times they did not get to the parachutists in time or turned a blind eye to the intentions of the mobs and allowed them to lynch or beat the captives to death.

Other military specialties were treated more in accord with international agreements: medical personnel, veterinarians, chaplains, and others who fell into the category of Protected Personnel. Most were repatriated home as quickly as possible.

Turning back the clock, even the Greeks, with their historic contributions to the philosophy of democracy, generally killed captives who were of no immediate use, serving as a warning to other belligerents. One of the Greek world's greatest philosophers, Aristotle, dismissed the fate of Greece's war prisoners with the simple dictum, "Those vanquished in war are held to belong to the victor."[4] Aristotle's student, the great philosopher Plato (427–347 B.C.), warned the soldiers of Greece that "If any fall alive into the enemies' hands we shall make them a present of him, and they may do what they like with their prey."[5]

Nor were the deaths of their prisoners particularly pleasant. During the Peloponnesian War in the late fifth century B.C., the Athenians and the Spartans, both Greeks, murdered each other with abandon for twenty-seven years. Battles were fought to the bitter end with no quarter asked or given. If prisoners were taken alive, and the odds were against it, the captives were treated as cruelly as any situation reminiscent of the notorious confederate war prison, Andersonville, or the Nazi concentration camp at Dachau. The plight of Athenian prisoners after the Syracusan defeat, for instance, saw the prisoners crammed into an open quarry, starved and left to die. At the battle of Corcyra, prisoners from the Spartan side were shut in a large building and groups of twenty were tied together and forced to run between two lines of heavy infantrymen from the Athenian side to be whipped and stabbed. None survived.[6]

The early Romans were no better. While it is true that the Romans conquered and ruled much of the known world and created wonders of architecture, literature, and political stability that would not be equaled for 1,000 years, their treatment of POWs was primitive. In warfare the ancient Romans were as ruthless as the barbarians they fought. Generally, an enemy soldier captured by the Roman legions knew his days were numbered. He was led through the streets of the Roman town or village in celebration of victory, or to entertain the public, and then used for target practice or as a gladiator for the arenas. Most, however, were simply strangled in nearby cellars. In the city of Rome itself, war prisoners were usually strangled after the parade in dark underground passages at the base of Capitoline Hill, ironically now located below the church San Giuseppe dei Falegnami, where burly servants waited with leather ropes to stand behind the kneeling prisoners.

Brutality against prisoners knows no bounds. The Danish Vikings, around 840 to 980 A.D., for example, came ashore in search of prisoners and booty along the Irish coast, as well as northern France and the southeastern coast of England. The Danes scoured the landscape, wielding heavy axes and broad swords, protected by little more than brightly painted circular shields and leather helmets, killing Christians and pillaging farms and villages. Curiously, their roving bands were often repelled and defeated by larger armies, but when they did take prisoners the captives were in for a horrible end. The Vikings had a predilection for a brutal punishment called "pitch-capping," or "blood-eagling"—a grisly ritual where the prisoner was tied facing a stake, his ribs hacked away from his spine with a sword and pulled outward like wings, revealing his lungs which were pulled out like balloons. Being an aristocrat or a rich prize did not always protect you. In fact, such was the fate of King Edmund of East Anglia in 870 A.D. at the hands of marauding Danes, who offered him peace on the condition that he would rule as their vassal and forbid the practice of Christianity. Legend has it that he refused and was "blood-eagled" by the Viking chieftain Ivar the Boneless in 869. His defiance on behalf of his faith earned him sainthood.[7]

Prisoners were often killed because they were simply too much trouble to bring along. After the historic battle of Agincourt in 1415, for example, Henry V of

England ordered all French prisoners killed expressly so that their guards could be released for combat duty. The sixteenth-century English chronicler Holinshed described the cruelty this way:

> When this dolorous decree, and pitiful proclamation was pronounced, pitie it was to see how some Frenchmen were suddenlie sticked with daggers, some were brained with pollaxes, some slaine with malls, other had their throats cut, and some their bellies panched, so that, in effect, hauing [having] respect to their great number, few prisoners were saued [saved].[8]

Five hundred years later during the Second World War, American soldiers in the Pacific routinely killed Japanese prisoners. While the Japanese rarely surrendered voluntarily and those who were captured were either unconscious or on the verge of starvation, few made it back to the rear lines alive. American, British, and Dutch soldiers despised their Japanese captives, a loathing that was reciprocated by the Japanese, but, realistically, combat in the jungles of the South Pacific did not lend itself to the care of prisoners on either side. In fact, the U.S. Army had to offer a reward of a quart of ice cream to anyone who brought in a living enemy prisoner before the first captured Japanese soldiers were brought in alive. Once behind the lines and headed for POW camps, the majority were treated decently, if with exaggerated security, and were shipped to camps in Australia and New Zealand, as well as to distant Camp Clinton, Iowa, and Camp McCoy, Wisconsin. In some camps they were passive and relatively cooperative since their culture never prepared them for becoming prisoners; in very few camps the prisoners fell under the control of political firebrands and were aggressive and uncooperative. Their greatest punishment lay ahead: the terrifying prospect of returning to Japan at the war's end, back to an unforgiving culture which saw war prisoners as soulless.

Fighting the Nazis in Europe was a bit safer for war captives, but occasionally not much. Prisoners were killed on all sides, sometimes as a result of combat hysteria or anger over lost comrades, but most often to lighten the load. Guarding enemy prisoners took men away from combat and weakened their units. An American officer recalled the following experience:

> The two men who had taken the prisoner to the rear returned. They had made a quick trip.
> "Did you get him back OK?" I asked.
> "Yessir," they answered and turned quickly toward their platoons.
> "Wait a minute," I said. "Did you find A Company? What did Lieutenant Smith say?"
> The men hesitated. One spoke out suddenly.
> "To tell you the truth, Cap'n, we didn't get to A Company. The sonofabitch tried to make a run for it. Know what I mean?"
> "Oh, I see," I said slowly, nodding my head. "I see."[9]

The Germans reluctantly killed their American, British, and Canadian prisoners as well, despite their general compliance with the Geneva Accords, presumably to reduce the drag on their forces as events moved quickly around them. Groups of Allied prisoners were found massacred in the wake of the Normandy Invasion in June 1944, many shot execution-style with their hands wired behind their backs. Since they were dispatched without torture and over a short period of time, one assumes that they murdered to lighten the enemy's ability to retreat speedily and without encumbrance. Again, it makes little difference to the victims if they were killed in anger or to improve battlefield efficiency. Overall, the murder of Allied POWs in German hands was sporadic, unlike the consistently barbaric treatment and murder of prisoners by the Japanese in the Pacific Theatre. Indeed, motivated by concerns for the reciprocal treatment of their prisoners in Allied hands, the Germans tried to adhere to the Geneva Convention of 1929. Of the 93,941 American servicemen taken prisoner in the European Theater, 1,121 died in captivity—a death rate of only 1.1 percent[10]

Sometimes prisoners were murdered just for the savagery. When Napoleon invaded Russia in 1812 and retreated after pillaging Moscow, he reduced more than 3,000 Russian prisoners to eating dead horses by the side of the road, and legend has it, eating their own dead, as well. The Russians, for their part, buried French prisoners alive, used them for target practice, cut off their tongues, ears, noses, and genitalia. While various Russian generals treated their prisoners differently, some with almost medieval chivalry, others personally ordered that prisoners be bayoneted. Polish soldiers found among the French were treated with special ruthlessness, despised as traitors to the Slavic cause. A hundred and fifty years later in the Philippines in 1942, Japanese soldiers bayoneted, stabbed, and brained 77,796 ragged and starving Filipino and American prisoners in the notorious Bataan Death March. Thousands of limping, emaciated survivors were marched the length of the Bataan Peninsula to waiting Japanese ships and years of starvation, disease, and brutality in Japanese prison camps. Once in captivity, 1,500 American prisoners who had survived the march across Bataan died within forty days, and 25,000 Filipinos were murdered by the Japanese by July 1942. Put a different way, 95 percent of the Japanese POWs held in Australia, New Zealand, and the United States survived the war, whereas only 49 percent of the Allied prisoners held in Japanese camps lived to return to their native lands. Simply surviving the battle wasn't enough; it made a great deal of difference where you were held.

Similar savagery was evident in the European Theatre during the same war when the ordinary German Army—not just the sinister and oft-responsible SS—murdered some 3.3 million Russian POWs out of the 5.7 million in its hands, routinely working them to death and tormenting them in such horrific ways as medical experiments and the Zyclone-B gas program.

Captives throughout history were often murdered on a whim. During Napoleon's catastrophic retreat across the frozen steppes of Russia in 1812, for example, Russia's Grand Duke Constantine and his senior officers happened to see a distinguished French officer among the prisoners. Appearing to ignore the mutually accepted rules protecting war prisoners, Constantine asked the officer if he would prefer death to his current humiliation. According to eyewitnesses, the officer answered,

> There are those in France who would lament my fate—for their sake I should wish to return; but if that be impossible, the sooner the ignominy and suffering are over the better.[11]

To everyone's horror, the Grand Duke drew his saber and killed the man.

War prisoners are sometimes brutalized to send a signal to one's enemies. One of the most striking examples is the act of the Byzantine Emperor Basil II "the Bulgar Slayer" (958–1025 A.D.) at the Battle of Kleidion in July 1014, as he fought to extend the influence of the Byzantine Empire over the Balkans, Mesopotamia, Armenia, and Georgia. Basil II triumphed over the Bulgarian Czar Samuel's army and, although Samuel managed to escape, Basil captured some 14,000 Bulgarian prisoners. He used his prisoners, all 14,000 of them, to send a message that the Bulgarians wouldn't forget, saying, in effect that "This is what happens to anyone who rises up against the empire." Basil had ninety-nine out of every hundred blinded. The hundredth man in each group was blinded in only one eye so he could lead his sightless comrades home. The column of almost 14,000 blind soldiers conveyed an unmistakable message to the Czar Samuel and Bulgarians. According to legend, when his blinded soldiers returned to Macedonia he collapsed and died at the sight, although his official biography notes that he actually died eleven years later.[12]

Lastly, on at least one horrible occasion, prisoners were murdered to prevent possible future problems. In late 1939 and 1940, as many as 28,000 Polish military prisoner officers were rounded up from Russian POW camps after Poland was divided up between the Germans and the Russians and, with their hands tied behind their backs, herded toward deep pits surrounded by bored gunmen cradling automatic weapons. They were transported to the Katyn Forest twelve miles west of Smolensk, Russia, while thousands more were taken to prisons in Moscow and other Soviet cities. There they were turned over to the Soviet Secret Police, the dreaded NKVD, and executed. Their bodies were stacked in layers, sometimes twelve layers deep, and the crime covered up and forgotten. The military prisoners who were murdered at Katyn included an admiral, fourteen generals, twenty-four colonels, nine lieutenant colonels, 258 majors, 654 captains, seventeen naval captains, 4,022 warrant officers and NCOs, not to mention chaplains and thousands of enlisted men. A scant 395 prisoners survived the slaughter. The mass graves were discovered by the Germans in 1943 during a German advance and, given the Wehrmacht's murderous treatment of Poles and Russians, the world assumed they had orchestrated the killings. Each side blamed the other and the issue was debated for decades. Begrudgingly, on April 13, 1990, on the forty-seventh anniversary of the discovery of the mass graves, the U.S.S.R. formally expressed "profound regret" and admitted that they did it after all.[13] Stalin assumed that Poland would fall under the Russians by the end of the war, and that Polish officers and intelligentsia might someday work to oppose him.

In this case, Stalin murdered hundreds of thousands of POWs not to send a message to the other side, or on a whim, or to discard unwieldy groups of captives—but to prevent possible *future* problems, to smooth his occupation of Poland an unknown number of years away.

Interestingly, war prisoners weren't generally hated except in Asian cultures where captives in battle are considered to be less than human and are viewed as "soulless" by having surrendered. In most cases in the Western world, war prisoners became "things," slaves, gladiators, laborers, soldiers, or propaganda fodder: things to be exploited. In nearly every conflict, war prisoners were considered booty or trophies to be displayed to the cheering crowds. Death or a lifetime of slavery waited for them. It was not an enviable end to the risks involved.

Nor were POWs always men. Female soldiers and military nurses have appeared among the captives in almost every conflict from medieval times to World War II and the more current Gulf War of 1990 and beyond. Like their male counterparts, women prisoners were held in POW camps of both sides in the American Civil War; indeed, during the Civil War, Union medical doctor Mary Walker was held for four months in a Confederate prison camp and became the only woman to have been awarded the Congressional Medal of Honor. On the other side, Nancy Hart served as a Confederate scout, guide, and spy, carrying messages between the Southern Armies. She was twenty years old when she was captured by the Yankees and jailed. Nancy gained the trust of one of her guards, got his weapon from him, shot him, and escaped. On at least one instance a "she" masqueraded as a "he." Florena Budwin, wife of a Pennsylvania soldier of the Civil War, disguised herself as a man and enlisted in the Union Army to be near her husband. Both husband and wife were captured and imprisoned at the infamous Andersonville Prison where her husband died. Florena was then transferred to another Confederate camp in Florence, South Carolina, where her true gender was finally discovered. She remained at the prison to care for Union soldiers, eventually dying of disease in 1865. She was buried at Florence National Cemetery and is believed to be the first woman buried in a National Cemetery.

Women prisoners were captured during World War I, and two women, in particular, Edith Cavell and Mata Hari, were executed as spies. During the Second World War, more than one hundred Army and Navy lieutenant (jg) nurses were captured by the Japanese at Guam and Corrigidor and spent the duration tormented and malnourished at places like Santo Tomas Internment camp in Manila and Zentsuii Prison on Shikoku Island.

American military women in Europe were occasionally captured by the Germans. One such prisoner was Lieutenant Reba Whittle, Army Nurse Corps, who, together with her crew, was shot down on her fortieth medical evacuation flight in September 1944. She was imprisoned in a POW camp where she continued to minister to other wounded prisoners. After repatriation, Lieutenant Whittle was awarded the Air Medal and the Purple Heart.

During the Vietnam War, American military nurses who often tended wounded soldiers close to the front line were captured by enemy guerrilla units. Eleanor Ardel Vietti was captured at a leper hospital in Ban Me Thuot on May 30, 1962. She was never heard from again. Another nurse, Betty Ann Olsen, was captured during a raid on the same leprosarium during the Tet offensive in 1968. She died in 1968 and was buried somewhere along Ho Chi Minh Trail. She is still listed as POW. Monika Schwinn, a German nurse, was held captive for three and a half years—at one time the only woman prisoner at the notorious "Hanoi Hilton."

Operation Desert Storm in 1991 saw the capture and imprisonment of Army Flight Surgeon, Major Rhonda Cornum, and an Army Transportation Specialist, Sp4 Melissa Rathbun-Nealy. Dr. Cornum, wife, mother, physician, and pilot, was on a search and rescue mission when her helicopter was shot down. She took a bullet in the shoulder, had a shattered knee, and could not move her badly broken arms. She was raped by Iraqi soldiers.

The current Operation Iraqi Freedom of 2003 has seen several high-profile women captives (PFC Jessica Lynch, 19, a supply clerk from Palestine, West Virginia, was taken prisoner in Iraq after her unit was ambushed. Ten days later, she was freed in a daring raid by U.S. Marines. Army Specialist Shoshana Johnson, 30, of Fort Bliss, Texas, and six of her fellow soldiers were rescued on April 13, 2003).[14] Despite the Geneva Convention's clear protection of the "dignity and modesty" of female POWs, a recent article indicates that sexual assault is a very real threat for American POWs in the Iraqi conflict, men as well as women.[15]

Whether men or women, prisoners throughout history have been brutally treated and often used in surprising ways. In the rarest of opportunities, prisoners were offered the chance to change sides and live to fight again. The Thirty Years' War, 1618–1648, is an excellent example. The war began as a religious conflict between Catholics and Protestants and deteriorated into a series of political battles which saw Catholic France join with Protestant Sweden against the Catholic Hapsburgs, which, in turn, threatened France. Nearly every army relied on mercenaries who, when captured, were welcomed into the ranks of the other side. Even prisoners who were not mercenaries by trade, but ordinary citizens, were occasionally offered a chance to change sides. During the American revolutionary war, for example, American colonial prisoners were freed from imprisonment if they were willing to fight on the British side. History tells us that few accepted the offer.

Normally, the inclusion of enemy forces into one's army was a dangerous risk, since they might have changed sides but not their loyalty. Mercenaries are somewhat safer to have change sides than prisoners who fought for an ideology or cause. Genuine mercenaries have no loyalty except to the side that pays their salary. Once ensconced into the winner's army, one must only hope that the other side won't outbid their new comrades for their services. Incidentally, the ability to change sides may have been beneficial to the captured mercenaries but it was the tragedy of the Thirty Years' War. Armies didn't wear down significantly because professional soldiers were allowed to change sides, and little was solved by the three decades of war.

Several striking recent examples of POWs who were allowed to change sides occurred during World War II. For instance, the German Army, locked in mortal combat with the Red Army in Russia and desperate to end the stalemate, combed its bulging POW camps for Russian volunteers willing to fight against Stalin under the German flag. Thus was created the so-called Vlasov's Army, some 50,000 Russian prisoners led by General Andrei Vlasov, a lifelong Soviet officer who was captured at the battle of Leningrad. He had survived Stalin's purges of his fellow officers during the 1930s and hated the Russian ruler. Mistrusted by Hitler and now on Stalin's death list, Vlasov's Army, named the Russian Liberation Army (POA), played a minor military role in the war, curiously changing sides once again to help liberate Prague, Czechoslovakia, from the Nazis. With Germany's surrender on May 8, 1945, it was time for Vlasov and his army to face the duplicitousness of the Allies who ruthlessly handed them over to Stalin. On August 2, the Soviet press announced that Andrei Vlasov had been hanged for treason. His men were loaded onto boxcars and sent back to Russia where they were machine-gunned as they got off the trains. The Germans recruited another group from among ex-Russian POWs in 1941–1942, a unit of killers who called themselves the Kaminski Brigade. The Kaminskis earned a gruesome reputation fighting partisans in the Bryansk region and were elevated into a Waffen-SS division in 1944. They were anticommunist Russians wearing German uniforms and often fighting their former comrades in the Red Army. They were not trusted by the Germans, whose racial lunacy relegated Russian Slavs to the bottom of the racial totem pole. Nor were they trusted to fight the Red Army with the necessary ferocity, although the Russians knew that by taking up arms against their own army they were considered traitors. Capture meant immediate death. All of these came into focus at the same time when Kaminski and his Waffen-SS division were assigned to subdue the resistance movement in Warsaw. Think of the irony: a unit of Russians in German uniforms who came to Warsaw to exterminate the largely communist resistance, while the Red Army paused on the other side of the Vistula River to move against the survivors. Their brutal treatment of Poles during the uprising did not end the resistance and the mission failed. Kaminski himself was eventually shot on Himmler's orders and his men folded into the Vlasov Army.

Even among the Japanese soldiers during World War II, perhaps the most dedicated soldiers in modern history, there are cases when Japanese POWs in Allied camps actually aided their American enemy. The curious problem facing them was that once in captivity, they simply had no concept of what it meant to be a prisoner. They knew their roles as warrior or head of household or teacher or student, but becoming a prisoner was never considered. When finding themselves in such an unthinkable situation, they became malleable to the point that several volunteered to fly with American bombers to point out Japanese refineries.[16]

Fortunate prisoners were merely enslaved, although the prospect of a lifetime of brutal servitude might hardly be considered fortunate. At best, he was the "forgotten man" herded into compounds far from home, abandoned by his homeland, and shunned by his captors. From biblical times the enslavement of war prisoners was a common outcome of any battle, and indeed, wars were often fought for the sole purpose of capturing slaves. Rome, in particular, grew to see the value of keeping its captives alive as galley slaves, and they were killed only when they were no longer able to pull an oar. Prisoners of war were developing value.

Why did soldiers over the centuries put themselves at such risk? There are as many reasons as conflicts. Some soldiers fought because it was their profession; others joined an army to make extra money after the harvest. In naval countries military service was often involuntary. Sailors were shanghaied while drunk—pressed into service by groups of thugs. More often, however, men who went to war did so as true believers in a cause, ideological, religious, or political.

Tragically, more wars have been fought in the name of God than for any other cause in history Whatever brought the soldier to the battle, life was simple for such men: they spent much of their time training and practicing their fighting style, living life as they found it, and praying to their gods for victory, personal bravery, and hopefully a share in the winners' rewards. "Onward for God and Country" is doubtless the most common rallying cry of an attacking army throughout history. Soldiers on every side understood the risks and weighed them against the money, orders, or ideology that drove them. Most tried not to dwell on the very real prospect of a lost limb, a painful death on the field, or a future life in slavery. Such constant fears hardened the soldiers of all sides and stiffened their resolve to win. However difficult to imagine from this distance, soldiers of past ages knew that losing the next battle was a distinct possibility and should that happen, a mortal blow or dismemberment was nearly assured.

Officers or aristocrats among the prisoners generally had the best chance of survival and repatriation. They represented the richest families of their nations, landowners, and aristocrats who could buy their way to safety. Simply put: wealthy prisoners were held for ransom and their families were squeezed for as much as the market would bear. Rich or powerful families redeemed their relatives promptly, especially if other rich or powerful families were looking on. In fact, many wealthy or aristocratic officers carried gold coins into battle to buy their lives or freedom. British officers in the many conflicts of the eighteenth century greeted most reversals in the tide of the conflict by holding out their purses and watches. Opponents increasingly saw battle and the prisoners it produced as a source of income either personally or to raise money during a protracted war. In addition to being promising sources of ransom, the prisoners had value during treaty negotiations as "bartering chips" to be used to get better terms; or they might be used in a prisoner exchange or to threaten the enemy. The prospect of watching large groups of one's countrymen die in enemy captivity often prompted rapid compromises.

But what if your army has the unbelievable good fortune to actually capture the enemy's king? On rare occasions an enemy prisoner might turn out to be a monarch or leading general and the rules went by the wayside. A captured king was a breathtaking opportunity to reap the greatest wealth and to exert enormous influence on the enemy's politics and its military. The haggling might go on for years and nearly bankrupt nations. England's "Richard the Lionheart" is a good case in point. Richard II was taken prisoner by the Austrians on his return from the Third Crusade to wrest Jerusalem from the Muslims in 1189. What a prize! The King of England had wandered into the hands of Britain's continental enemy, Austria. After lengthy negotiations between Austria's allies, Richard's ransom was set at the outrageously high sum of 150,000 marks—equal to three tons of silver. Richard languished for several years in a remote Austrian mountainside prison while England suffered under his brother John's dictatorial yoke and brutal taxation. The English were ruinously burdened, doubly so since they had been taxed to support the Crusade in the first place. The story of Robin Hood and his "merrie band" was set in this moment—a legend about happy English forest brigands who banded together to resist the tax collector and King John's evil Sheriff of Nottingham.

> Capturing a king or high-ranking aristocrat, while rare, was a momentous opportunity. The ransom of Jean II of France in 1360 was set at a jaw-dropping 3,000,000 crowns (£500,000), equal to twenty years of ordinary revenue by the British government. The Duke of Alençon netted his captors £26,666; and Bertrand du Guesclin, clearly lower on the knightly scale, brought only 100,000 francs (or £11,000). The phrase "worth a king's ransom" remains in common use today.[17]

Lest one extend too much sympathy for the imprisoned King Richard, it might help to recall that he slaughtered 3,000 Muslim prisoners a year earlier near Jerusalem when he grew tired of waiting for the Muslim leader, Saladin, to act on an agreed-upon prisoner exchange. One Muslim observer recalls that the Franks, on reaching the middle of the plain stretching between this hill and that of Keisan, close to which place the sultan's advanced guard had drawn back, ordered all the Musulman prisoners, whose martyrdom God had decreed for this day, to be brought before him. They numbered more than 3,000 and were all bound with ropes. The Franks then flung themselves upon them all at once and massacred them with sword and lance in cold blood.[18]

Several hundred years later, it was a Muslim king who was captured in battle. During the war for Spain between 1481 and 1492, as the Moors fought their crusade across Christian Granada, the young Moorish prince Boabdil [also known as Abu Abdallah and Mohammad XII] was captured in battle by an astonished, and much rewarded, common Spanish soldier. Given the ferocity of the war, the life of the captive prince hung in the balance. And all knew it. However, when he was marched to the court of the Count of Cabra he was astonished to be treated with the utmost hospitality and provided the finest food and entertainment that circumstances would permit. Behind the scenes, however, Spanish sovereigns knew the economic value of the Muslim prince and hoped for a better deal from the Moors if they treated their prince well, rather than killing him and creating a martyr. After haggling among themselves over their shares of the ransom, they turned to the Moors. Eventually he was exchanged for an annual payment of 12,000 doblas of gold, the release of 400 Christian captives, and the promise to permit free passage to enemy troops passing through his territories to continue the war for the Moorish conquest of Spain. His childrens' children were held to insure his compliance. The huge cost of his release was humiliating to the Moors, to be sure, but Boadbil's treatment after his capture indicates the range of possibilities facing a war prisoner in battle. The murder or ransom of captive leaders was capricious and depended on the nature of the battle, the personalities of the leaders, the history of their relations, and the amount of money in question.

The capture of kings and princes was one thing, but the fate of nonaristocratic prisoners was quite another. Ordinary officers held little monetary value or influence on enemy policy. They were just as costly to guard and feed as ordinary captives, perhaps more so since they were often better educated and could argue their cause or plan complicated escapes. Their demands were greater than those of common soldiers.

As wars progressed through the medieval and early modern periods, both sides in a battle began to develop an appreciation for the value of experienced or talented officers. They were not easily replaceable. Soldiers who knew their trade and could lead others became increasingly important as warfare grew more technical and multitiered. Battles that once were decided by two dozen men now involved and consumed thousands. The conduct of war required professionals who could decipher intricate maps as well as understand their opponent's culture and anticipate probable decisions. Officers had always been required to rally their men, but as armies grew larger so did the difficulties. There was a dramatic need for officers who were trained specialists while still being warriors.

New foot soldiers could always be recruited or conscripted but an officer who could accurately convey the orders of his superiors to the men under his control was not easily replaceable. In modern times nations have trained officers at national military academies—St. Cyr in France, Britain's Sandhurst, America's West Point or U.S. Naval Academy—renowned institutions where officer candidates were infused over four years with a carefully crafted education combining technology, policy, sport, and leadership. Since governments now invested so much time and money in the creation of young military leaders, it was foolish to allow them to languish or perish in the hands of the enemy. Their safe return was the key to winning future battles.

Commissioned officers became so important to the military that they formed a class unto themselves. They maintained a code of chivalrous behavior and treated fellow officers, even those of enemy armies, as members of the club. During World War I, for example, senior British flying officers held in German prison camps were routinely invited to dine with the German commandant. Non-officers or enlisted men ate in their POW barracks. Segregation of officers from their men became so ironbound that the armies in the Great War maintained separate bordellos—one type for officers and another, presumably less clean and ornate, for enlisted men. As recently as World War II American pilots shot down over Germany were held in relatively safe German *Luftwaffe* POW camps. While it was a miserable experience filled with loneliness, freezing cold, hunger, and ever-present danger, their American enlisted men, and those of any other army in captivity, had it far worse. In the United States German prisoners in many of the 650 POW camps maintained by the American Army during World War II could purchase beer in the evenings at the POW canteen. At Camp Trinidad, Colorado, during World War II, *Afrika Korps* officers could stroll miles away from their POW camp, unescorted, restricted only by their promise as officers to return. They always did. Overall, it was good to be an officer, not the least because you were of value to your country and family and consequently stood the best chance of being exchanged or treated reasonably well.

Increasing the value of common soldiers, however, took much longer. The history of warfare is crowded with battles where the common soldiers were routinely dispatched. Death was very much a part of combat, with no quarter expected or given. On occasion, as at the Spanish siege of Prato, near Florence in 1512, 12,000 Tuscan common soldiers were killed after being overwhelmed by 8,000 Spaniards who breached the medieval defenses of Prato—but not before they were tortured for three weeks to extract any ransom possible.

A frightful butchery followed, and not only murder but also rape and plundering. Those prisoners still alive after they had given up everything were tortured by the Spaniards for three weeks in order to force ransoms from their relatives living at some distance. The Florentines complained to the Spanish commander, Cardona, about the unprecedented size of the ransoms being demanded. He himself admitted that the demands were too high but said that he was powerless against his troops.[19]

As if to compound the importance of the prisoners, when the news of their plight reached nearby Florence, the great Republic of Florence promptly surrendered. The fall of Prato was the end of the Republic of Florence.

Life as a common soldier was clearly brutal and unprotected, and the treatment of war prisoners changed regularly. Once the soldier had surrendered to his enemies, he could not know what fate awaited him. Execution was still very much a possibility, whether to lighten the burden of the enemy or to send a pointed message to the other side or for the sheer savagery of killing a hated captive or, finally, at the whim of the enemy commander. If the prisoner's life was somehow spared, years of crushing servitude would surely lie ahead. Centuries would pass before the fate of individuals would be granted some protection. It would be slow going.

Notes

1. Quoted in the *Observer*, 1952.
2. Quoted in Richard Holmes, *Acts of War: The Behavior of Men in Battle* (New York: The Free Press, 1985), 382–385.
3. Ernst Jünger, *The Storm of Steel: From the Diary of a German Storm-Troop Officer on the Western Front* (New York: Howard Fertig, 1975), 262–263.
4. Aristotle, *Politics*, 1225a, pp. 6–7.
5. Plato, *Republic*, V, p. 468.
6. Helen H. Law, "Atrocities in Greek Warfare," *The Classical Journal*, 15(3) (December 1919), 132–147.
7. A.H. Smith (ed.), Anglo-Saxon Chronicle. *The Parker Chronicle 832–900* 2nd ed., Exeter Medieval English Texts (Exeter: University of Exeter Press, 1980). It has been suggested that Ivar the Boneless was a not-so-veiled reference to his impotence.
8. *'Holinshed' Chronicles* (London, 1808), III, 81–82, cited by Henry J. Webb, "Prisoner of War in the Middle Ages," *Military Affairs*, 12(1) (Spring 1948), 48.
9. Charles B. MacDonald, *Company Commander* (New York: Ballantine Books, 1947), 142.
10. "Theater Casualties," *VFW Magazine,* (August 1991), 29, and "Behind Barbed Wire: POWs in the Pacific and Europe," *VFW Magazine,* (November 1991), 64. The best source of information available in English is Robert C. Doyle, *Voices from Captivity: Interpreting the American POW Narrative* (Lawrence: University Press of Kansas, 1994), especially the Appendices.
11. Dubrovin, 325; Wilson, Invasion, 257–8; Zamoyski, 403. Adam Zamoyski, *Moscow 1812: Napoleon's Final March* (Harper Perennial, 2005), 384–405.
12. Sir Steven Runciman, *A History of the First Bulgarian Empire* (London: G. Bell and Sons, 1930).
13. "CHRONOLOGY 1990: The Soviet Union and Eastern Europe," *Foreign Affairs*, 1990, 212. See the press release online, Warsaw, November 30, 2004: (http://www.ipn.gov.pl/eng/eng_news_high_katyn_press.html).
14. Among the hundreds of relevant articles, academic dissertations, and books on the subject of women in the military and prisoners of war, available on http://findarticles.com/p/articles/mi_m0EXI/is_3-4_20/ai_113230464/pg_1, the best books are: Rhonda Cornum as told to Peter Copeland, *She Went to War: The Rhonda Cornum Story* (Novato, CA: Presidio, 1992); Elizabeth M. Norman, *We Band of Angels: The Untold Story of American Nurses Trapped on Bataan by the Japanese* (New York: Random House, 1999); Barbara Angell, *A Woman's War: The Exceptional Life of Wilma Oram Young* (Sydney: New Holland, 2003); Lavinia Warner and John Sandilands, *Women Beyond the Wire* (London: Arrow Books, 1987); Theresa Kaminski, *Prisoners in Paradise: American Women in the Wartime South Pacific* (Lawrence: University Press of Kansas, 2000); Celia Lucas, *Prisoners of Santo Tomas: A True Account of Women POWs under Japanese Control* (London: Cooper, 1975); and Rick Bragg, *I Am a Soldier, Too: The Jessica Lynch Story* (New York: Alfred A. Knopf, 2003).
15. Gretchen Cook, "POWs Likely to Endure Sexual Assault," *Women's ENews*, October 15, 2006.
16. See Arnold Krammer, "Japanese Prisoners of War in America," *Pacific Historical Review*, 52(1) (February 1983), 67–91.

17. Clifford J. Rogers, "The Military Revolutions of the Hundred Years' War," *The Journal of Military History*, 57(2) (April 1993), 256.

18. Beha-ed-Din, his account appears in Thomas Andrew Archer, *The Crusade of Richard I—1189–92*, selected and arranged by T.A. Archer (New York: AMS Press (1978); John Gillingham, *Richard I* (New Haven, CT: Yale University Press, 1999).

19. Hans Delbruck, *The History of the Art of War Within the Framework of Political History, Vol. IV: The Modern Era* (Westport, CT, Greenwood Press, 1985), 105.

CHAPTER 2

A Search for Legal Protection

Concern for war prisoners began haphazardly and as early as the Hammurabic Code in Babylon, eighteen centuries before Christ. The Hammurabic Code makes no direct provision for the treatment of war prisoners, assuming perhaps that such matters are left in the hands of the enemy. However, the fate of the prisoners' wife and children are under control of the community, and the following decisions are inscribed in law:

Clause 133: "If a man is taken prisoner in war, and there is sustenance in his house, but if his wife leaves house and court, and goes to another house, she shall be judicially condemned and thrown into the water."

Clause 134: "If any one be captured in war and there is not sustenance in his house, if then his wife go to another house this woman shall be held blameless."

Clause 135: "If a man be taken prisoner in war and there be no sustenance in his house and his wife go to another house and bear children, and if later her husband return and come to his home, then his wife shall return to her husband, but the children follow their father."

From these codes it would appear that soldiers taken as prisoners of war (POWs) were not always killed and sometimes returned, and that the issues of marriage and paternity were of paramount importance.

The issue of POWs was considered in legal arguments, military debates, and literature—from Shakespeare's "Henry the Fifth,"[1] to the formation of English Common Law, and the philosophical questions posed by St. Augustine and St. Thomas Aquinas. But, little changed. The rules for the protection of war prisoners differed from conflict to conflict, depending on the vagaries of the battle and the type of war.

Prisoners in the English Civil War during the 1640s, for all the deplorable torture and executions endured by both sides, saw halting steps toward their protection. Parliament's often-violated rule that "None shall kill an Enemy who yields and throws down his Arms" was vaguely matched by the Royalists. Along the way, both sides spared prisoners who willingly swore an oath to cease fighting, while others swore an allegiance to fight on the side of their captors. Prisoners were also held in custody as a bankable commodity for future exchanges, and exchanges were increasingly based on the equivalency of rank. If no equivalency of rank or importance could readily be found, high-ranking captives were sometimes passed from commander to commander until an exchange was feasible. Food quality for the prisoners varied widely, as did their treatment, although on balance, it was still largely barbaric.[2]

In the seventeenth century the highly-respected Dutch legal theorist Hugo Grotius (Huig de Groot), appalled by the chaotic warring world around him, proposed that moral laws be applied to the individual and state equally, and that all nations be subject to international law. In his major work *On the Law of War and Peace* (1625), Grotius described rules for every imaginable situation which a monarch or the ruling class might face. Of particular concern to the Dutch philosopher was the fate of war captives.

Grotius argued against the legality of reprisals against prisoners, except in cases where the prisoner had committed a crime normally punishable by law. He emphasized that "wars, undertaken to maintain national honor, should be conducted upon principles of moderation." With regard to war prisoners, he said that "after a place has surrendered, and there is no danger to be apprehended from the prisoners, there is nothing to justify the further effusion of blood."

What a bold statement for the year 1625! This was the era of the violent Civil War in England, Copernicus had not yet charted the movement of the planets, and the Puritans were only now leaving for the New World. Here was a renowned legal thinker who advised that wars should be approached with moderation and that prisoners must not be killed once they are rendered harmless. Grotius acknowledged that war captives, like citizens, had a recognizable humanity which could not be legally violated except in cases where a normal civilian might receive similar punishment.[3]

Yet, however brilliant the legal argument or progressive the foresight, Grotius' views reached only a small circle of philosophers and legal scholars. For the next two centuries war prisoners continued to be tortured, enslaved, or slaughtered.

The Enlightenment changed everything. During the 1700s, Europeans developed a growing sense of pride that they were entering into a period in which the light of reason would free all from the darkness of superstition and ignorance. Fueled by the burst of liberating scientific inventions and the hugely influential publications by such philosophers as John Locke and Thomas Hobbes, who wrote that everyone has the right to life, liberty, and the pursuit of property, the value of individuals—even POWs—began to improve. It was in this context that America's successful revolution in 1776 further advanced the rights of individuals and the later French Revolution of 1789 championed the concept of the Rights of Man and proved it by killing the king of France.

Should one think that this upward humanitarian climb substantially benefited the POWs of the era, reality tells us otherwise. Indeed, during the American

Revolutionary War, the British treated their POWs no differently than the wars of the past thousand years. Following the Battle of Long Island in August 1776 and the fall of New York City soon thereafter, the British found themselves holding thousands of American prisoners. The prisons of New York were overcrowded with American POWs so the British seized sixteen ships and turned them into floating prisons. Conditions were horrific, "sinkholes of filth, vermin, infectious disease, and despair. The ships were uniformly wretched, but the most notorious was the *Jersey*," which held as many as a thousand American prisoners below deck. In 1778, a Robert Sheffield escaped one of these prison ships and described the condition of his fellow prisoners to the *Connecticut Gazette* on July 10, 1778.

> Their sickly countenances and ghastly looks were truly horrible. Some swearing and blaspheming; some crying, praying, and wringing their hands, and stalking about like ghosts; others delirious, raving, and storming; some groaning and dying—all panting for breath; some dead and corrupting—air so foul at times that a lamp could not be kept burning, by reason of which the boys were not missed till they had been dead ten days. [4]

The surviving prisoners were not freed until 1783, when the British abandoned New York City.

So many dead bodies were thrown overboard every day that for years after the British surrendered, the bones of former prisoners washed up along the shores of Brooklyn and Long Island. These bones were collected by patriotic Brooklynites and eventually interred in a large memorial crypt called the Prison Ship Martyrs Monument that stands today in the center of Fort Greene Park—a nearly unknown memorial to the approximately 11,000 prisoners who died on Britain's floating POW camps, a startlingly high figure when compared to the total number of 4,435 battle deaths during the Revolutionary War itself. [5]

One of the first orders of business for the new United States was to indict the British commander of the prison ships and hang him.

As the illumination of the Enlightenment began to imbue human beings with value, the final remaining obstacle in the upward path of concern for war prisoners was the establishment of some sort of international agreement. This was probably the most difficult obstacle of all. All sides had to agree to some level of prisoner treatment, but the signing of such an agreement necessitated a modicum of trust in an atmosphere of dark suspicion. Once reassured by international agreement, warring countries entered into a tenuous balance: the well-being of one set of prisoners, or the lack thereof, would swiftly be felt by the prisoners held by the other. All that remained was to establish the level of treatment to which prisoners were entitled, and agree to the various aspects of their captivity which could or should be regulated. The final product of so many centuries of concern for the treatment of war captives was a mosaic of numerous large and small pieces.

Interestingly, a growing concern for the Rights of Man and the improved treatment of war prisoners forced the western world to look at slavery. Within decades, Britain liberated its slaves in the sugar islands in 1832, Russia freed its serfs in 1861, and America emancipated its slaves in 1863. Philosophers spoke of "certain inalienable rights" and politicians introduced stirring phrases about "all men being born equal." Suffrage was extended to more and more people as barriers fell to the participation of women and minorities previously excluded from the decision-making process. Prisoners of war had families at home who could now voice their concerns for the safe return of their sons and husbands at the election polls, and politicians ignored the angry voters at their peril.

During the American Civil War, President Lincoln asked Francis Lieber, professor of history and law at Columbia and a wounded veteran of three major European battles including Waterloo, to draft instructions for the U.S. armies during war. In a farsighted effort, Lincoln persuaded the Confederacy to abide by Lieber's Code. According to the new Code, enemy prisoners were recognized as fellow human citizens caught up in the chaos of war, not "outlaws," "pirates," or "bandits," and required their captors to feed, doctor, and shelter their prisoners. Prisoners were protected against torture or mistreatment to obtain military information, and specifically, denied the captors the right to execute prisoners who attempted to escape. The Lieber Code became the basis for numerous international agreements for the humane treatment of war prisoners well into the next century.

Almost at the same time, another major step occurred from an unlikely source when Henri Dunant, a Swiss banker, stumbled across the end of a major battle between the French and Austrians in Solferino, Italy, in 1859, during Napoleon III's effort to drive the Austrians from Italy. The stunned Henri Dunant was so moved by the thousands of dead and dying scattered across the smoking battlefield that he wrote an account of the savage battle, entitled *A Memory of Solferino*, and proposed the creation of a civilian volunteer relief corps to care for the wounded, now known as the International Committee of the Red Cross. An energetic Dunant then organized a conference to draft an agreement on the treatment of battlefield casualties which led to the first Geneva Conference in 1864. Soon, it became almost fashionable for Europe's diplomats to meet at famous spas and watering holes, often in Geneva, Switzerland, and The Hague, Netherlands, where they hammered out rules "civilizing war." In 1874, a meeting in Brussels, Belgium, specifically based its published code on Lieber's and established the precedents for the critical Hague Conventions of 1899 and 1907. These, in turn, formed the basis for the Geneva Conventions of 1929 and 1949.

Everything collapsed in 1914 with the eruption of the First World War. The Great War witnessed the violation of every "civilizing" rule, from the use of poison gas and so-called "dum-dum" hollow-point bullets, to the random execution of prisoners. Millions of deaths later, the world realized that it was crucial to create an ironclad body of rules, and in 1929, the diplomats met again in Geneva, this time with particular concern for the protection of POWs, Grotius' words from 1625 were revisited for possible wisdom. [6]

The Geneva Convention has ninety-seven separate articles covering every foreseeable problem faced by POWs and stands as the central monument to the modern protection of war captives. As examples,

Article 2: They must at all times be humanely treated and protected, particularly against acts of violence, insults, and public curiosity. Measures of reprisal against them are prohibited.

Article 3: Prisoners of war have the right to have their person and their honor respected. Women shall be treated with all the regard due to their sex. Prisoners retain their full civil status.

Article 5: No coercion may be used on prisoners to secure information to the condition of their army or country. Prisoners who refuse to answer may not be threatened, insulted, or exposed to unpleasant or disadvantageous treatment of any kind whatever.

Article 10: Prisoners of war shall be lodged in buildings or in barracks affording all possible guarantees of hygiene and healthfulness. The quarters must be fully protected from dampness, sufficiently heated and lighted. All precautions must be taken against danger of fire. With regard to dormitories the total surface, minimum cubic amount of air, arrangement and material of bedding—the conditions shall be the same as for the troops at base camps of the detaining Power.

Article 11: The food ration of prisoners of war shall be equal in quantity and quality to that of troops at base camps. Furthermore, prisoners shall receive facilities for preparing themselves additional food which thy might have. Sufficiency of potable water shall be furnished to them. The use of tobacco shall be permitted. Prisoners may be employed in the kitchens.

And so on for eighty-six additional articles.

It is well known that during the first years of World War II Washington paid little attention to the plight of the American prisoners in enemy hands. Ninety thousand Americans survived in remote camps scattered across Germany, crowded, guarded, fed at a subsistence level, and left largely to their own devices. Camp conditions in Germany were deplorable—except for Allied pilots, who always seemed to be accorded somewhat gentlemanly treatment, and, of course, high-ranking officers. Germany's military tradition carried a rather deep respect for military rank, and high-ranking American officers were treated like aristocrats. Washington saw no such value in the thirty-five German POW generals who spent the war years in a remote camp in Clinton, Mississippi. To their astonishment, they were not interviewed for military information or used for propaganda purposes.[7]

Jewish American soldiers, if found among the prisoners and whatever their ranks, were often shipped to concentration camps where they were worked to death.[8] Lest one think that Americans were the only victims, a recent memoir by a British POW captured in North Africa reveals that a number were shipped to Auschwitz, where they worked and died alongside the hundreds of thousands of European Jews singled out for extermination.[9] Strangely, neither London nor Washington became seriously involved in protecting its soldiers in enemy hands.

The War Department was caught in a Catch 22. It was convinced that the two best ways to protect the 90,000 Americans prisoners in German hands was by adhering as closely as possible to the Geneva Accords and hoping that the enemy would do the same. As a result, the 371,000 German POWs in American hands were fed and treated exactly like America's own soldiers, sometimes to the point of foolishness, as when American guards were moved out of their barracks into tents to match the conditions of the unfinished POW barracks. The Germans did not respond in kind.

The second premise in America's care for its prisoners in enemy hands was to tread lightly in applying diplomatic pressure on the Germans. Washington felt that holding the German government accountable might have angered the German authorities. As curious as it sounds, Washington was too concerned about jeopardizing the conditions of its soldiers in enemy hands to complain about the conditions of its soldiers in enemy hands.

Moreover, the international POW inspection system placed America's interests in the hands of the Swiss—substantially pro-Nazi—so that Swiss inspections of American captives in German camps overlooked numerous violations. Washington knew, of course, but continued to follow the path of least resistance. In fact, the War Department regularly lied to angry relatives who were pushing the State Department to be more aggressive on behalf of their young men in German captivity that, "there was an average surplus at the major German POW camps housing American prisoners of at least a fifteen-week supply of Red Cross parcels"[10] — patently untrue.

It wasn't until the approaching election in November 1944, that politicians, whether for or against Franklin Roosevelt's fourth term, began to "sympathize" with the problems of their constituents. By the end of the war, families were contacting their congressmen regularly to complain about the government's slow efforts to protect or feed their husbands, sons, and brothers. But, again, little actually changed.

Not until April 12, 1945, when the end of the war was only weeks away, did Secretary of War Henry Stimson and Secretary of State Edward Stettinius concede that the government was aware of the "deplorable conditions" suffered by the American prisoners in Germany. They said, however, that, "the American Red Cross through the International Red Cross has been doing and is doing everything within their power to get relief to the American prisoners." The American people, the two secretaries promised, "'will not forget' the criminal Nazi treatment of the prisoners."[11] The records indicate that no particular effort was made to punish Germany's mistreatment of American prisoners. In fact, even the seventy-four SS murderers responsible for the execution of eighty-one American POWs at Malmédy, Belgium, during the Battle of the Bulge—every convicted killer, including twenty-nine year old SS-Lieutenant Colonel Joachim Peiper and SS-General Sepp Dietrich—were free within eleven years, despite Washington's bombastic threats against anyone who treated American prisoners badly.

One atrocity led to another. Lest it be overlooked by history, the news of the Malmédy Massacre spread rapidly through the American ranks. On January 1, 1945, an American unit in the nearby Belgian town of Chenogne murdered sixty helpless German POWs in retaliation. An eyewitness account by John Fague of B Company, 21st Armored Infantry Battalion, described the so-called Chenogne Massacre of German prisoners by American soldiers in the following words.

> Some of the boys had some prisoners line up. I knew they were going to shoot them, and I hated this business.... They marched the prisoners back up the hill to murder them with the rest of the prisoners we had secured that morning.... As we were going up the hill out of town, I know some of our boys were lining up German prisoners in the fields on both sides of the road. There must have been 25 or 30 German boys in each group. Machine guns were being set up. These boys were to be machine gunned and murdered. We were committing the same crimes we were now accusing the Japs and Germans of doing.[12]

Their guilt went unpunished.

While American prisoners in Germany were held in "deplorable conditions" and survived on Red Cross parcels, German prisoners in American hands, more than 371,000 of them from 1942 to 1945, were treated extremely well. Officers occasionally received wine and beer with their evening meals, sports events, and theatre productions occupied their weekends, and while enlisted men were employed at nearby farms, former prisoners held in the United States recall their experiences as "the best time of their lives."[13] They were returned to Europe, one and all, between 1945 and 1946. The single four-year experience, between 1942 and 1946, was the pinnacle of POW treatment in recorded memory. Not before the Second World War nor any war since have several hundred thousand POWs been as consistently well treated by the enemy so long a period.

Prisoner conditions deteriorated substantially during the later Korean War, 1950–1953, and the Vietnam War, 1954–1974, partly a result of the changes in warfare, the racist antagonism between the enemies, and America's reliance for POW treatment on its South Korean and, in a later conflict, South Vietnamese allies.

Thus, POWs have clearly been treated vastly differently from century to century and from battle to battle. Sometimes they were ransomed or treated with chivalry, more frequently they were tortured, enslaved, or murdered. While it would be comforting to imagine that the care and protection of war prisoners has steadily improved over the centuries, the facts indicate otherwise. While the Roman legions routinely slaughtered its prisoners, so also did the Soviet Army kill its German prisoners (and vice versa) 2000 years later during World War II. Prisoners during the Hundred Years' War of the fourteenth century were beaten, starved, and murdered, as were Allied war prisoners of the Japanese 600 years later during World War II.

Given the wide variation in the treatment of POWs throughout history, from torture and cruel death to courtesy and entertainment, the question is:

Is there any indication about how a prisoner might be treated in wars, past, present, and future? And the answer is a very cautious "Yes."

Clearly, there is no way to calculate the many factors influencing the outcome of a prisoner's fate—the weather, the personalities of their leaders, the duration of the battle, etc.—but, broad generalizations are quite informative. The benefit of such speculation is to examine the differences in the treatment of POWs in search for patterns of behavior and the odds of a prisoner's survival in a given type of war. The key is not in the era or weapons used but, to a certain extent, in the type of war being fought.

Wars are not alike, of course. Nations and armies clash for many reasons, religious or ideological or for territorial aggrandizement, and it is these various categories of wars that will generally predict the prisoner's future.

Racial Wars

Wars that pit one race against another, whether for dominance, extermination, or exploitation, offer the worst outcome for a prisoner of either side. One cannot change one's race, of course, so any conflict between races which might produce war prisoners also affords those prisoners no protection from a continuation of the racial war. That is to say, the racial hatreds which led to the conflict between two races will affect the prisoners, regardless of the color of the winner ror loser.

One need go no further than to examine America's own conflicts with Native Americans, the Indians. Although there are doubtless exceptions, whites and Indians massacred their prisoners in most skirmishes, rather than enslave, parole, or offer them an opportunity to change sides. There are plenty of examples: the Fetterman Massacre in December 1866, saw eight Sioux killed and mutilated, or the Sand Creek Massacre on November 1864 in which 150–200 Cheyenne killed, or, for that matter, the Battle of Little Bighorn on June 25, 1876, in which Lieutenant Colonel George Custer and all his 211 men were killed and their bodies mutilated by Sioux and Cheyenne—prisoners stood little chance of survival.

A shift in public policy during the Civil War years saw the government refrain from killing Native American prisoners, rather taking them to reservations. It began slowly enough. For example, a band of Nez Perce Indians, led by Chief Joseph, were tracked down by the U.S. Army on October 5, 1877, and captured just forty miles from the Canadian border. They were shackled but allowed to live. Although decades earlier they would surely have been killed, they were now exiled to reservations in Kansas and Oklahoma. Eventually, the Nez Perce were resettled on the Colville Reservation in Washington Territory, nearer their traditional homeland.

Two years later a group of Cheyenne Indians, led by Chief Dull Knife, escaped from a holding pen at Fort Robinson, Nebraska, on January 9, 1879; thirty were killed, but the remaining prisoners were herded to a reservation in Montana.

In another case, at the end of the Apache Wars (1870–1886), a band of Chiricahua and Warm Springs Apaches were subdued but not killed; instead, on September 3, 1886, they were shipped off to prison in Florida. Eventually, the last remaining band of Warm Springs Apaches, led by Geronimo, turned themselves in to the U.S. Army 10th Cavalry, and they were shipped to reservations in Oklahoma. Thus, until public opinion began to soften toward America's native Indians in the 1880s and 1890s, prisoners in racial conflicts stood little chance of survival.

The American Civil War, fought over the issue of slavery as well as states' rights, often evolved into a racial conflict. Although both sides were primarily white, the Northern Army fielded numerous units of black soldiers, some former slaves but most were free born blacks living in the North. The Confederacy, however, found the prospect of black men in uniform unthinkable and openly unprotected by any military agreement. Negro soldiers wearing Northern Blue were more than simply war prisoners; in the eyes of Southern whites they were armed former slaves spreading a revolutionary doctrine. They were generally murdered when captured by Confederate troops.[14]

Perhaps most notorious was the massacre at Ft. Pillow in 1864. On April 12, two Confederate cavalry brigades totalling 1,800 men, commanded by General Nathan Bedford Forrest, stormed a garrison near Memphis, Tennessee, slaughtering an unnecessarily large number of captured Union soldiers. Despite earlier assurances of decent treatment, the 580 Federal soldiers—295 white and 262 black—were attacked by frenzied Confederates and randomly murdered. It is true that both whites and blacks were indiscriminately killed, but the black soldiers among them were chased down and tortured. They were drowned, nailed to barn walls and wooden tent floors, and burned alive. Some thirty black soldiers were found in the fort hospital and shot, after which the building was burned to the ground. "A number of Negro troops were drowned while they were trying to escape," admitted a defiant Tennessee historian, "but it was a proper military act to fire upon these men in the water, because there had not been an [official] surrender."[15]

Of those black soldiers who survived, a dozen were returned to their white "owners" in Tennessee and two unfortunate free Negro prisoners from Massachusetts were sold into slavery in faraway Texas. The numbers have been challenged by several Southern historians. That General Forrest's name is associated with slave trading as well as the creation of the Ku Klux Klan only heightens the conviction that black prisoners were singled out and intentionally killed. The cause is understandable, according to a Tennessee historian, since

> While the truce was in effect some of the Negro troops discharged their pieces and used language that was offensive to the attackers and also made offensive gestures with their hands. Forrest's men now seethed with anger.... The sworn testimony of a large number of honorable and trustworthy men established this fact.[16]

One thing is clear: while both whites and blacks were murdered, black troops suffered the worst:, 77 percent were killed or wounded to 43 percent of the white soldiers.[17]

Another dramatic example may be cited during the same period in Africa, where a series of wars and skirmishes between the advancing British army and the Zulu tribes automatically spelled death for the prisoners of either side. For instance, in the Zulu victory at the Battle of Isandlwana (on January 22, 1879), only sixty whites out of 800 somehow managed to survive and 400 blacks, of a total of 900, escaped with their lives. Similarly, in the British victory at the Battle of Khambula (on March 29, 1879), British troops chased the retreating Zulus for twelve miles across the open scrubland, killing any blacks who attempted to hide or surrender along the way. About 3,000 Zulu warriors were killed during or after the battle.

Black prisoners did no better in the German battles to subdue revolting Herero tribesmen in South West Africa in 1904. Germany's Kaiser, Wilhelm II, turned the matter over to the German General Staff who turned to General Lothar von Trotha. After the battle of Waterberg, von Trotha chased the Herero from waterhole to waterhole, murdering stragglers and driving them by the thousands into the Omaheke Desert. A majority of the Herero men, women, and children, were killed. Armed or unarmed, captive or not, the German troops rode them down. On July 9, 1904, von Trotha issued orders to his troops that "no quarter was to be given to the enemy. No prisoners were to be taken, but all, regardless of age or sex, were to be killed. We must exterminate them, so that we won't be bothered with rebellions in the future." [18]

Such brutality toward war prisoners was hardly restricted to the nineteenth century or before. In the mid-twentieth century, for example, the Second World War in the Pacific was racial at its heart for both parties. The death rate was high for white Europeans, Australians,[19] and Americans in Japanese hands, just as few Japanese prisoners in Allied hands made it from the front lines to the intelligence interrogators alive.

The Japanese treated the Chinese, Filipinos, and Koreans with undisguised racial revulsion, and the propaganda of all sides hammered home their racial superiority while ridiculing the other.

The Korean War (1950–1953) saw the notorious brutalization of American and British prisoners. Four months after the war began in Korea in June, 1950, the entry of Chinese troops increased the ferocity of the fighting and introduced a relatively new concept: war of ideologies, for which the United Nations prisoners were wholly unprepared. They had expected brutal treatment if they were captured, but did not think of themselves as students of politics. Returning veterans brought back stories of torture and disease, being squeezed into small boxes for weeks and months, forced to march in the snow without shoes for fifty miles and more, held in prolonged darkness, and notoriously, brainwashed. Chinese "re-education" was based on the premise that there was only one truth, communism, and a prisoners' refusal to accept it was his choice, and warranted increased prolonged torture.[20]

Indeed, the Chinese, as well as the North Koreans and the North Vietnamese—all formally known as People's Republics—convinced themselves, and sometimes their victims, that the torture they were undergoing was their own fault. A favorite scenario was to force the POWs to stand on tiptoe with a tightening noose around their necks or hold them under water, while reminding them that they were able to stop the pain and terror with a simple confession of their political errors.

Such treatment was usually a distraction, however. Executions were more efficient and final. North Korean and Chinese soldiers massacred American prisoners. On October 20, 1950, for example, approximately seventy-five Americans were shot dead by North Korean soldiers at what became known as the Sunchow Tunnel Massacre. A year later, at Kujang-dong, thirty American pilots were bayoneted and shot by North Korean soldiers. Of the 7,190 American soldiers who fell into North Korean hands as POWs, only 4,428 lived to return home. An astonishingly high 2,730 died in captivity, which translates to a death rate of 38 percent (compared to a 45 percent death rate for WW II German POWs in Soviet camps, and a 65 percent death rate for WW II Russians in German camps). In fact, 2,195 American servicemen are still missing in action and presumably a percentage died at the hands of the enemy.[21]

And, the American government hardly cared. Washington's lack of concern for its POWs, evident during World War II, extended to the Korean conflict and beyond. Recently declassified documents show that the Pentagon knew as early as December 1953 that more than 900 American troops were alive at the end of the war but never released by the North Koreans.

Historians of the Korean War have implied that the Eisenhower Administration decided not to tell the American public for fear of provoking a war with China or the Soviet Union by pressing them on the issue. In 1992, the U.S. Senate Select Committee on POWs and MIAs (Missing in Action) revealed that "The Government 'has covered up what it knew through a pattern of denial, misleading statements and, in some cases lies,' and asserted that the American prisoners had been transferred to China and the Soviet Union after the Korean War ended in 1953, and suggested that some might still be alive."[22]

North Korean prisoners were not particularly well treated. In the case of America's treatment of North Korean prisoners, America solved the problem by passing the problem to its South Korean ally. Given the language barrier and the knowledge of one another's cultural vulnerabilities, the South Koreans seemed best for the job. But their brutality toward prisoners was startling, even to their American combat comrades.

American POWs in the Vietnam War, 1954 to 1975, suffered similarly barbaric conditions at infamous prisons like Bang Liet (nicknamed "Skid Row"), Son Tay ("Hope"), Xom Ap Lo ("Briarpatch") and Hoa Lo (the infamous "Hanoi Hilton"), and at least fifteen others. There they were subjected to chronic malaria, dysentery, starvation, insufficient shelter and food, torture, and such notorious punishments as being hanged from the ceiling or dragged on the ground with a broken leg. Some former prisoners such as U.S. Senator John McCain managed to survive as much as five years of such torture and isolation.

The "brainwashing" of American POWs in Vietnam was nearly identical to the political indoctrination of American prisoners during the Korean War two decades earlier, and both were learned from the Chinese. According to the noted management psychologist Edgar H. Schein, American captives were told that they were misguided innocents who had been "tricked into fighting for an evil capitalist society" in a faraway civil war. They were promised leniency, encouraged to discuss politics, values and beliefs, and write an autobiography. They were fed carefully controlled world news. Recalcitrant prisoners were subjected to the increasing terror of intimidation and torture.[23]

An authoritative source states that 771 American servicemen were held as POWs in Vietnam, 113 of whom died in captivity, for a death rate of roughly 15 percent.[24] However, when the war ended and American forces were withdrawn in 1973, an additional 2,214 American soldiers remained unaccounted for, and were assumed to be POWs. Both Washington and Hanoi maintain that no POWs remain in Vietnam, despite some 1,600 first-hand sightings over the past thirty years. Controversy about their fate is still debated in the United States and black M.I.A. flags continue to flutter from flagpoles across the country.[25]

"If the Vietnamese communists were fully cooperating as purported," roared Michael D. Benge, a civilian POW in Vietnam for five years, to a Congressional Committee in November 1999, "they would have told us the true fate of the 173 U.S. servicemen who were last known to be alive and in the hands of the North Vietnamese communists. . . . [They would also] . . . reveal the names of the Cuban [interrogators]. . . . 'Fidel,' 'Chico,' and 'Pancho,' who were responsible for the torture of nineteen American POWs; beating one so severely that it resulted in his death." Even worse, "upon their return to the U.S., the POWs in the 'Cuban Program' were told by [the American] government not to tell of their torture by the Cubans, but they resisted, as they had in the 'Cuban Program,' and some broke the silence. Regardless, the 'Cuban Program' was swept under the rug by the U.S. Government."[26]

In fact, many governments have swept POW matters under the rug. Crimes against POWs often make it difficult to resume diplomatic relations after the war. It is sometimes easier to look the other way and ignore troublesome complaints of torture or malnutrition. According to noted U.S. military historian, Frederick Kiley, "the French cannot account within 10,000 how many of its forces were actually POWs during the earlier Indochina War. The Pakistanis might come within 100,000 for their fighting with the Bengalis and the Indians. There is no calculating the number of Central Africans who have died in captivity in the past thirty years."[27]

The National Liberation Front (NLF) and North Vietnamese enemy prisoners were treated somewhat better by the American forces, but only marginally. They were generally trussed up, blindfolded, and slapped or prodded along as they were moved to the rear to be interrogated. On occasion an enemy prisoner was killed by an overzealous intelligence officer or by angry, frustrated soldiers. Officially, however, all enemy prisoners were supposed to be turned over to America's South Vietnamese allies and were not technically America's responsibility.

Religious Wars

One of man's most primitive instincts revolves around religion. Indeed, few causes evoke as much passion or cruelty as religion. More wars have been fought in the name of God than for any other reason in history. It doesn't seem to matter whether the conflict revolves around two different religions, such as the crusades of the eleventh century which pitted Europe's Christians against the Muslims in Palestine, or warring factions of the same religion such as the current violent Middle Eastern struggle between the Shiite and Sunni Muslims. True believers cannot tolerate compromise in matters of faith and the clash of two religious certainties will not bode well for the losers. The relationship between Man and his gods is sacrosanct; religion provides the rules of life, of behavior, and promises of life eternal. It is a deeply personal relationship and in many cultures religion defines the individual. In a conflict between different religions or factions within the same religion, each side portrays the other as satanic and a heretic false faith. If both sides are committed enough to their religions to go to war, what is one to do with the losers? Having lost the struggle indicates that one god has triumphed over the other and the religion built around the weaker god is suspect, if not defunct. The war prisoners from the losing side, if they wish to survive, must be willing to convert, and quickly. If not, they would continue to represent the hated enemy religion, and it is doubtful if the representatives of a defeated god would be treated well or even dispatched with humanity.

In cultures such as the Aztecs in Middle America, POWs did not have an opportunity to be redeemed or converted in any way. They were captured to be used in a religious ritual—in which they were eaten. When Cortez and his men arrived in Mexico in 1519, they were stunned to see what the Aztecs had been doing for untold centuries, a surprising revulsion coming from Spaniards whose own culture sanctified the breaking of bones on the racks of the Inquisition, the tearing apart of limbs by horse tugs-of-war, and burnings at the stake. However, when Moctezuma, the last Aztec king, invited his Spanish guests to climb the 114 steps to the top of the pyramid at Tenochtitlan (today located in the center of Mexico City), to witness the endless ritual murders to please their gods, Cortez was, instead, distracted by the enormous wealth and power of the Aztec empire spread out before them. The Spaniards also learned that the main source of food for the Aztec gods were war prisoners. Cortez and his men stared dumbly at the panorama of thousands of people who patiently marched up to the pyramid in lines sometimes two miles long, to be seized by four blood-soaked priests, spread-eagled backward over the stone alter while a fifth priest cut open the prisoner's chest with an obsidian knife to wrench out his beating heart. The heart was pushed through the gaping mouth of the god Uitzilopochtli to fall to the packs of dogs waiting below, and the lifeless body was kicked down the steep slope of the pyramid to the Aztec population who cooked and devoured it. The entire event took only minutes to complete.[28]

To be taken prisoner by the Aztecs—or, for that matter—any of numerous cultures from Brazil to the Iroquois Indians of the American Great Lakes—often meant that you ended in the stomachs of your captors.

Civil Wars

Civil wars are particularly brutal. When a nation is torn apart by an internal war in which both sides share the same nationality or language or culture, the result is a particularly angry struggle. The situation is made worse when both sides are evenly matched and the conflict is protracted. If the civil war is brief, such as the relatively short civil war in Austria, from February 12 to February 16, 1934, hatreds do not have enough time to solidify or amplify, although even in Austria's short uprising between the socialists (represented by the Social Democratic Party of Austria) and the conservatives (Christian Social Party), which took place principally in the cities of Vienna and Linz, several hundred people died in the armed conflict.

The best civil war, from the point of prisoners' ability to survive, is one which reaches a conclusion, any conclusion, as quickly as possible. Unfortunately, history leans toward prolonged civil wars, producing hurts and hatreds that extend for generations. Examples abound. The English Civil War of the 1640s, fought between the supporters of absolute monarchy and the supporters of the Parliament determined to bring the monarchy under its control, is peppered with prisoner atrocities. Prisoners were routinely skinned, burned, had large amounts of urine forced down their throats through a funnel, a rope was twisted around the forehead until the victim's eyes burst from their sockets. In some cases, such as the mass surrender of the garrison of Hopton Castle in March 1644 to the Royalist troops, the assumption was that their lives would be spared. However, the prisoners were " bound together, stripped naked despite the cold and their wounds, and turned over to the common soldiers who presently fell upon them, wounding them grievously. They drove them into a cellar unfinished, wherein was stinking water, the house being on fire over them, when they were every man [. . .] presently massacred. Most of the victims were clubbed to death.[29]

Costa Rican Civil War of 1948

On the other hand, even brief civil wars, such as the Costa Rican Civil War which lasted only six weeks (March 12–April 19, 1948), witnessed the deaths of more than 2,000 people. The bloodiest war in twentieth century Costa Rican history began after the ruling National Republicans annulled the election, in which Otilio Ulate Blanco of the Social Democratic Party was elected. Jose Figueres Ferrer, an exiled businessman, along with about 700 revolutionaries calling themselves the Caribbean Legion planned to overthrow the Costa

Rican government. Jose Ferrer and the Caribbean Legion, with arms supplied by the Guatemalan government, successfully took over the government in forty-four days. The Battle of El Tejar was the bloodiest conflict of the war with 400 casualties and 190 dead. The Caribbean Legion only lost fourteen at that battle. In fact, of the 2,000 soldiers killed throughout the entire war, fewer than a hundred were from the Legion. The revolutionaries captured no prisoners; they were simply killed.

Pakistan Civil War of 1971

In the 1970 Pakistani elections, the East Pakistani Awami League won a clear majority: 167 out of 169 seats in the East Pakistan parliament. Because West Pakistan had the political power, the victory was ignored. With a history of injustice and discrimination from West Pakistan, this event was the last straw that forced East Pakistan to revolt and declare its independence. The Pakistan Civil War lasted for roughly nine months, from March 26 until December 16, 1971. On March 27, 1971, the Prime Minister of India, Indira Gandhi expressed full support for the Bangladeshi war of liberation. The war turned into a conflict between India and Pakistan. At the same time, the Pakistani military, composed largely of West Pakistanis, embarked on a program of mass arrests and murder, systematically killing a large number of doctors, teachers, and students—the Hindu minority who made up the urban educated intellectuals. While the war resulted in the independence of East Pakistan, now called Bangladesh, the genocide of 1,500,000 East Pakistanis by the West Pakistani government on March 26, 1971, is considered one of the bloodiest events of the twentieth century.

Russian Civil War (1917–1921)

The Russian Civil War began after the Bolshevik takeover in 1917. An opposition army, the Whites, arose immediately, made up of a wide spectrum of anti-communists, monarchists, Cossacks, and military expeditionary forces from America and Japan. German troops and Czech prisoners of war and bandits of every political stripe wandered the vast war-torn country. In the resulting chaos, prisoners from any side were generally shot out of hand, or put to work as forced laborers. Thousands were pressed into service into the army of whoever captured them. Diaries of the participants are peppered with entries like the following: "We drag prisoners with us all the time, then hand them over to the authority of escort troops. Some did not make it that far, as it was not uncommon for the soldiers to murder prisoners without inquiries." From the same diary we read, "Prisoners were brought in, one, completely fit was then shot . . . by a Red Army man for no reason at all . . . . The prisoners are rounded up, made to undress, a strange scene, they undress quickly, shaking their heads, all this out in the sun, a bit embarrassing, all the commanders are there . . . but who cares, shut your eyes to it.... I couldn't look at their faces, they bayoneted some, shot others, bodies covered by corpses, they strip one man while they're shooting another, groans, screams...."[30]

From another diarist, "Krasotkin had been taken prisoner in 1918, after the rout of the Second Caucasian Army. He had survived mass shootings of prisoners; he himself was maimed during some sort of excesses taken with prisoners. His fingers had been cut off, he was wounded in the forearm, and one hand no longer functioned.[31]

The war between the Red Army and White Army continued until 1921, when the Red Army won and established the Soviet Union.

The Algerian Civil War 1991–2002

The Algerian Civil War was particularly brutal. In 1990, the Islamic Salvation Front (FIS) won local elections, and it was projected that they would win the national elections by a landslide. Alarmed at the prospect, the Algerian government cancelled the elections and thus began the civil war. Thousands of Islamic FIS guerrilla fighters took to the hills, while the Algerian government rounded up and imprisoned thousands more. For the next bloody decade, the killing of captured guerrilla fighters was the norm, and witnesses testified to the torture of prisoners with electric drills by the Algerian army during interrogations in so-called "killing rooms." With stunning audacity, the police later ransomed their broken bodies to their relatives. After the passage of a clemency law by which several prisoners were released, the Algerian government simply ceased taking prisoners, killing any suspected guerrillas on the spot.

Conclusion

Regardless of the legitimacy of the issues, civil wars are especially violent. Whether due to the frustration of failing to win over the other side, the inability to distinguish between friend and foe, or the open-ended nature of the struggle, a civil war is especially ruthless. Prisoners captured during a civil war are rarely treated humanely. Prisoners are seldom spared, whether it is in the English Civil War 350 years ago, or more recent conflicts like the American Civil War between the Union and the Confederacy (1861 to 1865), the bloody Russian Civil War between the new Soviet government and the anti-communists and monarchists (1918 to 1921), or the civil war in Spain between the legally-elected Republic and the military rebellion (1936 to 1939), which claimed as many as one million lives.

Even those war prisoners who survived the battles were herded into the appalling poor conditions of the notorious prison camps of both sides. During the American Civil War, in fact, 26,436 Southern soldiers died in Northern prisons and 22,576 Northerners died in Southern prisons: indeed, more soldiers died in prisons than were killed in the battles of Shiloh, Chancellorsville, Gettysburg, Sharpsburg, and Chickamauga combined. Long periods of mistreatment were punctuated by unexpected pauses or, more often, by sudden and even more brutality.[32]

The key to survival in civil wars appears to be *when* a prisoner is captured. That is to say, the protection and care of captives in a civil war may be likened to a roller coaster: treatment breaks down, stops, starts again, and depending on the level of war hysteria, a captive's safety depends largely on when he got on the roller coaster.

Political or Nationalistic Wars

Nationalism is among the most stirring, unifying, and destructive forces of modern times. Ignited by a yearning for self-rule and the restoration of customs and traditions, nationalism sparked numerous revolts across Europe and produced wars of liberation and violent mass movements. Until the mid-1600s, people generally fought over religious differences, political domination, and plain greed, but seldom over matters of differing political or nationalistic ideologies. Nations fought nations or race fought race or "haves" and "have-nots" turned to war for a solution. Historians generally agree that the French Revolution in 1789 spawned the ethereal concept of "nation"—a cause worth dying for. Prior to the French Revolution people were willing to fight and die for their tribe or family, perhaps for their king. But, the concept of "nation" and its symbolic representation of a flag or anthem was intangible. Where is the "nation?" Is the national flag or anthem interchangeable with the nation? How did it become a criminal act to burn the nation's flag? Anyone who cannot imagine the power of nationalistic tribalism need only watch the antics of berserk fans at the international soccer matches. And who couldn't love the words of the French anthem, La Marseillaise, that "we will water our furrows with impure blood." When such passion is improperly harnessed it leads to war. And wars produce prisoners.

In addition to nationalism as a driving force for war, another recent motivation for conflict is political ideology. Political ideology is a world-view or, even better, a secular religion. Some call it revolution. The best examples in the twentieth century of nations driven by their political ideologies are fascism and communism—struggles between them litter the century. Like religious wars, if the captive recants his ideology, he may be freed. The Red Chinese spared captured Nationalists in 1949–1950 whenever the captives confessed, repented, and reformed. The Viet Mihn spared Algerians captured at Dien Bien Phu in 1954 because Ho Chi Minh considered them fellow victims of French oppression. Israel's treatment of Arab soldiers, especially Egyptians, has depended largely on the prisoner's level of aggression and potential danger, and the United Nations' decent treatment of captured North Koreans resulted in three-quarters of them refusing repatriation back to the North in 1953.

Sometimes, nations consider their own repatriated POWs as "infected" or "cowardly" and treat their returning citizens as untrustworthy or worse. Post-World War II, Japan considered its soldiers returning from Allied prisoner or war camps as profoundly shamed, at best, and "soulless" at worst. Decades were to pass before former POWs felt comfortable enough to acknowledge their wartime experience.[33]

Stalin's Soviet Union viewed its returned POWs not as "soulless ghosts" but as traitors and deserters. Stalin demanded the forcible return of all Soviet prisoners liberated from Nazi captivity in 1945, and with the full knowledge of the rest of the world, hundreds of thousands of Russian war prisoners were handed over to meet their doom. Most disappeared into the Russian slave labor system.[34]

Since the degree of worship to a cause is determined by the beholder, ideological or religious conflicts are often unregulated and especially bloody.

Wars for Territory

Wars for territory are the old-fashioned conflicts we are most familiar with—and we can point at random to the French attack of Britain in 1066, the German attack against Holland in 1940, or Italy's attack against Ethiopia in 1935. The goal—however cloaked in noble slogans—has been to seize the territory or the belongings (geographical or economic) of another country, permanently or temporarily. Territorial expansion was the hallmark of the nineteenth and twentieth centuries through two world wars and dozens of smaller conflicts. Wars were no longer fought to protect or defend the homeland, but to secure additional territory, and the execution, enslavement, beating, and incarceration of war prisoners saw few limits

More and more often, wars are fought between political ideologies, especially in the twentieth and twenty-first centuries—first between Nazism and Communism, then a lengthy Cold War between Communism and Capitalism, and currently between radical Muslims and the West—which dramatically complicates the chances of survival for war captives. The more variables, the more dangerous for prisoners. The struggle between Russia and Germany on the Eastern Front during World War II had *two* motives (territorial aggrandizement and political ideology). But this particular war added a *third* agenda: nationalism, where a population of wild-eyed and disciplined people committed their lives and future to a secular religion as determined by the dictatorial leadership of their nation. Millions paid the price for this lunacy.

Further, the Second World War had a *fourth* motive: racial hatred (since the Germans considered the Slavs to be subhuman). An example is the murderous treatment by the Germans of Soviet-Jewish POWs, combining anti-Semitism, anti-Slavic racism, contrasting political ideology, territorial expansion, and, nationalism, as well.[35] With *four* motives, much less *five*, the chances that war prisoners would survive dropped precipitously. The facts bear this out.[36]

The Soviets were equally as savage toward their captive German invaders as were the German occupiers to theirs. Most disappeared into the chaotic Soviet slave labor system. Thousands froze to death or were starved as they marched toward Siberia, long lines of emaciated men plodding into the blinding snow. Over the next years they were used to construct huge, labor-intensive projects ranging from railroad lines and power plants, to the Moscow Metro, and gold mines in Eastern Siberia. Of the 3,035,700 Germans taken captive by the Red Army during World War II, very few were released. When they did come home, it was in small batches yearly from mid-1947 until the final trainload was released by the Soviets in 1955 (following a last-chance visit to Moscow by Germany's Konrad Adenauer and a legendary vodka-soaked evening of negotiation with Khrushchev and Bulganin in September 1955). The cost to Germany was high: Bulganin only agreed to release the last POWs when the Adenauer administration was willing to establish diplomatic relations with the Soviet Union. The last 9,626 German POWs did not return home until 1956, more than ten years after the end of the war.[37]

Russian POWs captured by the Germans had it worse. Even before the first Russian winter descended on the conflict in 1941, millions of Soviet prisoners were dying in enormous open-air enclosures, subject to the weather and starvation and indiscriminate murder by the German army or being force marched or shipped by cattle cars to POW camps, and concentration camps, and the factories of Germany. Anyone who faltered along the way was executed without thought. According to the expert on the Eastern Front, Omer Bartov, casualty figures for groups of Russian prisoners never dropped below 30 percent and sometimes rose as high as 95 percent.[38] The survivors were, in essence, sentenced to death by slave labor. In point of fact, the Germans killed more Soviet women soldiers than the entire American losses in World War II

Russian prisoners were the "subhumans" used for every dirty job in the Nazi POW and concentration camp system; eventually they became guinea pigs for pseudo-medical experiments and to test the mobile gas vans and the mass gas chambers at Auschwitz. Russian prisoners were murdered or worked to death, although Daniel Goldhagen, author of *Hitler's Willing Executioners*, reminds us that however badly the Russian prisoners were treated the Jews were treated far worse, as unimaginable as that may be. Like a painting by the medieval artist Hieronymus Bosch, skeletal figures in shredded Russian uniforms hovered around flickering campfires, starved and covered with lice, sometimes seen feeding on the corpses of the dead and dying. "The total number of prisoners taken by the German armies in the U.S.S.R. was in the region of 5.5 million," write Peter Calvocoressi and Guy Wint in *Total War*.

> "Of these the astounding number of 3.5 million or more had been lost by the middle of 1944 and the assumption must be that they were either deliberately killed or done to death by criminal negligence. There are few records documenting the actual fates of those 3.5 million, but it is estimated that nearly two million died in camps and close on another million disappeared while in military custody [. . .] a further quarter of a million disappeared or died in transit [. . .] and specific records indicate that yet another 473,000 died or were killed in military custody in Germany or Poland."[39] In the end, of the estimated 5.5 million Russian POWs taken by the Germans, only about

1.8 million starved and brutalized. Russian prisoners were repatriated back to their homeland to face Soviet leader Josef Stalin's dreaded Order No. 270, which declared that all Red Army soldiers who had allowed themselves to be captured alive were "traitors to the Motherland" and were generally destined for the slave labor camps.

On the Western Front in the same war, however, the German Army in Belgium, Holland, and France treated POWs with tolerable care, with one eye on the requirements of the Geneva Convention.

In the past, most battles have resulted in the deaths of the majority of captives, but at least there was a possibility of survival. Their odds drop substantially, however, when the conflict is driven by more than one motive. A combination of, say, race and ideology, or nationalism and ideology, or nationalism and territorial aggrandizement complicates the prospect of survival. Add yet another motive, and the captives have little or no chance.

Clearly, there are numerous combinations of threats facing a prisoner of war and the more motives which drive the war, the less likely he is to survive. Yet, over the centuries, philosophers, theologians, and legal scholars have debated the need for some assurance of protection. Compared with other historic trends, the international concern for the humane treatment and general well-being of POWs has been exceptionally slow and punctuated by sudden returns to barbarism. The highwater mark came after the horrors of World War I with the writing of the Geneva Accords in 1929; those countries which signed the document pledged to abide by the rules. And, with a number of glaring exceptions during the Second World War, they did. In 1949, the Geneva Conventions were updated to cover new or habitually violated situations. More recently, since the terrorist attack on September 11, 2001, war has evolved into a clandestine conflict in which nation-states are locked in combat with movements, not other nations, and requires a reconsideration of prisoner protection. For a short period, however, 1941 to 1946, modern history saw the most humane treatment of POWs—when America held 371,000 German POWs, 53,000 Italians, and 5,000 Japanese soldiers, in 650 main and branch camps across the United States.

Notes

1. Theodore Meron, "Shakespeare's Henry the Fifth and the Law of War," *The American Journal of International Law*, 86(1) (January 1992), 1–45.

2. Barbara Donagan, "Prisoners in the English Civil War," *History Today*, Vol. 41, (March 1991), 28–35.

3. See Hugo Grotius *On the Law of War and Peace,* translated from the original Latin De Jure Belli ac Pacis by A.C. Campbell, A.M. (Kitchener, Ontario, Canada: Batoche Books, 2001), 323–324. Also Theodor Meron, "Shakespeare's 'Henry the Fifth' and the Law of War," *The American Journal of International Law*, 86 (1) (Jan. 1992), 37.

4. George DeWan, "The Wretched Prison Ships," *Newsday*, July 4, 2006.

5. See Larry G. Bowman, *Captive Americans: Prisoners during the American Revolution* (Athens: Ohio University Press, 1976), also see Report of a Committee, Massachusetts Historical Society, Exchange of Prisoners, The American Revolutionary War, Presented on December 19, 1861 (Boston: Printed for the Society, 1861).

6. George G. Phillimore, Hugh H.L. Bellot, "Treatment of Prisoners of War," *Transactions of the Grotius Society*, Vol. 5, Problems of Peace and War, Papers Read before the Society of the Year 1919, (1919), 47–64. Edna Jo Hunter, *Families in Crisis: The Families of Prisoners of War* (Center for Prisoner of War Studies, Naval Health Research Center, San Diego, CA). Dr. Edna Jo Hunter, expert on military families and prisoners of war, is the first woman named as distinguished military psychologist of the American Psychological Association; she served on the faculty of the U.S. Military Academy at West Point, where she was awarded the Living Legacy Award in 1992.

7. Arnold Krammer, "The Treatment of German Generals in America during WW II," *Journal of Military History,* 54(1) January 1990, 27–46.

8. Roger Cohen, "What the Nazis Did to Jewish G.I.s," *The New York Times Magazine*, February 27, 2005, 46–51, 82, 90, 111–112. See also, Hal Lister, *Krautland Calling: An American POW Radio Broadcaster in Nazi Germany* (Austin, TX: Eakin Publisher, 1990); and Daniel B. Drooz, *American Prisoners of War in German Death, Concentration, and Slave Labor Camps* (Lewiston, New York: Edwin Mellon Press, 2003).

9. Colin Rushton, *Spectator in Hell* (Berkshire, England: Pharoah Press, 1998), pp. 51–53; 63–130.

10. Arieh J. Kochavi, *Confronting Captivity: Britain and the United States and their POWs in Nazi Germany* (Chapel Hill: University of North Carolina Press, 2005), 92.

11. "Brutal Neglect of Prisoners Known to U.S.", *New York Times*, April 12, 1945. Families of American POWs were especially vulnerable. See Edna Jo Hunter, *Families in Crisis*, op. cit.

12. John Fague, *B Company 21st Artillery Observation Battalion* (Thunderbolt Unit Histories, 2006).

13. Arnold Krammer, *Nazi Prisoners of War in America* (Lanham, MD: Scarborough, 1996).

14. Gregory J.W. Urwin, "'We Cannot Treat Negroes...as Prisoners of War': Racial Atrocities and Reprisals in Civil War Arkansas," *Civil War History*, 42(3) 1996, 193–210; Richard J. Sommers, "The Dutch Gap Affair: Military Atrocities and Rights of Negro Soldiers," *Civil War History*, 21(1) (1975), 51–64.

15. John L. Jordan, "Was There a Massacre at Ft. Pillow?" *Tennessee Historical Quarterly,* (March–December 1947), 119.

16. Jordan, "Was There a Massacre at Fort Pillow?" op. cit., 108.

17. James Ford Rhodes, *History of the United States of America*, Vol. 5, Chapter 29, (New York, 1904, 1920 ed.), 512. See also, Gregory J.W. Urwin, "'We Cannot Treat Negroes...As Prisoners of War': Racial Atrocities and Reprisals in Civil War Arkansas," *Civil War History*, 42(3) (1996), 193–210

18. Isabel V. Hull, *Absolute Destruction* (Ithaca and London: Cornell University Press: 2005), 45–46.

19. See Hank Nelson, *P.O.W. Prisoners of War; Australians Under Nippon* (Sydney: ABC Enterprises, 1985).

20. See especially, Ministry of Defence, *Treatment of British Prisoners of War in Korea* (London: Her Majesty's Stationery Office, 1955), 41. Also Lewis H. Carlson, *Remembered Prisoners of a Forgotten War* (New York: St. Martin's Press, 2002), and Richard M. Bassett,

And the Wind Blew Cold: The Story of an American POW in North Korea (Kent, OH: Kent State University Press, 2002).

21. See John S. Edwards, ed., *American Ex-Prisoners of War* (Paducah, KY: Turner 1991), 2, 78; POW-MIA Fact Book (Washington, D.C., Department of Defense, July 1991).

22. Steven Holmes, "Hearings Opened on Korea M.I.A.'s," *The New York Times*, November 11, 1992; Philip Shenon, "U.S. Knew in 1953 North Koreans Held American P.O.W.s," *The New York Times*, September 17, 1996; Jill Stewart, "U.S. Families Claim Some Korean POWs May Be Alive," *Los Angeles Times*, July 8, 1990; R. Cort Kirkwood, "Kidnapped!", *Washington (Seattle) Times*, October 19, 1990; and Mark Sauter, "U.S. Government turns its back on POWs," *Washington (Seattle) Times*, October 22, 1990.

23. See Edgar H. Schein (with Inge Schneier and Curtis H. Baker), *Coercive-persuasion: A socio-psychological analysis of the "brain-washing" of the American civilian prisoners by the Chinese Communists* (New York: W.W. Norton, 1961).

24. Frederick Kiley, *The History of American Prisoners of War in Southeast Asia, 1961–1973* (Washington, D.C.: Office of the Secretary of Defense, 1998), Appendix 1, 597.

25. Rod Colvin, *First Heroes: The POWs Left Behind in Vietnam* (New York: Irvington, 1987), 19.

26. Michael D. Benge before the House International Relations Committee Chaired by the Honorable Benjamin A. Gilman, November 4, 1999.

27. Frederick Kiley, "A Survey of the Treatment of Prisoners of War Since World War II" (Office of the Secretary of Defense), December 1977. American Historical Association Conference, Dallas, TX. December 28–30, 1977.

28. Marvin Harris, *Cannibals and Kings: The Origin of Cultures* (New York: Random House, 1977), 110–124.

29. Barbara Donagan, "Atrocity, War Crime, and Treason in the English Civil War," *The American Historical Review*, 99(4), (Oct. 1994), 1152. The conflict finally ended in 1649 with the monarchy's defeat and the execution of Charles I—shocking events in Europe—but of enormous importance in the years to follow.

30. Isaac Babel, 1920 Diary, edited and with an Introduction by Carol J. Avins, trans. By H.T. Willetts (New Haven, CT: Yale University Press, 1995), xxv, 39, 73.

31. Eduard M. Dune, *Notes of a Red Guard*, trans. and edited by Diane P. Koenker and S.A. Smith (Urbana: University of Illinois Press, 1993), 185.

32. Robert W. Glover, Camp Ford: Tyler Texas, C.S.A. Ann and Lee Lawrence, *East Texas History Series*, Vol. 2 (Nacogdoches, Texas: Stephen F. Austin State University, 1998), 34.

33. Ulrich Straus, *The Anguish of Surrender: Japanese POWs of World War II* (Seattle and London: University of Washington Press, 2003).

34. Nicholas Bethell, *The Last Secret: The Delivery to Stalin of over Two Million Russians by Britain and the U.S.* (New York: Basic Books, 1974).

35. Jonathan North, "Hitler's Forgotten Victims," *World War II Magazine* (January/February 2006), 26–32, 80.

36. Pavel Polian, "First Victims of the Holocaust: Soviet-Jewish Prisoners of War in German Captivity," *Kritika: Explorations in Russian and Eurasian History*, 6(4) (2005), 763–787.

37. G. F. Krivosheev, *Grif sekretnosti sniat: Poteri vooruzhennykh sil SSSR v voinakh boevykh deistviiakh I voennykh konfliktakh* [Losses of the armed forces of the USSR in wars, combat actions, and military conflicts] (Moscow:Voenizdat, 1993), 384–392. Felix von Eckardt, *Ein unordentliches Leben* (A Disorderly Life), (Dusseldorf, Wien: Econ-Verlag,

1967), 367, 409, 411, 413. See also Simon Rees, "German POWs and the Art of Survival," *Military History*, May 2007, 46–53; and Jonathan F. Vance (ed.), *Encyclopedia of Prisoners of War and Internment* (Santa Barbara, Calif.: ABC-CLIO, 2000), 332.

38. Omer Bartov, *The Eastern Front: German Troops and the Barbarism of Warfare* (Basingstoke, Hampshire: Macmillan, in association with St. Anthoney's College, Oxford, 1985), 110.

39. Peter Calvocoressi and Guy Wint, *Total War: The Story of World War II* (New York: Pantheon Books, 1972). See also, *The German Army and Genocide: Crimes against War Prisoners, Jews, and Other Civilians, 1939–1944*, ed. Hamburg Institute for Social Research, New York, 1999.

CHAPTER 3

The Best and the Worst

When America went to war in December 1941, following the Japanese attack on the United States' fleet at Pearl Harbor, Hawaii, the country was left reeling. Four days later, on December 11, Nazi Germany and Italy also declared war on the United States, and the nation mobilized like never before in its history. Everyone realized that this war—named the "Second" World War—might be more costly and last longer than the First, only twenty-five years in the past. Factories geared up for the long haul, and millions of workers—men and women—left the unemployment lines of the Great Depression behind them and rushed into the swelling work force. The military worked feverishly to draft, train, and equip hundreds of thousands of soldiers overnight and ship them to battlefields on two sides of the globe. Industries had to retool, and consumer goods had to be sidelined for war production. New government agencies popped up like mushrooms.

Among the last things of concern to the nation at that time were prisoners of war. Nobody was thinking that far ahead. Moreover, there weren't any precedents. America had hardly any experience with POWs. When America entered World War I in April 1917, a handful of German ships were impounded and their crews placed in camps. Before that, American planners had nothing to learn from except Civil War horrors like Andersonville and Camp Grant.

Yet, the reality was that enemy prisoners would soon be pouring into the United States as the Allies chased Hitler's Afrika Korps from Egypt across North Africa. They were about to participate in the best treatment of large numbers of enemy POWs in recorded history. Between 1942 and 1946, America's superb treatment of some 370,000 German POWs was the pinnacle of the historic development of prisoner protection.

But first, the question was where would Washington put them all? The Provost Marshal General's Office (PMGO), which was in charge of POWs, first turned to abandoned Civilian Conservation Corps camps from the Depression years, unused sections of military bases, fairgrounds, auditoriums, high school gyms, and even tent cities if necessary. As the pith helmeted Afrika Korps troops found themselves caught between the British forces closing on them from the east and American forces from the west, German prisoners were surrendering by the thousands and held in large, sprawling POW camps in North Africa, awaiting shipment to Britain or the United States.

After filling out a Red Cross post card assuring their families that they were alive and in Allied hands, as required by the Geneva Accords (or Convention), each German prisoner was assigned a serial number which would be used throughout his captivity. The first component designated the theater in which he was captured: eighty-one meant North Africa, five indicated the Western Defense Command, and thirty-one meant the European Theater. A German prisoner captured in North Africa, for instance, would therefore have a number that began with 81G, an Italian would have the number beginning with 81I, and an Austrian's number would begin 81A. The rest of the number for any of them was a sequential series, such as 81G-1234.

For the thousands of prisoners who were transferred to the United States in haste, before a number could be assigned, each was given a number beginning with the American Service Command, 1–9, followed by a "W" for War Department, and the first letter of the country which he served. Thus, an incoming German POWs who found himself processed in Oklahoma or Texas, would have a number which might read: 8WG-1234. In April 1943, a bare trickle of 2,146 German POWs arrived in the United States, crammed aboard empty Liberty ships and troop transports returning from North Africa. The very next month, May, the number of incoming German prisoners soared to 22,110, and Italian fascist prisoners to 13,911.

Meanwhile, the number of Japanese military prisoners from the war in the Pacific, always miniscule, rose to sixty-two (as opposed to the roundup and imprisonment of 120,000 innocent Japanese and Japanese-American citizens on the West Coast by the War Relocation program). The incoming prisoners disembarked at Camp Shanks, New York, and from there were marched aboard heavily-guarded plush Pullman trains and transported to hastily-built makeshift camps. No one could know that the numbers would soar to a jaw dropping 422,871 prisoners by mid-summer 1945 (371,683 Germans, 50,273 Italians,[1] and 5,413 Japanese military prisoners), but it was clear that America needed to prepare for the worst. And quickly.

On September 15, 1942, the War Department opened a number of existing military posts which had extra space to contain the arriving prisoners. These included Camp Forrest, Tennessee (capacity for 3,000 prisoners); Camp Clark, Missouri (3,000); Fort Bliss, Texas (1,350); Fort Bragg, North Carolina (140); Fort Devens, Massachusetts (1,000); Fort Meade, Maryland (1,680); Fort Oglethorpe, Georgia (948); Camp McCoy, Wisconsin (100); Fort Sam Houston, Texas (1,000); Camp Sheby, Mississippi (1,200); and Fort Sill, Oklahoma (700).

Meanwhile, the Army's Corp of Engineers shifted into high gear. Rural communities sold or donated tracts of land to the government in the hopes of bringing economic prosperity to their towns, and the Corps of Engineers went to work. The ideal campsite was an area of about 350 acres, five miles from a railroad line, and no less than 500 feet from any important roadway.

Each new camp was constructed according to a standard plan and designed to hold between 2,000 and 4,000 Axis prisoners. The camp was divided into four separate compounds of approximately 500–750 men each. The compounds, in turn, usually had four barracks, built on concrete slabs to deter enthusiastic diggers. The barracks were wooden frame buildings covered with tar paper, with rows of army cots, footlockers for personal items and a potbellied iron stove in the center of the aisle. Each compound of four barracks was surrounded by barbed wire fences. The POW camps were, in effect, camps within camps.

With some variation in camp size, most of America's 155 main POW camps looked remarkably similar.[2] The remaining 450 branch camps and work camps were built to suit the landscape and the size needed. Most were rural but some branch camps were constructed to be close to factories or military bases, such as Camp Crockett which was built in the middle of downtown Galveston Island, Texas. The camp was about four blocks wide and eight blocks long, designed for a total of 650 German POWs. It cut directly across the city's prominent Seawall Boulevard, across the beach, and into the water. Galvestonians frequently watched the German prisoners cavorting in the surf. It's little wonder that people often referred to the compound as "The Fritz Ritz."

Every camp had a mess hall, workshop, canteen, office, shower house, and recreation hall. A wide, flat area served as a combination inspection ground, processing center, and soccer field. All in all, the POW camp looked like any hastily constructed Army training center, except for the barbed-wire and chain-link fences everywhere and guard towers equipped with searchlights at opposite corners. Most POW camp fences had an 8–10 foot "Caution Zone" (or so-called "Death Zone") where any prisoner who strayed too close to the perimeter was liable to be shot.

Lest one think that these "Death Zones" were cosmetic only, consider the following. On October 15, 1943, at Camp Concordia, Kansas, for example, a German prisoner was shot to death while trying to retrieve a soccer ball. Witnesses to the shooting stated that the POWs had been warned several times against chasing the ball beyond the caution line. Adolph Huebner continued to defy the guard's warning and, according to the authorities, deliberately kicked the ball into the forbidden area. He hopped over the rail and ran after the ball, looking back over his shoulder and taunting the sentinel. The guard fired once, shooting him through the head. Another incident occurred at Fort Knox, Kentucky, in November 1944, when two POWs were shot to death by an American guard.

In another case, under different circumstances, a mentally unbalanced German prisoner was shot as he was being transferred from Camp Robinson at Little Rock, Arkansas to Mason General Hospital, a psychiatric institution at Brentwood, Long Island, New York. Traveling aboard a Pennsylvania Railroad passenger train and guarded by two military policemen, Hermann Mattschutt evidently went berserk among the crowded civilian commuters and was shot as he fought to climb through a window of the speeding train.[3]

By the end of the war, a total of fifty-six German prisoners had risked the odds to taunt their guards or escape and were shot to death. Being a prisoner of war, even in wonderful America, could be serious business.

The worst part of being a prisoner of war, particularly prevalent in America where security was relatively light and the outside attractions were many, was boredom. Once the POWs settled in to camp life and took stock of their situation, time would begin to weigh heavy. Washington realized the dangers if the prisoners had too much free time, and provided plenty of comforts and distractions. Each camp maintained handicraft rooms, a library that would usually do credit to a small high school, and a POW-constructed canteen, where the men could buy Cokes, cigarettes, and beer in the evening while they gossiped, wrote letters home, and played ping-pong or checkers. Camp Campbell's (Kentucky) canteen-recreation room boasted a record player and a collection of fifty phonograph records including "Home on the Range," "Missouri Waltz," "Whistling Cowboy," "Tuxedo Junction," "Friendly Tavern Polka," and "Can't Get Indiana Off My Mind." The most popular record at Campbell, as well as at nearly every other camp, was Bing Crosby's "Don't Fence Me In."

The larger camps maintained makeshift theaters for weekly movies, the most popular being grade "B" westerns, gangster films, and cartoons. All had to be approved by the camp authorities for their non-Nazi content. A typical evening would consist of three films: (cartoon): "Andy Panda Goes Fishing," (scientific): "Fire: The Red Poacher," and (feature): "The Gentlemen from West Point," to an audience of as many as 1,000 men. Attendance increased substantially when scantily-dressed stars like Rita Hayworth or Jean Harlow were shown, also giving rise to a spirited but harmless black market in pictures pirated from individual frames by enterprising POW projectionists with photographic experience.

Sports, however, were the most popular pastime. At Camp Opelika, Alabama, POW Alfred Klein recalls that:

> Sports started right after breakfast, and our camp had a whole slate of outstanding teams in soccer, handball, volleyball, etc. Athletic activities were taken very, very seriously. The Camp Championships, especially in soccer and handball, were so exciting that even our guards participated as cheerleaders from their towers and attended games on weekends with their families shouting from the sidelines. Many of our athletes, as a matter of fact, went on to sports careers in Germany after their release.

Next to sports, the most popular pastime was the production of plays and theatrical performances. Every camp had a makeshift theater, usually at the end of the mess hall, in which the POWs performed everything from uproariously funny skits with burly men cavorting about in women's clothing to highly sophisticated three-act plays complete with props and orchestration. A crudely-built electrical system, fashioned from tin cans, controlled the lighting features. Ceiling light fixtures were made by using inverted glass jars. On any Friday or Saturday night at any large prison camp, an enthusiastic audience of several hundred POWs would have been treated to a theatrical performance of some sort; laughing at a little skit set in a French café; hooting and wolf-whistling at a group of hairy and muscular men in Polynesian grass skirts; or listening in rapt attention as Cyrano de Bergerac wooed lovely Roxanne from beneath her balcony. German officers and American camp administrators were always preferential guests, and the occasional visits by representatives of the War Department, Swiss Legation, YMCA or International Red Cross signaled an impressive evening.

The arriving German prisoners were cautious at first, finding their treatment and especially the availability of food beyond their highest hopes. While German prisoners in Russian camps were often reduced to eating rodents and drinking melted snow, the German POWs in America were eating better than they might in their mothers' kitchens at that moment. A bill of fare at Camp Clinton, Mississippi, for example, was as follows:

Breakfast:	Corn Flake
	Cake or Bread
	Marmalade
	Coffee, Milk
	Sugar
Lunch:	Potato Salad
	Roast Pork
	Carrots
	Icewater
Supper:	Meat Loaf
	Scrambled Eggs or Boiled Eggs
	Coffee, Milk
	Bread

Most of the prisoners had grown up being propagandized by their Nazi government and were much relieved to find that they were safe in enemy hands. POW Reinhold Pabel, whose book *Enemies Are Human* chronicled his life as a POW and his legendary escape, recalled that when he arrived at Camp Grant, Illinois

We found our first permanent home. Our shelters were regular army barracks, clean and fairly roomy, with plenty of showers, and a PX, well-stocked with merchandise. What a world of difference between these quarters and those inadequate facilities in Africa!

The 'old' inmates of the camp showered us upon our arrival with icecream, candy, cigarettes and other goodies. When we gathered in the mess halls for our first dinner at camp, we at first suspected that the Yanks wanted to make fun of us. Such a menu: soup, vegetables, meat, milk, fish, grapes, coffee and ice-cream! Never before in our military career had we been served a meal like that.[4]

In fact, they were still in German hands. In order to free as many American soldiers as possible for overseas service, control inside the POW camp was turned over to the german officers. German enlisted men were required to snap to attention when their officers crossed their path. Ironically, the American guards were also instructed to show the same respect to German officers, partially as a military courtesy and partially in the vain hope that American officer prisoners in German hands might be shown reciprocal courtesy.

Discipline at the more than six hundred German POW camps across America was maintained by the German officers themselves; Washington believed that the prisoners would respond better to their own officers, while freeing up American guards to be sent to the frontlines. Periodic inspections of the camps reported that discipline was fair, although troublemakers among the prisoners were no strangers to restricted diets of bread and water, or 10-day stints in the stockade. American authorities sent prisoners to the guard house for infractions like refusing to obey orders, avoiding work details, "laxness" during the morning flag-raising and playing of the National Anthem, or just creating "trouble."

Officers lived apart and, like officers in any army, enjoyed benefits not available to the enlisted men. They often lived in bungalows rather than barracks, sometimes had beer or wine with their evening meals, and could order flowers for their tables. At some camps, and depending on their rank, German officers cultivated elaborate gardens, developed serious hobbies like carpentry, or strolled about the camp with a pet on a leash.

Moreover, the prisoners received their regular military pay. However incongruous that POWs should receive their monthly salaries, the Geneva Convention requires it. And while few if any other countries honored that rule, America did. The amounts were not particularly out of line with American military salaries, but indicate Washington's adherence to the Geneva Accords. German POW officers received the following monthly salaries:

> Second Lieutenant . . . . . . 72 Reichsmarks or $28.80
> First Lieutenant . . . . . . 81 Reichsmarks or $32.40
> Captains . . . . . . 96 Reichsmarks or $38.40
> Majors . . . . . . 108 Reichsmarks or $43.20
> Lt. Colonels . . . . . . 120 Reichsmarks or $48.00
> Colonels . . . . . . 150 Reichsmarks or $60.00

Since War Department rules (and common sense) prevented hard currency from falling into the hands of the prisoners, both officers and enlisted men were paid in script, redeemable in the camp canteen, or on repatriation.

Officers used their time to read or keep diaries and others painted murals or portraits. At Camp Hearne, Texas, they supervised the construction of an elaborate miniature concrete castle, waist-high, complete with turrets and a moat. Those with special skills in foreign languages or mathematics or physics volunteered to teach at mini-universities within the camp, complete with homework assignments, examinations, and grade certificates. At Fort Devens, Massachusetts, for example, the sweeping educational program included nine English courses, three Russian courses, two Spanish courses, one French course, and courses in physics, basic chemistry and organic chemistry, statistics, construction engineering, stenography, art history, figure drawing, sculpture, and business law. Not only that, but POWs could petition to enroll in extension courses from nearby universities and community colleges. Reinhold Pabel remembers that:

> At Camp Ellis, Illinois, I decided to take full advantage of the educational facilities that were provided. I got together with some other linguistically inclined men for small classes in foreign languages. Among others, we purchased a Persian Linguaphone Course and learned enough to be able to read and listen to an excerpt of the Rubaiyat in the original. I concentrated my efforts finally on Russian and completed two correspondence courses in that language with the University of Chicago Extension Division. Sometime later, I conducted two Russian courses for beginners for my fellow prisoners, making up my lessons myself and mimeographing them for class use.[5]

Thousands of former prisoners returned to postwar Germany with an admirable education under their belts. They climbed the corporate ladder and many German CEOs in the 1950s and 1960s could thank their POW Camp education. A few who completed their correspondence courses today sport class rings from American schools.

More than a dozen camps actually held social receptions with local American girls, arranged with the best of motives by local churches or YMCAs. At POW Camp Trinidad, Colorado, German officers were allowed to roam the beautiful Colorado hills on their promise to return to camp in the evening, and they always did. A group of Afrika Korps POWs received permission to build a fishing cabin on a nearby lake, where they were allowed to spend occasional weekends. In the special case of particularly high-ranking German prisoners, like the forty generals and three admirals who were kept in a special compound at Camp Clinton, Mississippi, they lived privileged lives, under the circumstances. Each had his army valet, and as generals from a militaristic German culture, they demanded—and received—the courtesies, salaries, and better-than-average food due their rank. The War Department agreed to give the generals anything they wanted—after all, American generals were in prisoner of war camps in Germany, too. Without question, these big-wigs could have had enormous influence on the German military, and in governmental circles, as well. In British hands, such high-ranking prisoners were "wined and dined," entertained and interrogated with care. But not in the United States. For some reason, the generals at Camp Clinton, Mississippi, were all but ignored for the duration of the war; they weren't even exploited for their propaganda value.

The Provost Marshal General's Office encouraged each camp to maintain its own newspaper. The logic was simple: first, it provided an outlet for the prisoners to practice democracy, to demonstrate its superiority to Nazism. The prisoners could write anything they pleased without fear of retaliation or censorship. Second, it provided weekly schedules for sports events and camp announcements. The newspapers were surprisingly sophisticated, carrying such things as poetry and short stories; crossword puzzles and word games; a weekly calendar of events such as concerts, plays, and films, comic strips, and a detailed classified page with items for trade or needed. Last, routine close examination of the camp newspapers by the American commanders revealed changes in the level or intensity of Nazism or anti-Americanism among the inmates. It allowed the camp authorities to "take the temperature" of the changing politics inside the barbed-wire. By mid-1943, nearly every camp in the country had its own newspaper. Camp Shelby put out the *Mississippi Post*; Camp Carson, Colorado, *Die PW Woche* (*The PW Weekly*); Camp Campbell, Kentucky, *Der Europäer* (*The European*); Camp Crossville, Tennessee, *Die Brücke* (*The Bridge*); Camp Houlton, Maine, *Der Wächter* (*The Watchman*); and so forth. Camp Maxey's (Texas) literary-minded prisoners published no less than three newspapers: *Echo*, *Der Texas Horchposten* (*The Texas Listening Post*), and *Deutsche Stimme* (*The German Voice*).[6]

The key to America's prisoner of war program, and the overarching reason for its success, was the War Department's almost religious adherence to the Geneva Accords of 1929. The country, after all, had never held POWs in any large number, and had few precedents to look to. The Geneva Accords, thrashed out in the wake of the Great War, was surprisingly thorough. For instance, prisoners were protected from everything ranging from aggressive treatment of any kind, and the theft of their medals, to the size of their barracks space or the amount and quality of food. The Geneva Convention required that the prisoners be accommodated with the same amenities as American soldiers—including military salaries—which included providing them with running water, laundry and bathing facilities, electricity and sufficient leisure time, as well as the ability to work for the host country on strictly nonmilitary tasks. The PMGO always leaned toward the most liberal interpretation of the regulations in order to insure the best protection for American POWs in German hands, although the State Department was otherwise notoriously deaf to their plight. The PMGO went so far as to require that the POWs were treated to the same Thanksgiving and Christmas turkey dinners as their American guards. Rules governing care of the prisoners were taken so seriously that if existing facilities did not include these requirements, the War Department had to locate alternate housing or acquire land to build new facilities. This meant that when the POWs did without, as was the case in several early makeshift camps when they had to sleep in tents while construction was being completed, then so too did the guards!

The Geneva regulations required that each compound elect a prisoner spokesman who transmitted prisoner complaints to the American authorities and explained the authorities' requests to the Germans. To ensure that the regulations of the Geneva Convention were being followed to the letter, inspectors from neutral Switzerland visited each American camp periodically to interview the German spokesmen and follow up on any complaints. The most common complaint was that their food did not reflect their German or Italian diets—too much spaghetti and not enough meat and potatoes or vice versa. The German POWs were usually complaining about something or other. American white bread was declared inedible when compared with the hearty whole-grain bread in Europe, American coffee was compared to dishwater, and ketchup was unfamiliar—but underneath they knew that they were eating better in American captivity than war prisoners anywhere. The German prisoners may have delighted in their clout, but the appearance of the Swiss inspectors was always a tense time for American camp administrators. Washington realized that POW complaints, whether true or not, were reported back to Berlin with possible adverse consequences to the more than 90,000 American captives in enemy hands. All sides understood the Principle of Reciprocity: the level of treatment done to one set of captives will be reflected by the other side.

The quality of the American guards was a decidedly mixed bag. Some were trained Military Policemen, highly-motivated and professional, but a portion of the rest were "dead-enders," men with alcohol problems and long transfer records from unit to unit. During the last days of the war, at the branch camp at Ovid, Colorado, an American guard, newly returned from combat overseas, killed three German prisoners after "they had made threatening remarks and were acting as though they intended to attack him."[7] Similarly, at the branch camp near Parma, Ohio, an American guard shot and killed a German prisoner who threatened him and advanced toward him after being ordered to stop singing a song which ridiculed American servicemen.[8]

On July 8, 1945, when Private Clarence V. Bertucci, an American guard at Fort Douglas, near Salina, Utah, went berserk and machine-gunned eight German POWs asleep in their tents, the Camp Commander Colonel Arthur A. Ericsson admitted that Bertucci had "twice been tried before a summary court-martial and had been in several Army hospitals in the last years."[9]

Both the POWs and the guards were isolated by the scarcity of German-speaking American guards since qualified translators were in high demand at the frontlines in Europe. Guards were also drawn from soldiers who were being recycled from the war zone overseas—edgy combat veterans who sometimes panicked when faced with menacing groups of German POWs. Overall, however, the guards were often well-intentioned and professional; former prisoners look back with some fondness at their American guards who are viewed as being generally fair and even-tempered. On the downside, the guards are also remembered as being naïve, unprepared to argue issues such as America's treatment of its own minority citizens, and easy to manipulate, please, or anger.

By June 1943, with the collapse of the North African theater and the surrender of several hundred thousand Germans and Italians, prisoners poured into the United States. In June, 36,688 German POWs arrived on American shores; the number doubled in July to 65,058, and thousands more were right behind them. In the spring of 1943, just a year and a half after the attack on Pearl Harbor that embroiled American in the war, the Afrika Korps surrendered, and more than 150,000 German prisoners filled every available military transport arriving from the battlefields. After that, an average of 20,000 POWs arrived each month.

Clearly, the War Department was facing a crisis. Hordes of prisoners were arriving weekly, and at the same time, America was starved for labor since the military was taking every able-bodied man for service overseas. The War Department in Washington, DC, decided to ease the labor shortage by putting the prisoners of war to work. Not only would it help American farmers and small businessmen, but heavy work would keep the prisoners too preoccupied and too fatigued to escape. By the Geneva Accords, officers were not required to work and seldom volunteered. The details of employing POW labor were spelled out in Articles 27 to 34 of the Geneva Accords, and once the legal kinks were worked out it was relatively easy to put the prisoners to work. Eventually, local farmers were only required to call the camp a day or two before the men were needed with the facts about the task: the number of prisoners wanted, the time required to complete the job, and the assurance that the necessary tools and bologna sandwiches for lunch would be available. The German POWs generally worked well, although not as quickly or efficiently as free labor. However, it was a nearly self-sustaining program: the farmers paid the government the going local rate for each prisoner, and the government, in turn, paid the POW only eighty cents per day—in paper canteen coupons. Prisoners were paid in coupons rather than cash to prevent them from pooling their cash to bribe a guard or purchase a bus ticket in the event of an escape. Eighty cents was more reasonable than it might seem today. In those years, a bottle of beer cost ten cents, and a pack of cigarettes just a nickel. In fact, POWs could purchase a long list of items at their camp canteen, from art supplies to handicraft tools, none of which exceeded seventy-five cents.

Officers, were exempted by the Geneva Accords, but the enlisted men and noncommissioned officers (sergeants) were put to work. The majority saw physical labor as good exercise and as a welcome distraction from the mind-numbing boredom. Some, however, resented being put to use by the enemy, especially if their work could be viewed as aiding the Allied war effort. Many were simply troublemakers. On occasion, they participated in work slowdowns, when small detachments of eight or ten men worked in slow motion picking potatoes in Idaho, or added rocks to the long bags of picked cotton on the way to the weigh stations in the Mississippi cotton fields, or nailed colored shingles in the shape of a Nazi swastika while roofing a Massachusetts factory building which was only accidentally spotted by a low-flying pilot.

By October 1943, the Provost Marshal General's Office, in charge of POW affairs, grew so frustrated with the hundreds of minor incidents of work slowdowns and stoppages at camps across the country that it reinterpreted Article 27 of the Geneva Convention to permit the detaining power to use reasonable pressure to encourage prisoners to comply with a work order. Called the policy of "Administrative Pressure," the reinterpretation authorized the camp commander to impose restricted diet and reduced privileges. The new slogan became "NO WORK—NO EAT." Now, if prisoners defied official orders or did willful damage to the farmer's tools or equipment bordering on sabotage, it was off to the camp stockade for a month on bread and water.

An examination of the Punishment Records for the first two months of 1944 provides a representative picture of the average violations and punishments:

1/21/44 20 POWs	Unsatisfactory work slow, refused to work	7 days confinement bread and water
1/20/44 20 POWs	Carved swastikas on trees; poor workers	7 days confinement bread and water
1/21/44 1 POW	Poor worker; exceeded rest period; gave guard false name	No beer or shows for one month
2/09/44 3 POWs	Refused to work; refused to give names to guard	7 days confinement bread and water
1/29/44 1 POW	Stole file and pliers. Tried to smuggle into Compound in rags.	1 month on "Ash & Trash" no pay No shows 3 months
2/16/44 1 POW	Violation of Art. 96. Refused order from POW Sgt. Lang	Court-martial Hard-labor for 3 months.[10]

The warning in the government's official Handbook for Work Supervisors of Prisoners of War exhorted all guards and work supervisors to "Be aloof, for the German respects firm leadership. Allow them to rest only when necessary. DRIVE!" American Lieutenant General Wilhelm D. Styer grunted the order that "We must overcome the psychology that you cannot do this or that. I want to see these prisoners work like piss ants!"[11] Despite such orders from the top, the POW and guard relationship usually evolved into more lenient custodial care.

Guards accompanied the POWs, although they often only straightened up and shouldered their rifles when giggling young girls waved from passing pickup trucks. Every former German POW recalls funny stories about their American guards, who often spent the days asleep under a tree while a selected prisoner was assigned to march around the work-site with his empty rifle. "I remember a number of occasions when I was set to work at Camp Rucker, Alabama, and the guard would ask me to hold his rifle until he had climbed in or out of the truck.

Almost as an after-thought, he would ask me to hand it up to him a few minutes later," recalls Alfred Klein.[12]

According to the official policy, prisoners were forbidden from approaching within fifteen feet of the guards, but these rules were seldom followed. While there were exceptions, of course, the relationship between the German POWs and American farmers was often quite cordial, and it was not unusual for the POW to eat lunch with the farm family, or for the prisoner to give the farmer or his children a handmade gift. Former guards and former prisoners recall many warm friendships, many lasting well into the postwar years. The Buxton family, from Hickory, Oklahoma, petitioned the State Department to allow the POWs who worked on their ranch to enter the United States after the war. One Kansas farmer died without leaving a family and willed his farm to the POW who worked for him twenty-five years earlier. At Camp San Augustine, Texas, a German POW named Otto Rinkenauer fell in love with a local girl, Amelia Keidel. He was repatriated to Germany after the war, but not long afterwards, he returned from Germany and they married. They built Keidel's Motel in San Augustine, Texas, which stands to this day.

Regardless of the state in which the prisoners were located, they were used primarily to harvest crops. In Louisiana, for example, prisoners were used to plant and harvest rice, cotton, and sugarcane (harvesting more than 246,000 acres of cane in 1944 alone). In Missouri, POWs harvested potatoes and shucked oats and wheat. They harvested tomatoes in Indiana, potatoes and sugar beets in Nebraska, wheat and seed crops in Kansas, and more than 1,075,000 stacks of peanuts on 58,000 acres in Georgia. In Pennsylvania, the prisoners were used primarily for nursery and orchard work; in Maryland they harvested fruit, corn, hay, grain, and tobacco; in Maine they harvested over 4,890,000 bushels of potatoes in 1945 alone; in New York State they harvested and helped process over 2,000,000 tons of fruits and vegetables. In Illinois they cut asparagus, and in Texas the POWs gathered pecans, picked peaches and figs, and harvested record amounts of cotton. In Mississippi, in the three months from October to December 1943, the POWs picked over 6,675,000 pounds of cottonseed; and in Idaho, they harvested sugar beets, fruits, and vegetables. Spinach growers of Muskogee County, Oklahoma, used German prisoners from nearby Camp Gruber to harvest more than 4,000 acres during the single month of December, 1943. And so it went across the country. From the end of 1943 to early 1946, war captives were employed on every major agricultural crop in nearly every state in the union.[13]

But not all the prisoners were pleased with their surroundings. Some POWs took the opportunity to point out America's racial problems, often, perhaps, to justify their own racial philosophy. POW Corporal Hans Gurn, at Camp Roswell, New Mexico, recalls that:

> There was a plumber who came to work in the camp. His name was Gutier-rez, and he was Mexican. He was a very nice guy. When he went to the barbershop, he stood in the corner, he did not move, and, as he was

"colored," he had to wait until all the Whites were done. You know, things like that upset us very much.[14]

And from Corporal Willibald Bergmann, at Camp Sheridan, Illinois:

Me, I was in peas: picking and canning factory. The farmers liked me, and wanted me to stay after the war, but I wasn't sure ... I met some old people of German origin one day, and these poor old people told me: "We feel alone here. It's sad. It's too big. If we could, we would walk back to Germany on foot ..." And the Blacks! They were always saying: "We are just like you: Prisoners: Oppressed; Second-class men ..."[15]

The issue of race discrimination in the United States remained the constant target of many German prisoners and a keen source of embarrassment to the War Department during later efforts to "democratize" the POWs. Yet as deplorable as such discrimination was, the fact that it was exploited by the soldiers of a government which was, at that moment, exterminating people by the millions, was ludicrous.

Without question, the central issue to the War Department was the concern about prisoner escapes. The prospect of hundreds or thousands of enemy military men, trained in the use of weapons and explosives, sabotaging and raping their way across the United States during wartime, was at the top of the list. Camps had rows of barbed-wire fences, patrolling war dogs, monthly shakedowns, internal military discipline, and often guards with itchy trigger fingers. Therefore, the government was tiring them out with heavy agricultural work and distracting them by an impressive array of camp educational and handicraft programs.

Nonetheless, a number of prisoners wanted to escape. Some tried because they felt it was their duty. Every army orders its soldiers to escape, if possible. Others wanted to get out and walk through the woods, or meet girls, or enjoy some privacy from the thousands of POWs in each teeming camp. Very rarely, a few prisoners were tempted by the thought of sabotaging a train or industrial target— their countries were at war, after all—but of the many thousands of prisoner escapes, there are only nine cases of attempted damage on record by escaped prisoners, none more dangerous than a broken latch on a railroad car, laundry stolen off a clothes line, or the "appropriation" of a boat or getaway car. (Theft or intentional damage by an escaped POW during wartime constituted a federal offense and changed an average seven days in the camp brig, when captured, to four years in a federal penitentiary).

There are exactly 1,036 escape attempts on record, and while that number seems alarming at first glance it should be remembered that of the average number of German POWs in America's care, around 360,000, the monthly rate of escape was approximately only three escapees per 10,000—a ratio better than that achieved by the nation's penitentiary system.

Most of the 1,036 escape attempts were motivated by nothing more sinister than the availability of opportunity. In other words, someone might leave a gate unlocked, or a guard was distracted or their worksite was unsupervised and freedom was only a few steps away. Indeed, the earliest escape was just such a moment. On November 5, 1942, two German prisoners fresh from North Africa, Karl Kuft and Hans Jourat, jumped from the train carrying them from Cincinnati, Ohio, to their new homes at Camp Forrest, Tennessee. They were picked up two days later outside Bowling Green, Kentucky.

"It was not complicated to escape," recalls former Afrika Korps Major Tilman Kiwe in reflecting on his many escape attempts from Camp Trinidad, Colorado, and Camp Alva, Oklahoma. About his third attempt, he recalled:

> The [escape] organization first obtained an American uniform for me that the guards must have traded for our military decorations or pretty wood sculptures. A tailor in the camp fashioned a very smart civilian raincoat. The problem was that it was grey-green, but we were not short of chemists in the camp. With boiled onions they obtained a marvelous shade of orange-yellow, and with tea they darkened it a bit to a perfect inconspicuous color. Before leaving this time I worked to perfect myself in English, especially in American slang. There was a prisoner in the camp who had spent twenty three years in America; he was an interpreter and he took me well in hand. I could soon pass absolutely for an American . . . The organization furnished me with the necessary money—about a hundred dollars . . . The day was set for the escape . . . I slid under a barrack. They were all on blocks; although there wasn't much room, I changed clothes and stepped out in the uniform of an American Lieutenant. I waited until around 10:30 and went to the guard post. The sentinel must have thought I was taking a walk, I gave him a little sign with my hand, said "Hello," threw him a vague salute, and hop! I was outside![16]

Major Kiwe, like the overwhelming majority of escaped prisoners, was picked up and returned to camp within two days. Since he was captured wearing a makeshift American military uniform, he was fortunate not to have been charged with being a spy.

Once on the loose, the escaped prisoners resorted to virtually the same tactics. They slept in the woods or fields by day and tramped the highways at night. They foraged for food in orchards and gardens, and attempted to get to the Canadian or Mexican borders, or slip into the anonymity of large, sprawling cities. Yet, however ambitious their plans, they seldom got far. Prisoners were generally tripped up by small details, or a lack of English or knowledge of American customs, and still others by totally unforeseen circumstances. In mid-1944, for example, a German escaped from Camp Hearne, Texas, and was found a day and a half later huddling in a railroad boxcar, hungry and thirsty, in an unused spur line in the middle of the downtown area. He was unaware that neither the car nor the spur line was in use. In another escape from the same camp, a prisoner sprinted away from an agricultural work party and cut across a fenced-in pasture. He was soon run up a tree by an angry Brahman bull. When the guards who were searching for him along the highway were attracted by his cries for help and rescued him, he was enormously grateful to get back to the safety of his prison camp. At yet another Texas stockade, Camp Barkeley, outside of Abilene, the few escape attempts invariably found the German prisoners sleeping in the bandstand in Abilene's central park.[17]

At Camp Atterbury, Indiana, an escapee was captured by an eight-year-old boy who was playing with a toy pistol and ordered an imaginary "bad guy" to come out of an abandoned shack near the boy's home in Columbus, Indiana. No one could have been more surprised than he when Franz Wilming stepped out to surrender.[18]

On another occasion, an escapee from Camp Grant, near Rockford, Illinois, made it to Chicago in time to celebrate New Year's Eve, 1946, at a local tavern. When the drunken party moved to a private home for sandwiches, Paul Stachowiak went along too. Everybody thought he was the guest of someone else, but when he began to boast that he had just escaped from a POW camp, one of the more sober partygoers called the police.

The prisoners cut wire fences, smuggled themselves out of camps aboard commercial delivery trucks, climbed out of hospital windows, and tunneled like moles. At Camp Mexia, Texas, a group of prisoners constructed dummies which their comrades stood up at the back of the line during morning inspection so that none of the guards would realize that the men had bolted. "It worked fine," said former POW Werner Richter, "until one of the dummies fell over." At Camp Somerset, Maryland, a prisoner made several "practice escapes" in which he actually left the camp and returned, before making his final, short-lived escape.[19]

At the Texas camp at Hearne, three German prisoners spent part of every day constructing a makeshift boat in a hidden area along the Brazos River; it was a remarkable craft made of waterproof GI ponchos with canvas for sails. One night they escaped and sailed their improvisation down the Brazos, hoping to reach the Gulf coast. It was an ambitious project, but they were spotted by a startled fisherman two days later fifteen miles downriver from the camp.[20]

One of the most spectacular escapes occurred on December 24, 1944, from Papago Park camp, not far from Phoenix, Arizona. While the guards were preoccupied with controlling a volatile POW demonstration with tear gas and clubs, 25 German prisoners, mostly submarine officers, escaped through a sophisticated 200-foot tunnel, cut through rocky soil with makeshift tools. All were captured, some carrying packs of nearly 100 pounds of spare clothing, canned goods, medical supplies, maps, and cigarettes. The complete story of the escape was described in a suspenseful book called *The Faustball Tunnel*.[21]

One of the more ludicrous escape attempts saw a pair of Germans slip away from their worksite and dash headlong across the southwest to freedom. According to the news report[22]:

> One was more than 6 feet tall and of sturdy frame; the other short, broad-shouldered, big tummied. They wore khaki shirts and shorts...they hailed a truck and climbed into the seat beside the driver.

> "Where are you headed?" asked the driver.
> "We're Boy Scouts," was the reply, "going to an international jamboree in Mexico."
> The driver, suspicious of the men's accent and the hairy muscle-knotted legs extending from the shorts, halted at the nearest town, and turned the brawny "Scouts" over to the authorities.

Prisoner escapes, it is evident, were as varied as imagination and circumstances allowed. They did, however, have one thing in common: the overwhelming majority were recaptured within three days. For Major Tilman Kiwe, now transferred to Camp Alva, Oklahoma, success was still elusive:

> This time I prepared my escape more seriously. For three months I let my beard grow, and completely transformed my appearance. I now had lacquered hair, parted in the middle, and glasses. And a real civilian suit this time. And in order not to make the same mistake twice, I obtained a real American suitcase, so I would look less like a foreigner... This time I almost made it into Mexico, but was arrested by the Border Patrol at the Rio Grande River... And once again I found myself back in the prison camp, with my thirty days in jail as expected.[23]

There is an important point here. America's interpretation of the Geneva Convention of 1929 protected war prisoners to such a degree that a POW who attempted escape—even if it was his 3rd or 4th attempt—could expect only thirty days in the brig. Punishment might include a diet of bread and water for a week or two, on the authority of the camp commander, but it would not be excessive. Periodic visits by the Swiss inspectors ensured that the Geneva Convention was being respected. Indeed, POWs were protected better in America than anywhere else, before or since World War II. Captured German prisoners, being marched back into camp after several days on the outside, were almost always greeted by their comrades as nearly-triumphant heroes and treated to a well-needed meal and slaps on the back.

As the European war ground to a close in May 1945, German prisoners in America were funneled from small branch camps to main camps, and from the west toward the largest camps on the East Coast, and eventual repatriation. As trainloads of prisoners were being shifted around the country during the summer and fall of 1945, several segments of American society were squaring off about the future of the POWs.

Labor unions wanted the prisoners out of the country. "Our boys shouldn't come back from overseas and find their jobs taken by enemy POWs," thundered union leaders. At the same time, American farmers wanted to hold on to the cheap labor; where else could they find hard workers willing to chop cotton or pick fruit for eighty cents a day? To complicate the developing conflict, the American general in charge of postwar occupation, Lucius Clay, refused to accept 370,000 additional German prisoners, all well-nourished and many still unrepentant Nazis.

The log jam was broken by President Truman. Never one to mince words, Truman weighed the issues and barked that the only remaining option was to ship the prisoners to our Allies, Britain and France. Thus began a dark passage in American history as the thousands of war prisoners were transported into the not-so-gentle care of England and France, both of which had suffered grievously at the hands of the Germans in two world wars and intended to make the German prisoners pay. For the next several years, America's German POWs labored in the French mines and cleared rubble in bombed English towns. Most lost an average of 35 lbs. from their years in the United States. For many german POWs, repatriation was delayed until 1948!

Yet, however difficult the experiences of the German POWs, particularly in the hands of Britain and France, they were still head-and-shoulders above the experiences of other nationalities. American POWs in German hands, for example, not to mention American POWs in Japanese hands, were poorly treated. Although Germany was a signatory to the Geneva Convention of 1929, it did not respond at the same level. Yet, by all accounts, the Germans treated their prisoners, British or American, as well as scarcity, military losses, mismanagement, and anti-American feelings would allow. This translates to mean that Allied POWs were held near starvation level, Red Cross packages were often hoarded and pilfered by the German guards, and the danger of disease or an angry guard or the appearance of volatile and deadly SS-men, in their black uniforms with a death's head insignia, always hovered menacingly nearby. But, despite the inequitable level of treatment, America continued to adhere to the Geneva Convention.

The oft-cited reasoning was to protect America's POWs, although it is feasible that the motivation was also an absence of any other model, or that the Germans, unlike the Japanese, looked much like the majority of Americans. Today, military historians widely believe that America's submission to the Geneva Convention caused German soldiers to surrender more often, especially when faced with the advancing Russians, thus ending the war sooner. Moreover, the decent treatment of prisoners may well have laid the foundation for the postwar atmosphere of trust between the United States and the new Germany which both countries today enjoy.

World War II, with its many horrors, also became the only conflict in which the German captives in American hands were treated better than POWs had ever been treated in the past. Unfortunately, that high level of protection and care would soon become a distant memory.

Notes

1. Louis E. Keefer, *Italian Prisoners of War in America, 1942–1946: Captives or Allies* (Westport, CT: Praeger, 1992).

2. In Germany, by comparison, there were a total of fifty-seven large *Stalags* (*Stalag* was the abbreviation for *Stammlager* or permanent army camp for enlisted men), Stalag

Lufts (any POW camp operated by the *Luftwaffe*, or air force, for downed Allied fliers was simply called a *Stalag Luft*, whether for POW officers or enlisted men), and *Oflag* (*Oflag* was the abbreviation of *Offizierslager* or permanent officers camp) in Germany during the war, many holding 3,000 to 5,500 men or more.

3. "Nazi Shot Twice Trying to Escape," *The New York Times*, July 29, 1944, 19.

4. Reinhold Pabel, *Enemies Are Human* (Philadelphia: The John C. Winston Company, 1955), 148.

5. Pabel, *Enemies Are Human*, 159.

6. For a complete list of every POW newspaper, see John Arndt (ed.), *Microfilm Guide and Index to the Library of Congress Collection of German Prisoner of War Newspapers Published in the United States from 1943–1946*, (Worcester, Massachusetts: Clark University, 1965).

7. "Guard, a Veteran, Kills 3 War Prisoners. Declares They Seemed Ready to Rush Him," *The New York Times*, August 2, 1945, 9.

8. "Cleared in Shooting of Nazi," *The New York Times*, February 12, 1945, 13.

9. "Eight Germans Slain, 20 shot by Guard at Prison Camp," *The New York Times*, July 9, 1945, 1, 20.

10. Farrand Collection, Stanford University. See Arnold Krammer, *Nazi Prisoners of War in America* (New York: Stein and Day, 1979, 1991, 1996), 111–112.

11. Minutes, Conference held in General Styer's Office, October 1, 1945. Subject: Conference on Employment of Prisoners of War, Military Police Command, AEWESPAC, 383.6 Prisoners of War. Book 3, DPRB, TAG, as quoted in *Lewis and Mewha, Prisoner of War Utilization*, 254.

12. Letter from Alfred Klein, Munich, Germany, May 20, 1976.

13. For a summary of the agricultural harvests brought in by the German POWs, see Krammer, op. cit., 88–89.

14. Daniel Costelle, *Les Prisonniers* (Paris: Flammarion, 1975), 116.

15. Ibid., 116.

16. Ibid., 153–157.

17. Ibid., 153–157.

18. "Jim Citizen Helps FBI Catch Runaway Prisoners of War," *Kansas City Star*, September 3, 1944.

19. "POW Camp was Mexia Attraction," *Mexia [Texas] Daily News*, June 30, 1971, and "World War II POWs Come Back to Texas," *Dallas Morning News*, October 10, 1971.

20. See the outstanding book by Michael R.Waters, et al., *Lone Star Stalag: German Prisoners of War at Camp Hearne* (College Station" Texas A&M University Press, 2004), 84–85. "Stalag Hearne—A Reminder of the Home Effort," *Bryan [Texas] Eagle*, October 14, 1973. See also Norman L. McCarver and Norman L. McCarver, Jr., *Hearne on the Brazos* (San Antonio: San Antonio Century Press of Texas, 1958), 83.

21. John Hammond Moore, *The Faustball Tunnel* (New York: Random House, 1978).

22. *Kansas City Star*, September 3, 1944.

23. Costelle, *Les Prisonniers* op.cit., 83.

CHAPTER 4

The Rules Have Changed

The German, Austrian, Italian, and Japanese prisoners of war who were held in American hands during World War II experienced the best treatment of any nation's prisoners in that conflict or probably any other. Never before had the key ingredients come together: the Geneva Convention of 1929, which anticipated and regulated nearly every facet of prisoner life; the fresh psychological scars of a horrific world war only two decades earlier; European enemies who looked and acted much like their captors; and the lack of any model other than the Geneva Convention. During their captivity in America, the public grew to like the German prisoners for their efficiency, cleanliness, and hard work, and American women, in particular, were often smitten by the handsome, Mediterranean charm of the Italian lads. Farmers regularly invited their German workers to share lunch with the family and allowed them to play with their children. Such concern for the welfare of the prisoners, however, evaporated at the end of the war. Aside from some American families who continued to send CARE packages to their former POW laborers, people simply weren't concerned about them.

The reasons for the initial disinterest are clear and entirely human. People were tired of hearing about the war. It had consumed the last four years of everyone's lives. Fresh opportunities and new products called to the public from all sides. The stunning educational benefits offered by the G.I. Bill enabled an entire generation of veterans to attend college, lifting millions of Americans into the Middle Class. New home-owners flocked to the new suburbs.

If they were interested in the war, however, the book stores were flooded with stories of major battles, generals, weapons, and biographies of Churchill, Hitler, Rommel, Eisenhower, MacArthur, and Nimitz. The few portraits of ordinary soldiers were to be found in brilliant fiction and autobiographies by returning combat veterans like Norman Mailer (*The Naked and the Dead*), James Jones (*From Here to Eternity*), Robert Lee Scott (*God is My Co-Pilot*), and James Michener (*Tales of the South Pacific*).[1]

The number of books about the experiences of POWs could be counted on one hand: Edward Beattie's raw and anguished *Diary of a Kriegie* (1946), Alan Newcomb's *Vacation with Pay: Being an Account of My Stay at the German Rest Camp for Tired Allied Airmen at Beautiful Barth-on-the-Baltic* (1947) whose caustically humorous title parodies his ill-treatment as well as his nation's lack of support. The following year, 1948, saw publication of *Paratrooper Padre*, a conflicted account by Francis Sampson, whose experiences in an elite combat unit challenged his calling as a man of the cloth. Finally, in 1951, an excellent account by John Vietor appeared as *Time Out: American Airmen at Stalag Luft I*. Still, a half-dozen books about POWs in five years does not indicate intense public interest.

The second reason for the early lack of interest in the story of POWs stemmed from the traditional military view of soldiers who fall into enemy hands. Since biblical times, war captives had been considered property and counted as war booty to be enslaved or killed. The army that lost prisoners viewed the loss as acceptable and considered its former soldiers as potential turncoats who might be pressured into revealing military information to the enemy. Captured war prisoners were considered cowards by both sides, undeserving of concern or further interest. Neither side was moved to allocate precious resources for their care or upkeep. War hysteria and cultural attitudes further influenced their poor treatment, as evidenced by the fate of Allied prisoners in World War II in Japanese hands or Germans in Russian captivity. For many, captivity was little more than a slow death sentence. Until very recently, medals or public accolades for former war prisoners were unthinkable. It was the Vietnam War, media-driven and polarizing, that caused the American public to reevaluate the plight of its sons and brothers, heroic and clearly loyal, as they fell into the hands of an inscrutable and apparently unyielding distant enemy.

Otherwise, the public was first confronted with the POW issue in 1953, when it was thrust onto the screen in an Academy Award-winning movie, *Stalag 17*. Although the plot is vintage McCarthy-era fare about a German spy working from within a group of American POWs secretly disclosing their escape plans to the enemy, the public was forced to face the spartan conditions of POW life and the often life-and-death problems facing brave and stereotypical American soldiers in a nameless prison camp. That year the reading public snapped up two new books, *P.O.W.*, by a former B-24 gunner, Edward Dobran, who spent a year in Stalag Luft IV, and a general, wide-ranging book by Eric Williams, *The Book of Famous Escapes*. The public was clearly ready to take the next step. That step came in the form of the blockbuster movie about the brutality of life in a remote Japanese POW camp, *Bridge on the River Kwai* (1957). Alec Guinness and Sessue Hayakawa play an eyeball-to-eyeball cat-and-mouse game of devotion to duty and hubris in the form of building a crucial bridge that is ultimately destroyed, together with the chance of Japanese military success and the honor of the Japanese commandant. The movie garnered seven Academy Awards, opened America's eyes to the horrors of prison camp life, and gave the public a whistling marching tune that remained popular for decades.

Prisoner of war movies were almost becoming fashionable. One, like the 1962 Cold War thriller, *The Manchurian Candidate*, utilized brainwashed American POWs during the Korean War to point out the dangers of international Communism. The trend was clearly to focus on life in enemy prison camps, shorn of politics. In 1963, another blockbuster hit the screens: *The Great Escape*, with Steve McQueen. The film is based on the true story of seventy-six Allied POWs who escaped from Stalag Luft III in March 1944 after a year of digging tunnels, counterfeiting documents, tailoring enemy uniforms, and maintaining a camp security system as complicated as the proverbial Swiss watch. Indeed, *The Great Escape* is still among the most popular movies available.

No sooner had the dust settled from *The Great Escape* than yet another excellent POW film appeared in 1965: *King Rat*. In this movie, based on James Clavell's real experiences in a Japanese camp, an undisciplined American corporal (George Segal) rises from a camp scrounger and wheeler-dealer to a successful entrepreneur who cultivates a secret rat farm under the barracks, unbeknownst to his starving officers who buy the meat disguised as a local delicacy. The American public was now clearly ready to face the experiences of the ninety-five thousand U.S. prisoners who spent part or all of the war years in enemy captivity. What the public got, however, was a ludicrous television series called *Hogan's Heroes* (1965–97).

Hogan's Heroes was a zany situation comedy in which American Air Force Colonel Hogan leads a small band of misfit POWs in a nameless German camp to befuddle and corrupt the ever-confused Colonel Klink and his jovial Sergeant Schultz. Sidestepping a torrent of criticism from every direction, particularly from former POWs who were outraged at the trivialization of their experiences, *Hogan's Heroes* flourished for six years and, in fact, continues in syndication to this moment.[2]

The 1960s witnessed a growing interest in the experience of American POWs following the release of such popular films and the ongoing lunacy of *Hogan's Heroes*. More books appeared, two of the best being *Name, Rank, and Serial Number* (1969) by Florimond Duke, and *Prisoners of War* (1975) by James F. Stone, a former bombardier. In 1967, the theme of prisoners was viewed through the psychedelic lens of the Age of Aquarius to produce a quirky British-made TV show starring Patrick MacGoohan called *The Prisoner* (1967). Although the convoluted, dark story about the interrogation of agent "Number Six" lasted only seventeen episodes, the show has achieved cult status today.

The Vietnam War "humanized" POWs. By the mid-1960s, the heavily televised war in Vietnam brought home the plight of American POWs in Southeast Asia, and the public began to see them as individuals rather than as a category of expendable or cowardly soldiers. It became fashionable to wear the name of a single POW on a metal bracelet. Prisoners who were fortunate enough to be released from captivity wrote their memoirs and many used their popularity to catapult themselves into local and national politics. Only one year after the end of the Vietnam War, an excellent book appeared from John G. Hubbell titled *P.O.W.: A Definitive History of the American Prisoner-of-War Experience in Vietnam, 1964–1973.* In 1976, Navy Captain John (Mike) McGrath wrote *Prisoner of War: Six Years in Hanoi* about the horrors of his lengthy experiences in enemy hands. He went on to become the authority for all accurate information about POWs in Vietnam. Three years later American television broadcast a major film, *When Hell Was in Session* (1979), based on the experiences of Navy commander Jeremiah Denton who spent seven and one-half years in a North Vietnamese POW camp and heroically united his fellow prisoners while maintaining their sanity under the most adverse conditions.

One of the best books about American POWs in the European Theater appeared from scholar David A. Foy, titled *For You the War is Over: American Prisoners of War in Nazi Germany* (1984). The following year, 1985, saw the publication of the notable book by E. B. Kerr about the Pacific Theater, *Surrender and Survival: The Experience of American POWs in the Pacific 1941–1945.* Pedestrian books appeared over the next several years until the publication in 1991 of the splendid recollection by David Westheimer (who also authored the taut escape story, *Von Ryan's Express*). The new book was called *Setting It Out: A World War II POW Memoir.* Westheimer had the additional worry that the Germans or his bigoted American comrades would learn he was Jewish. Finally, an incisive book appeared in 1993 which indicated, perhaps, that the initial literary phase of POW studies—the contribution of primary recollections—was evolving into a more mature, contemplative stage with the publication of Robert C. Doyle's outstanding *Voices from Captivity: Interpreting the American POW Narrative.*

Once again, moviemakers turned to POW stories as an untapped venue. Sylvester Stallone starred in a forgettable movie called *Victory* (1981), in which a group of Nazi officers devise a propaganda event to challenge their all-star Nazi soccer team against their POWs in a winner-take-all game. With the help of the Brazilian superstar, Pelé, in the role of a POW, the prisoners win and ultimately escape. In 1983, British rock star David Bowie gave a credible performance in *Merry Christmas, Mr. Lawrence*, a film depicting the complicated relationship between a British officer and his Japanese camp commander in a POW camp in Java. Finally, on November 8, 1985, the seemingly unthinkable happened; Congress passed Public Law 99–145 authorizing an official medal be awarded to every former POW dating back to April 1917. The subject of American POWs had entered the mainstream.

In 1993, a made-for-television movie, *Stalag Luft*, entered the nation's living rooms and the American public once again realized the importance of this aspect of the history of World War II. Most recently (2002), tough guy Bruce Willis discovered the potential of a POW setting in *Hart's War*, in which an American colonel, William McNamara, utilized a camp murder to demand a formal court-martial officiated by the German SS camp commandant while McNamara secretly plots the destruction of a nearby German munitions factory.

In the decades since the Second World War, numerous conflicts in nearly every region of the world have altered the international understanding of what constitutes an enemy, a prisoner of war. It has not been a peaceful sixty years. In fact, since the end of 1945, there have been a jaw-dropping number of conflicts. Consider the following: Burma, Tibet, Greece, Indochina, China, Korea, Albania, Hungary, Poland, Czechoslovakia, Israel, Lebanon, Yemen, India, Malaysia, Egypt, Congo, Kenya, Pakistan, Nicaragua, Panama, Grenada, El Salvador, Angola, Mozambique, Iraq, Iran, Algeria, Cuba, Algeria, Eritrea, Oman, Kuwait, Somalia, Indonesia, Dominican Republic, Vietnam, Cambodia, Syria, Rwanda, Sudan, Turkey, Nigeria, Ghana, Northern Ireland, Kurdistan, Romania, Philippines—to name the most glaring examples. Yet, people died—and, in many cases, are still killing one another—in conflicts around the globe. Whether the conflicts were lengthy civil wars in Greece, Turkey, China, Korea, Vietnam, Iraq, or local wars in any number of African nations like Angola or Nigeria—or short incursions into Panama or Grenada, or Somalia—the very issue of what constituted an enemy soldier has blurred.

The Vietnam War marks a major transition from the years when armies were in uniform, and therefore covered by the Geneva Convention, and contemporary times when all rules are suspended. Suddenly, an approaching woman or child with a gift for a soldier may well have been offering a deadly explosive.

The next major leap in the asymmetry of modern war came in December 1979. The much heralded Soviet Army invaded Afghanistan with an undersized force, poor equipment, and a euphoric and groundless belief that they would be greeted as liberators. Thus began a nine year bloody war that demoralized the Russian military and bankrupted the nation. The collapse of communism in 1989 waited at the end. The insurgent enemy—"Freedom Fighters" to the United States at the time—harassed and murdered Soviet soldiers. The decision makers in Moscow had simply failed to anticipate the influential role of Islam in Afghan society. Moreover, the Soviet troops had absolutely no anti-guerrilla training. For the first time since the Great Patriotic War, Russian mothers watched their sons and sweethearts coming home in coffins. At the same time, the Mudjahadin learned the techniques necessary to fight modern western armies. Their success in driving Russia out of Afghanistan in 1988 created the self-confidence to confront other superpowers. The war also brought fighters together into bands like Al-Qaeda [*the Base*], and lifted some, such as Osama bin Laden, to become future leaders. In fact, the Soviet Army fighting against Islam in Afghanistan contributed to a rapid rise of Islamic fundamentalism in the Central Asian republics and possibly to the start of the independence movement in Chechnya, both of which continue to pose major security threats to Russia today.

The last appearance of uniformed armies came in 1991 with America's campaign to drive the Iraqi Army out of neighboring Kuwait in "Operation Desert Storm"; the Iraqi Army and its Republican Guard and the American military were all in uniform, although most of the small number (twenty-three) of American POWs in Iraqi hands suffered badly.[3]

According to the *Washington Post*, "During the Persian Gulf War, Iraq brutally tortured U.S. POWs. Saddam Hussein's secret police broke bones; shattered skulls and eardrums; and whipped, burned, shocked, beat, starved, and urinated on [American] POWs.[4]

The face of warfare—indeed, its very nature, tactics, weapons, training, goals, and rules of engagement—was now different. Gone are set piece battles, flags and buglers, and the ethical treatment of POWs. However primitive the tactics, such as roadside explosives or kidnapped hostages, the weapons are often sophisticated and always deadly. Western armies have still not grasped the profound change in warfare, as shown by the recent 2006 Israeli conflict against Hezbollah fighters in southern Lebanon. The vaunted Israeli military, western in orientation and materiel, found itself fighting a guerrilla war for which it was unprepared.

This, then, brings us to a central question: Do enemy soldiers need to wear different uniforms, like opposing football teams? What about people who were not in the army, but who picked up rifles and shot from rooftops or fired rockets at foreign invaders? Are they considered soldiers, who warrant protection, or civilians? In years past, enemy soldiers captured in civilian clothes were considered "partisans," "irregulars," or just plain "spies," and most were promptly shot. It was one's uniform or identification "dog-tags" which proved whether one was a soldier and thus deserved to be protected. Or was simply carrying a weapon enough to signify an enemy's status and membership? How is it possible that a ragtag Taliban army in Afghanistan were dubbed "Freedom Fighters" when fighting Russian invaders, and given the most sophisticated battlefield weapons by the West, especially the United States, but when the Russians were driven out of Afghanistan and the Taliban turned against the West, they became "Terrorists?" Apparently, one man's freedom fighter is another man's terrorist, and their enemy/prisoner status depends on whom they are fighting.

During the Vietnam War, American forces were often faced with "shadow soldiers" generally lumped into a category called Viet Cong, North Vietnamese sympathizers living in the south who were indistinguishable from the South Vietnamese farmers living around them. Prisoners from all sides were brutalized throughout the twenty-year conflict (1954–1974). War was changing.

Then Came the Attack on September 11, 2001!

History turned on the suddenness and visual horror of the calamity and everything changed. Warfare changed. War had already become asymmetrical—one side might wear uniforms while the other side might not, POWs might be well-treated or held for ransom or beheaded—and the old rules were out-of-date.

One need look no further for asymmetrical warfare than the American Revolution. American colonialists—"Freedom Fighters" in this case—rose up against British in 1775. The uniformed English troops and their Hessian mercenary allies were conventional soldiers, while their rebel enemies were often indistinguishable from their loyal neighbors. Although the war's asymmetry did not deviate from the norm of the day to the degree seen in today's conflicts, it may have tipped the outcome in favor of the rebels and ultimately the establishment of an independent America.

The War on Terror, often called the "Global War on Terror," however murky its origins, has further departed from the paradigm of past wars. America and Western Europe were following the old features of war: uniforms, units, ranks, rules of engagement, and political control. The opposing side was an assortment of radical religious jihadists, nationalists defending their homes, and ideologues anxious to change the world. They fought without any consideration of boundaries or language or military organization. In fact, neither borders nor nationality mattered any longer. Guerrilla fighters now moved effortlessly across frontiers by foot or helicopter and blended in with any local population.

Passports and military papers are laughably absent in modern war, and citizenship rarely matters if the cause is deemed just. Not since the four decades of the Cold War after World War II has the world found itself embroiled in a conflict which encompasses nearly the entire planet. Somewhat reminiscent of the struggle between communism and capitalism before the fall of the Berlin Wall, participants are bound and motivated by religious passion rather than nationalist dreams of political expansion. Consistent with the passions of the Middle East, logic is seldom a determining factor in the actions of the participants.

The modern battlefield has changed as well. Far from the open battlefields of the past, where men and armies maneuvered for advantage, today's battlefield might entail suicide bombers, roadside explosives triggered from a distance, robot drone airplanes, kidnapping, beheadings, poison gas, uranium-tipped artillery shells, booby-trapped toilet seats, or feces-smeared bamboo spikes designed to promote immediate infection. The days of "ten'shun" and battlefield etiquette are past. "I want to fight in a war like World War II. I want to fight an enemy," said an American soldier in Iraq, Sergeant Christopher Dugger, to *Newsweek* magazine. "And this, out here . . . it's a faceless enemy.[5]

The problem is that no one foresaw the changes occurring on the modern battlefield, so creating new rules has been bewildering. Not only are the frontiers porous enough to allow the free flow of troops of various nationalities and weapons and, but in current warfare, information has no boundaries at all. Pundits who discuss military maneuvers and political options are enlightening an international audience. Friends as well as enemies are watching the same CNN broadcasts and the popular Arab satellite channels like Al-Jazeera and Al-Arabiya, and planning accordingly.

In the "War against Terror" uniforms are usually worn by one side only; the Western armies are identified by nation and rank, while the "Insurgents" are indistinguishable from the general population. Indeed, often they are the population. Little effort is made by either side to understand the enemy's culture, and each side's unfathomable culture, religion, and language only serve to heighten the perception of their danger. Battlefield conditions change as religious fervor widens to engulf entire regions, often driving moderates and nonviolent nationalists into the radical camp and stimulating new recruits in distant lands.. Not only must battlefield conditions change, but the treatment of POWs must also be considered anew.

First of all, prisoners are often captured with a level of indiscriminate urban violence startling to American military authorities. Because the captives are often ordinary citizens, their captures have been unorthodox. An American soldier of the 3rd Brigade, 2nd Infantry, recalls that after a ritual of strong coffee and a blaring CD rendition of Barry Sadler's "Ballad of the Green Berets" to get "pumped up," Army Specialist Colby Buzzell's squad went out into the night to find "evildoers."

> We arrived at the target individual's neighborhood...We crept silently through the dark shadows in these really narrow mazed alleys for almost half and hour before we finally located the target house...These people never knew what hit them. We bust in when they were sleeping. Scared the living shit out of them. Half a dozen little kids, a woman in traditional black Arabic clothing, and the target individual, all sleeping on the ground in the outdoor part of the house. The kids were screaming in fear and crying and so was the lady...We separated the target individual in another room, tied his hands with a plastic zip tie, and put a blindfold on him...They put the vapor sniffer up to the target individual's hands...and the test results showed that he come up positive for several types of explosives. So we had our guy.[6]

The level of public anger in America immediately after 9/11 had not been seen since the Japanese attack on Pearl Harbor a generation earlier on December 7, 1941, and there was little sympathy for captured "enemies." The fate of captives depended on rules that were made up as circumstances and the avoidance of prying eyes dictated. Language specialists were rare and indigenous personnel frequently served as interpreters, casting further doubt on the validity of any legal proceedings from all sides.

Some 500 detainees were determined to have some intelligence value and were shipped to an American military base at Guantánamo Bay in Cuba for further interrogation. Interestingly, not all were local Iraqis or Afghanis—by 2002 Guantánamo held eighty-five Yemenis, five Bahrainis, thirteen Kuwaitis, six from Bosnia-Herzegovina, one from Sudan, a Saudi, a Chadian, a Mauritanian, and a prisoner with both Turkish and German citizenship.

Several prisoners captured on the battlefield were not even Middle Eastern, and this deepened the dilemma about the treatment of prisoners of war. David Hicks, for example, was an Australian citizen, as was Mamdouh Habib, both of whom were picked up in Pakistan as a terrorist suspects and transported to Guantánamo where they languished for several years despite the rising tide of Australian anger to free David Hicks. Both Hicks and Habib were declared to be official POWs and supposedly protected by the Australian Section of the International Commission of Jurists, using the same Article 4 of the Third Geneva Convention that the Bush Administration used to determine that "terrorist detainees" were *not* protected. A leading law expert simply threw up his hands and concluded that the "Existing international law is simply incapable of application to the fight against international terrorism."[7]

But, what if any of the captives turned out to be American citizens? As unimaginable as it seemed that an American citizen might be found among captive Afghanis, Somalis or Indonesians, it might complicate POW treatment in the New Age of warfare. President Bush's Military Order of November 13, 2001, prepared for such an eventuality by exempting any U.S. citizens captured with the enemy from trial by military tribunal. If Americans were really among the enemy, they were to be tried by the American criminal justice system, and *then* thrown into legal limbo. In earlier centuries, any prisoner who turned out to be an enemy citizen would have been shot as a spy or a turncoat.

But, America citizens did show up. Yasir Hamdi was captured while fighting for the Taliban in Afghanistan, and shipped in routine secrecy to the U.S. base at Guantánamo Bay. There the startled American interrogators discovered that he was a U.S. citizen born in Louisiana, and thus entitled to somewhat different treatment. He was plucked from the group and transferred to the Norfolk, Virginia, Naval Station brig. Still considered an "unlawful combatant" without the rights of either a criminal defendant or a civil detainee, POW Hamdi was placed in solitary confinement in Virginia, without access to counsel, bail, or a speedy trial. After two and a half years in solitary confinement without visitors, much less legal counsel, a public defender filed a petition of *habeas corpus* on his behalf, with another petition filed by his father, and the case moved before the Fourth Circuit in Virginia. The case eventually reached the Supreme Court in *Hamdi v. Rumsfeld*.[8] The decision, maddening in its avoidance of confronting the real issues of open-ended detention or torture, simply concluded that Hamdi "could not be held indefinitely without some access to the legal system." Behind the scenes, the U.S. government stripped Hamdi of his American citizenship and shipped him to Saudi Arabia, thus establishing an unconstitutional precedent without a word of dissent from the Supreme Court.[9]

Another bearded, grimy fighter captured with the Taliban turned out to be a young American from Marin County, California. John Lingh (dubbed by the press, "Jihad Johnny"), was taken out of the pack and shipped to the United States where he was brought before a U.S. court. The government dismissed the terror-related charges against him; instead he was convicted of providing services to the Taliban government and carrying explosives on their behalf. "Jihad Johnny" received twenty years in a federal penitentiary. Whether he was threatened with the loss of his American citizenship and deportation isn't known. Efforts by his lawyer to have the sentence further reduced were rejected by the federal government. Barring early parole, he will remain in custody until the year 2019. Legally, the safety of captured "Insurgents" (now called "detainees") was being discarded and centuries of hard-won protection evaporated in the face of the new type of warfare.

Prisoners were moved from the battlefield where they were captured to a jail, police station, or local government building. One American soldier recalls that "I put them in separate cells."

> I'd say most of these guys were model detainees [. . .] Then one kept pulling down his blindfold, claiming his allergies were hurting his eyes. We compromised and told him we'd loosen the blindfold if he faced the wall and shut up. He only partially complied. He was warned and rewarned by the lieutenant and the interpreter. But like a child, he kept pushing the limit . . . I removed him from the cell, took his blindfold off, and put on a new one—a huge one made out of a first-aid cravat—and tied it as tightly as I could. I also flex-cuffed his hands behind his back, also tight enough for him to be uncomfortable. A half hour later, he had pulled the blindfold down with his teeth somehow. Last straw.[10]

In Iraq, prisoners were often funneled from these collecting points to a trans-shipment camp at Tallil Air Base, about 190 miles south of Baghdad, near the ancient city of An Nasiriya and the Biblical city of Ur (where Alexander the Great supposedly landed when he invaded Mesopotamia in 300 B.C.) Wherever the prisoners are taken the first collection point after capture is critical in the extraction of information. Prisoners reveal information more easily if they are disoriented by the capture experience. However, their value degrades as they regain their composure or, even worse, mingle together to adjust their stories. Military Intelligence people must bear down for information while determining if the POW has potential for a more detailed interrogation. Eventually, most of the prisoners ended up at Camp Bucca, in southern Iraq near the Persian Gulf and the ancient city of Umm Qasar. Camp Bucca, like many camps in Iraq, were named after NYC fire marshals (in this case, Ronald Bucca) who were killed on September 11. Camp Bucca is a sprawling, heavily-guarded American POW camp. Inside the fence are a number of "mini-camps"—compounds designed to hold 500 prisoners each and surrounded by triple stranded concertina wire. Since the camp itself was defended by multiple rows of razor wire, Bucca looked like a number of small camps within a larger one. That's not to say that the camp had no amenities at all; Bucca had portable lights, a mess hall with two air conditioners, and Spartan shower facilities. The number of detainees swelled to 8,000 before most of the unimportant and low-ranking Iraqi prisoners were released to return home. According to General Janis Karpinski, Commanding Officer of the 800th MP Brigade, "By the time I arrived, about 300 prisoners were left, mostly generals and foreign fighters who could be set free only by the permission of the secretary of defense."[11]

Depending on the suspected importance of their secrets, they could be shipped to Abu Ghraib prison in Baghdad (or the prisons at Tasferat or Russafa or the Kadamiya women's prison—Saddam Hussein had a large network of prisons), or turned over to the C.I.A. and clandestinely transported to countries where the rules against torture were not taken too seriously. Guantánamo Bay, Cuba, loomed as a perfect distant prison for special cases.

In Washington, all eyes turned to the Geneva Convention for prisoner guidance. On September 25, 2001, two weeks after the attacks of September 11, Deputy Assistant Attorney General John Yoo and fellow member of the Office of Legal Counsel, Robert Delahunty, itemized the many reasons that the President could assume broad executive powers in the war on terror. The last footnote of the Yoo-Delahunty Memo, chilling in its sinister potential, declared that, "In the exercise of his plenary power to use military force, the President's decisions are for him alone and are unreviewable."

On January 9, 2002, John Yoo wrote another detailed and secret memo explaining why a violation of POW care would not constitute a crime for the Bush administration. The Geneva Conventions of 1929 and 1949 were redefined to place Iraq and Afghanistan outside the jurisdiction of the Geneva regulations. The memo flatly asserts over and over that, "As a constitutional matter, the President has the power to consider performance of some or all of the obligations of the United States under the Conventions suspended." The Geneva Convention was suspended. Just like that.

The next step in the government's efforts to place prisoners outside the historical pale of protection came on January 19, 2002, when Secretary of Defense Donald Rumsfeld ordered the Chairman of the Joint Chiefs of Staff to inform combat commanders that "Al-Qaeda and Taliban individuals are not entitled to prisoner of war status for purposes of the Geneva Convention of 1949." Commanders were thus given permission (The Rumsfeld Order, January 19, 2002) to depart from the provisions of the Geneva Convention wherever they deemed it appropriate.

The government's immunity was further endorsed by Alberto Gonzales, then counsel to the President, and William Haynes, counsel to the Department of Defense, who both concurred with the Office of Legal Counsel to assure that "We conclude that customary international law does not bind the President or the U.S. Armed Forces in their decisions concerning the detention conditions of Al-Qaeda and Taliban prisoners." Not only were there no restrictions on the President's actions, but, according to Assistant Attorney General Jay S. Bybee, in a Memo dated January 22, 2002, anything which prevented the Administration from acting as it pleased was actually deemed to be unconstitutional. According to Mr. Bybee, "Any effort to apply Section 2340A (restricting torture or cruel treatment) in a manner that interferes with the president's direction of such core war matters as the detention and interrogation of enemy combatants thus would be unconstitutional."[12] In conclusion, the President/Administration could do as he pleased with enemy prisoners, and anyone who tried to stop him was acting against the Constitution. In other words, the Administration argued, it might actually be considered illegal for any misguided humanitarian to interfere with the torture!

Secretary of Defense Rumsfeld summed up this discussion with his Memo to the President of January 25, 2002, in which he concluded that the Geneva Convention's regulations on the treatment of POWs "does not apply to the conflict with Al-Qaeda and the Taliban [. . .] and renders obsolete Geneva's strict limitations on questioning of enemy prisoners and renders quaint some of its provisions requiring that captured enemy be afforded such things as commissary privileges, scrip (i.e. advances of monthly pay), athletic uniforms, and scientific instruments."[13] White House Counsel Alberto Gonzales further advised President Bush that a side benefit of denying the protection under the Geneva Accords to the prisoners "detained" in Afghanistan would be that it would be more difficult for U.S. personnel to be prosecuted under the U.S. War Crimes Act. After all, if the prisoners weren't protected by international agreement, what laws had American soldiers broken?

Assured by his "team" that Afghanistan was a failed state and that the Taliban did not represent the nation (and consequently were not covered by Geneva as representatives of that nation's army), Bush issued the Order of February 7, 2002. By this order, the President accepted the arguments of Yoo, Rumsfeld, and Gonzales, and denied Geneva Convention protection to captured members of Al-Qaeda and Taliban, saying:

> I accept the legal conclusion of the Department of Justice and determine that none of the provisions of Geneva apply to our conflict with al Qaeda in Afghanistan or elsewhere throughout the world because, among other reasons, al Qaeda is not a High Contracting Party to Geneva . . . and . . . I also accept the legal conclusion of the Department of Justice and determine that common Article 3 of Geneva does not apply to either al Qaeda or Taliban detainees, because, among other reasons, the relevant conflicts are international in scope and common Article 3 applies only to "armed conflict not of an international character."

Finally, the President declared that, "Based on the facts supplied by the Department of Defense and the recommendation of the Department of Justice, I determine that the Taliban detainees are unlawful combatants and, therefore, do not qualify as POWs under Article 4 of Geneva . . . Al-Qaeda detainees also do not qualify as POWs."[14]

Despite declaring the "jihadists" to be an "outlaw group" and not worthy of legal protection, and establishing legal immunity for actions which had not yet occurred, President Bush nonetheless assured his listeners that American military forces would live up to the highest level of civilized conduct, saying: "As a matter of policy, the United States Armed Forces shall continue to treat detainees humanely and, to the extent appropriate and consistent with military necessity, in a manner consistent with the principles of Geneva."[15]

There were several lonely voices of opposition to the government's assault on the Geneva Convention. One was the Administration's new Secretary of State, General Colin Powell. Powell reasoned that if American soldiers fell into enemy hands their captors would have no motivation to treat them with humanity. If an enemy did kill or maim American prisoners, he on she couldn't even be brought to justice for violating the War Crimes Act. Moreover, despite the "fig leaf" of the President's assurance that the U.S. military would "treat detainees humanely," the suspension of Geneva might cause a political rift, or the refusal of America's allies to hand over captives for interrogation. Finally, Secretary Powell warned about the erosion which unregulated brutality toward prisoners would have on the traditionally high standards of America's forces and society.[16]

Senator John McCain of Arizona, who knows something about torture, was adamant that such treatment is "cruel, inhuman and degrading" and often doesn't work since victims will generally admit to anything to halt the pain. In fact, on August 15, 2007, the American Psychological Association, the world's largest professional association of psychologists, issued a condemnation of the interrogation techniques employed by the U.S. authorities against detainees. Torture simply doesn't work.

Alberto Gonzales felt that "the arguments for reconsideration and reversal are unpersuasive." Senator McCain's efforts were momentarily blocked by the Bush Administration, but in the face of a rising tide of scathing editorials President Bush announced in December 2005 that he would no longer object to Senator McCain's anti-torture legislation and made it clear that his Administration would not tolerate such treatment of prisoners.[17]

The contest was not about the prospects of success, but rather the morality of such treatment. Many of America's allies used torture, after all, whether it was the British in Northern Ireland, the Israelis in the Middle East, or the French in Algeria. But should America stoop to such treatment of prisoners, and what might happen to Americans in enemy hands as a result? An excellent new book by Karen J. Greenberg, entitled *The Torture Debate in America*, analyzes various elements of the discussion, the pros and cons, and summarizes the costs and changes which the introduction of torture will make in future conflicts.[18] Another outstanding recent book examines the question of torture from the prospective of the torturers. Has it come to mean that the ends justify the means? James M. Olson, former chief of CIA counterintelligence, in *Fair Play: The Moral Dilemmas of Spying*, examines the moral ramifications of fifty distinct scenarios which might confront an intelligence agent. The scenarios range from election tampering, drugging a foreign diplomat, and the use of prostitutes, to hit teams, collateral damage, and interrogation and torture. Olson considers the moral issues: what difficulties face the interrogator, and what inhumanities are committed in the name of the nation. While a *Newsweek* opinion poll in November 2005 indicated that 58 percent of

Americans would approve of torture to prevent a genuine threat to the nation or the loss of American lives, Olson notes with interest, "that there is a greater revulsion on the part of Americans to torturing terrorists than to killing them."[19] Given this moral ambiguity, the Administration quietly continued to maintain that Insurgents weren't protected by either the Geneva Conventions of 1929 or 1949, and were thus subject to any pressure required to extract intelligence.

Besides, Administration supporters snorted, even if the Geneva Conventions were extended to the jihadists (or "Insurgents," or "terrorists"), the host nation (American) could not provide amenities, or salaries, or entertainment privileges, or any of the many comforts guaranteed by the Convention.[20]

Centuries of legal agreements designed to protect war prisoners were suddenly evaporating. War prisoners were no longer guaranteed protection. Clearly, the world was facing a new kind of war. Article 4 of the 1949 Geneva Convention determined that only lawful combatants are eligible for POW protection—a stipulation which the floating membership of Al-Qaeda, Taliban, Hezbollah, or any of the burgeoning number of terrorist splinter groups could meet. Despite the fact that "terrorists" often describe themselves as "soldiers" and "soldiers of God," they don't wear uniforms or represent any particular nationality. Even the International Red Cross, guardian of the wounded and war prisoners, found that captive "terrorists" fail to meet four official guidelines that determine official POW status: they must have been commanded by a person responsible for his subordinates, have a fixed distinctive symbol recognizable at a distance, carry weapons openly, and conduct their operations in accordance with the laws of war.

Lest one believe that the Geneva Accords are the only civilized rules protecting POWs, Islamic law governing POWs is both well-developed and generally humane. The rules are derived from a rich body of Islamic Law regarding international relations known as *siyar*, which divides wars into narrow categories like "defensive wars," and "wars in which one Muslim country aids another which is being impressed," and punitive wars to subdue rebellion or "those who break covenants," and finally, "wars to subordinate the non-Islamic sovereignty of God."[21] A prisoner's treatment was dependent on the category of their war. The captor's options are also clearly defined, whether execution, enslavement, or release with or without ransom.

The Koran has several interesting similarities and differences from the Geneva Accords. Both require that prisoners receive similar facilities as their guards, humane treatment, and absolutely no brutality. Islam also forbids forced labor for enlisted POWs, not just for officers as stated in the Geneva Accords. The biggest difference between Geneva and the Koran—and this is critical —is the question of reciprocity. The Geneva agreement is based entirely on reciprocity, the treatment of each side's prisoners has to be roughly equal. Not so with the Koran. *Siyar* requires that all Muslims honor these requirements for treatment of their war prisoners, regardless of what the other side does. It is a moral obligation for Muslims.[22] History indicates that adherence to the *Siyar* has been sporadic at best. In Iraq, according to the Council on Foreign Relations daily commentary on

International Law and POWs, of March 31, 2003, "U.S. officials worry that some American prisoners have been tortured or executed. British Prime Minister Tony Blair announced on March 20 [2003] that two British POWs had been killed after capture."[23]

By January 2002, with the war in Afghanistan underway and captured Taliban and Al-Qaeda war prisoners coming into American hands, the question was where prisoners could be placed and interrogated for information? It was also considered critical to hold them in private since the law was not yet clear on the flexibility of the international laws which protect prisoners. Initially, according to the International Committee of the Red Cross, the main places of internment where mistreatment allegedly took place included battle group unit stations; the military intelligence sections of Camp Cropper and Abu Ghraib Correctional Facility; Al-Baghdadi; Heat Base and Habbania Camp in Ramadi governorate; Tikrit holding area (former Saddam Hussein Islamic School); a former train station in Al-Khaim, near the Syrian border, turned into a military base; the Ministry of Defense and Presidential Palace in Baghdad, the former *mukhabarat* office in Basrah, as well as several Iraqi police stations in Baghdad.[24] The real solution came in the form of a remote American naval base at Guantánamo Bay, on the island of Cuba, nicknamed "Gitmo." Considered American territory by international agreement (despite Fidel Castro's surrounding communist regime), Guantánamo Bay was converted into a detention center supposedly beyond the review of American courts.

The obvious next question concerned the amount of physical and psychological pressure which their status outside of the protective arms of the Geneva Accords allowed—in other words, the explosive issue of torture. Bybee twisted the Geneva Convention to argue, in his memo of January 22, 2002 (noted earlier), that if the abuser is torturing a captive to get information and not merely for sadistic enjoyment, "even if he knows that severe pain will result from his actions," he's not guilty of torture. Huh? One would think that it wouldn't make much difference to the victim if he was being tortured to obtain information or to satisfy the interrogator's sadistic enjoyment.

In any case, Article 3 of the Geneva Conventions, which prohibits torture, cruel treatment, and, "outrages upon personal dignity, in particular humiliating and degrading treatment," would not apply to the "detainees." Therefore, nobody involved could be prosecuted under the U.S. War Crimes Act for that either. The government's policy, however motivated, dramatically changed the rules protecting POWs. Prisoners were no longer protected by international agreement, and their captors were legally blameless for inhumane treatment of the "detainees."

Secretary Rumsfeld and the Bush Administration had an important point here. As any soldier knows, intelligence is perishable. The key to the need for torture was to gain information from terrorists as quickly as possible. They had proven their enemy status, having been captured in battle, after all, fighting for what was seen as an unfathomable cause, for a religion little understood in the West, and perhaps in possession of knowledge about pending attacks on America. In short, because an unimaginable number of lives might hang in the balance (not an idle concern in the months after September 11), legal niceties were weighed against the potential threat. The use of force superseded negotiation. In fact, the government suggested the argument that torture might even be considered "self-defense" on the grounds that "the threat of an impending terrorist attack threatens the lives of hundreds if not thousands of American citizens." However, when asked about the value of torture, General John Vessey, battle-hardened veteran and chairman of the Joint Chiefs of Staff, said, "No information that we could obtain through cruel, inhumane treatment, or torture could in any way counterbalance the damage that's done to the image of the United States of America by doing it."[25]

The respected *Economist* magazine minced no words about Attorney General Gonzales's actions in saying that "had he an ounce of integrity, he would have resigned long ago for his role in commissioning a memorandum that amounted to a legal defense of torture."[26] The Administration's cavalier tolerance of torture in the new War on Terror soon included Rumsfeld's authorization to use dogs to intimidate prisoners and nudity to humiliate them. Beating prisoners was not considered torture either. Results were all that mattered. The use of hooding now became standard; the same goes for forced nudity, sexual humiliation, and brutal beatings; there have been incidents of rape and electric shocks. Many of the abuses were specifically selected to embarrass Arabs and Muslims, who are humiliated by being naked in public. Bybee offered a startling example, stating that kicking an inmate in the stomach with military boots while the prisoner is in a kneeling position does not by itself rise to the level of torture.[27] One can only wonder what might be considered torture.

To jeopardize what little protection the prisoners had left, nobody understood the rules. Policymakers in Washington as well as in the battle zone handed down conflicting instructions from their superiors, who often received equally conflicting memos from the State or Defense Departments about what constituted torture and what did not. Prisoners were different, as well. The battlefields of the world are littered with captives of all kinds. There are angry nationalists, jihadists, locals and professional, and agents of every political stripe. There are arms salesmen, religious militia members, highly-paid mercenaries, and professional security people, not to mention politicians, civilian contractors, and news reporters, and future revolutionaries benefiting from the hands-on training. Should every captive be treated the same? At what level of care? Is a captive mercenary the same as a soldier? Are professional jihadists who float from conflict to conflict more likely to have valuable information and face torture? What are the rules surrounding torture? "These young soldiers could not have had an inkling of [. . .] the conflicting and confusing rules for interrogation issued at various times, approved by White House legal counsel Alberto Gonzales . . . and implemented by Secretary Rumsfeld," says American General Janis Karpinski.[28] President Bush simplified matters by declaring that, "The gloves are coming off, gentlemen, regarding these detainees, [Col. Boltz has made it clear that] we want these individuals broken."[29]

How do you break these people? According to the International Committee of the Red Cross, approximately fifty allegations of ill-treatment included:

> hooding; tight handcuffing; use of stress positions (kneeling, squatting, standing with arms raised over the head) for three or four hours; taking aim at individuals with rifles, striking them with rifle butts, slaps, punches, prolonged exposure to the sun, and isolation in dark cells. ICRC delegates witnessed marks on the bodies of several persons . . . consistent with their allegations. In one illustrative case, a person . . . .arrested at home by the CF [Coalition Forces] on suspicion of involvement in an attack against the CF, was allegedly beaten during interrogation [. . .] He alleged that he had been hooded and cuffed with flexi-cuffs, threatened to be tortured and killed, urinated on, kicked in the head, lower back and groin, force-fed a baseball which was tied into the mouth using a scarf and deprived of sleep for four consecutive days. Interrogators would allegedly take turns ill-treating him. When he said he would complain to the ICRC he was allegedly beaten more. An ICRC medical examination revealed haematoma in the lower back, blood in urine, sensory loss in the right hand due to tight handcuffing with flexi-cuffs, and a broken rib.[30]

And another, in a detainee's own words:

> They threw pepper on my face and the beating started. This went on for a half hour. And then he started beating me with the chair until the chair was broken. After that they started choking me. At that time I thought I was going to die, but it's a miracle I lived. And then they started beating me again. They concentrated on beating me in my heart until they got tired from beating me. They took a little break and then they started kicking me very hard with their feet until I passed out.[31]

One Guantánamo detainee named Mohamed al-Qahtani, considered to have high intelligence value, seemed to resist the regular interrogation techniques. Secretary of Defense Rumsfeld authorized the "special interrogation plan." According to Amnesty International, al-Qahtani was

> subjected to extreme isolation for three months in late 2002 and early 2003. He was forced to wear women's underwear; was tied by a leash and led around the room while being forced to perform a number of dog tricks; was forced to dance with a male interrogator while made to wear a towel on his head "like a burka"; was subjected to forcible shaving of his head and beard during interrogation, stripping and strip-searching in the presence of women, sexual humiliation, culturally inappropriate use of female interrogators, and to sexual insults about his female relatives; was subjected to hooding, loud music, white noise, sleep deprivation, and to extremes of heat and cold; was made to stand for long periods; and was forced to urinate in his clothing when interrogators refused to allow him to go to the toilet. Mohamed al-Qahtani

was interrogated for 18 to 20 hours per day for 48 out of 54 consecutive days. During the period of his interrogation, Mohamed al-Qahtani was threatened with shipment to a foreign torture center, injected with tranquilizers, made to wear blackened goggles, and taken out of Guantánamo in a plane.

According to Amnesty International, a military investigation concluded that Mohamed al-Qahtani's treatment, while cumulatively "degrading and abusive . . . did not rise to the level of prohibited inhumane treatment."[32] Particularly important "detainees" were often shuttled to any number of hidden jails out of view of the Red Cross, in places like Egypt, Syria, Uzbekistan, Yemen Algeria, Morocco, Guantánamo Bay, Russia, Tunisia, and Turkey, where crucial information could be extracted as rapidly as possible. But torture is illegal by most nations' definition, and politically explosive. Thus, the Defense Department and the C.I.A. connived to outsource the problem to countries notorious for their brutal interrogators. The process is called "prisoner rendition" (or "deportation," "removal," "expulsion," or "extradition"). According to the recent report by the highly-regarded humanitarian organization Human Rights Watch, "*Still at Risk*,"[33] "there is substantial evidence that in the global 'war on terrorism,' an increasing number of governments have transferred, or proposed sending, alleged terrorist suspects to countries where they know the suspects will be at risk of torture or ill-treatment . . . where members of particular groups—Islamists, Chechens, Kurds—are routinely singled out for the worst forms of abuse." The path now led inexorably to the central Baghdad prison at Abu Ghraib, where detainees and suspects were brutalized and humiliated, to the horror of the civilized world.[34]

There are, doubtless, dangerous people among the "detainees"—people who intend to bring great harm to America and the West—over the years, America and Europe have learned to acknowledge their existence, despite the illogic of their hatred. Furthermore, some of those captives have critical information about nefarious plans underway to murder hundreds or thousands of innocent people. It would seem prudent, however inhumane the torture or the resulting erosion of democracy's foundation, to sacrifice principles for expediency. But, there are many who are guiltless, and in wars without rules, they have no protection.

News reporter Dana Priest wrote that, "Virtually nothing is known about who is kept in the facilities, what interrogation methods are employed with them, or how decisions are made about whether they should be detained or for how long." This is the border along which democracy blurs into tyranny.[35]

The world of war has changed forever. Prisoners may no longer be protected by the Geneva Conventions of 1929, the four 1949 Geneva Conventions, two additional Protocols, and four other treaties, such as the Hague Convention of 1907 which had combined to form a framework of legal rights for war prisoners. In the future, the care of any captive will likely depend on the circumstances of battle and the willingness of his captors to guard him—and the importance of the intelligence information which a captor *believes* the prisoner might have. The suspension of the Geneva Convention and the introduction of limitless detention and torture remove the very keystone of all previous international agreements: *reciprocity*. The past humane treatment of war captives has always rested entirely on the knowledge that each side's level of care would be reflected in the treatment by the other side. No one wants to be the first to break the agreement for fear that a similar fate would surely await one's own soldiers in the hands of the enemy.

The removal of legal restraints on the mistreatment of prisoners at the highest governmental level and the increasingly well-known shipment of "high-value" captives to foreign torture centers and interrogation prisons, virtually assures that similar mistreatment will befall the other side. And so it already has. In current conflicts, Western prisoners are routinely kidnapped and often mistreated, starved, tortured, or executed. For example, U.S. Navy SEAL Neil Roberts was captured in Afghanistan—and tortured and executed. An organization called the U.S. Veteran Dispatch in Kinston, North Carolina, lists twenty-five American POWs presumably executed by their captors. Dozens more are unaccounted for and presumed dead or being held for ransom or to be used as propaganda. In addition, there is a significant number of civilians, doctors, nurses, missionaries, journalists, and civilian contractors, who have been executed or have died of starvation, disease, or brutal mistreatment at the hands of "insurgents." Without rules to assure the protection of prisoners, warfare in the future can only revert back to the more primitive centuries.

Asymmetrical warfare is likely here to stay. Perhaps there is some consolation in knowing that the United States is not the only modern army facing the problem of asymmetry. The uniformed British Army in Northern Ireland faces civilian bombers and snipers from rooftops, and the Israeli Defense Force, also in uniform, is in conflict with suicide bombers. Israel has settled into a fragile POW relationship with its Arab neighbors in which both sides imprison their war prisoners for possible later exchange. Sometimes such prisoner exchanges involve the release of hundreds of Arab prisoners for one or two Israeli soldiers. Otherwise, the brutal treatment of prisoners is becoming more common as political or religious violence erupts in the Balkans or Sudan or the Philippines or East Timor.

This book addresses the treatment of POWs at the very moment in contemporary history when the clash of ideologies is forcing the world to confront the issue. War is changing. First of all, the uniformed side, easily identifiable, will probably suffer a higher proportion of casualties than the "insurgents," who can appear or disappear into the civilian population. Innocent civilians, however, will also be killed in larger numbers as those "insurgents" hide among them. Moreover, in an asymmetrical war, "insurgents" do not necessarily adhere to a chain-of-command. They may operate individually or in small groups, so each is equally deadly. Since war prisoners are no longer protected by internationally agreed-upon rules, they are most vulnerable. Torture has been redefined and the need for military intelligence seems to supersede all else. Intelligence aside, unless the prisoner has value as a hostage, as a propaganda message, or to obtain ransom, he (or she) is likely to be executed.

Reciprocity is gone, and each side can treat its prisoners as it likes. Without that foundation, the treatment of war captives depends largely on the whims of their captors and the cost of guarding them and bringing them along with the advancing army. In other words, without the assurance of reciprocity, POWs are as vulnerable now as during any time in history. The world has allowed confusion over ideologies and the demands of politics to place all future POWs in jeopardy. In the pointed words of historian Sally Marks on the issue of eliminating reciprocity, "Even the Nazis knew better."[36]

The history of POWs has been a long, cruel odyssey. Since biblical times, war captives have been murdered out of hand, enslaved, ransomed, or simply forgotten. An untold number of captives have suffered and disappeared into the mists of history. Centuries passed before soldiers were considered valuable enough to keep alive. As the philosophers and writers of the Enlightenment of the eighteenth century imbued Mankind with universal nobility, war captives found themselves in a world of increasing safety. Prisoners were not routinely executed without reason, starved unnecessarily, or left to endure the elements. This evolving concern for the safety of war captives was codified in such agreements as the Geneva Convention of August 1864; another signed by the President of the United States in March 1882; followed by later conventions of July 1906, July 1929, and August 1949. These conventions, accords, and agreements have formed the laws protecting prisoners and, in fact, influencing the conduct of war.

Without question, the best treatment in history for war captives occurred during World War II, when a total of 425,000 German, Italian, Austrian, and Japanese soldiers found themselves in camps across the United States. It was the pinnacle of humane treatment of war prisoners. Most could not believe their good fortune. However miserable the boredom and loneliness of incarceration, all knew that they were safe and would be well-fed, especially in contrast to the treatment of war prisoners by other nations. Even neutral Switzerland, long mythologized as an "international safe haven," held more than 1,000 American airmen in particularly brutal camps.[37] Still, the promise of reciprocity assured that each side's treatment of prisoners might be mirrored by the other side.

The deterioration of conflict in the latter half of the twentieth century into asymmetrical conflagrations in which only one side wears uniforms and the Geneva Accords are haphazardly followed has been the hallmark of post-modern warfare. The decision by the United States to tolerate brutal interrogation, humiliation, and open-ended imprisonment without access to visitors or legal counsel, has discarded any semblance of legal protection, and, with that decision, the safety-net of reciprocity. The treatment of war prisoners is now an issue of expediency—whatever is required to extract critical information, immobilize enemy fighters, or break the nationalist spirit or religious devotion of opponents. Whether necessary or not in the face of a new type of warfare, this change signals a sad return to earlier and more barbaric times.[38]

Notes

1. This section is reprinted, with permission of the University Press of Oklahoma, from Arnold Krammer, "Foreword," in Dawn Trimble Bunyak, *Our Last Mission: A World War II Prisoner in Germany* (Norman: University of Oklahoma Press, 2003), xi.

2. Believe it or not, the ubiquitous *Hogan's Heroes* currently flourishes on German television. The German-language version takes parody a step further. Now called *Ein Käfig Voller Helden* (*A Cage Full of Heroes*), Col. Klink and Sgt. Schultz have rural Gomer Pyle-type accents, stiff-armed salutes are accompanied by such witticisms as "this is how high the cornflowers grow," and bombs dropped on London are translated as "condoms." How rich the irony: German fans of a comedy that ridicules Germans, lionizes Germany's former enemies, and trivializes the gravity of the circumstances.

3. *POW-MIA Fact Book* (Washington, DC; Department of Defense, July 1991), 34.

4. John Norton Moore, "Forgotten POWs, Forgotten Honor," *Washington Post*, November 10, 2004, A27. To Washington's discredit, the attempts by the returned American POWs and their families to bring suit against the Iraqi government for their mistreatment (*Acree v. Republic of Iraq*), and to help outlaw future violations against prisoners of war, were quashed by the Bush administration.

5. *Newsweek*, December 25/January 1, 2007, 94.

6. Colby Buzzell, *My War: Killing Time in Iraq* (New York: G.P. Putnam, 2005), 237–239.

7. John Norton Moore, "Forgotten POWs, Forgotten Honor," *Washington Post*, November 10, 2004, A27.

8. *Hamdi v. Rumsfeld*, 296 F. 3d 278 (4th Cir. 2002).

9. Mike Whitney, "Deporting Yasir Hamdi: An Incalculable Victory for Despotism," *Al-Jazeerah*, October 13, 2004.

10. Jason Christopher Hartley, *Just Another Soldier: A Year on the Ground in Iraq* (New York: Harper Collins, 2005), 84–85.

11. General Janis Karpinski with Steve Strasser, *One Woman's Army: The Commanding General of Abu Ghraib Tells Her Story* (New York: Hyperion Books, 2005), 155.

12. Andrew Sullivan, "Atrocities in Plain Sight," *The New York Times*, January 23, 2005, Sec. 7,1.

13. Memorandum, Alberto R. Gonzales, "Decision Re Application of the Geneva Convention on Prisoners of War to the Conflict with Al Qaeda and the Taliban," January 25, 2002. Available on http://news.lp.findlaw.com/hdocs/docs/torture/gnzls12502mem2gwb.html

14. See also Daniel Kanstroom, "'Unlawful Combatants' in the United States: Drawing the Fine Line Between Law and War," *Human Rights Magazine* (American Bar Association), Winter 2003. http://www.abanet.org/irr/hr/winter03/unlawful.html

15. Memo, George Bush to Secretaries of State, Defense, Attorney General, and Joint Chiefs of Staff, February 7, 2002. Available on WashingtonPost.com/wp-srv/nation/documents/020702bush.pdf

16. Memorandum, Alberto R. Gonzales, "Decision Re Application of the Geneva Convention on Prisoners of War to the Conflict with Al Qaeda and the Taliban," January 25, 2002 and November 21, 2005. Op. cit.

17. See "The Debate Over Torture," *Newsweek*, November 21, 2005, 26–33.

18. Karen J. Greenberg, *The Torture Debate in America* (New York: Cambridge University Press, 2006).

19. James M. Olson, *Fair Play: The Moral Dilemmas of Spying* (Washington, DC: Potomac Books, Inc., 2006), especially pp. 65–66.

20. Senator John Cornyn, "Vindicating Gonzales," *National Review online*, February 2, 2005. Accessed: 10 May 2007. http://www.nationalreview.com/comment/cornyn200502020746.asp

21. Syed R. Hassan, *The Reconstruction of Legal Thought in Islam* (Lahore, Pakistan: Law Publishing Company, 1974), 171.

22. Troy Thomas, "Jihad's Captives: Prisoners of War in Islam," *USAF The Journal of Legal Studies*, 12 (2002–2003), 87–101.

23. Council of Foreign Relations (CFR.org), IRAQ: International Law and POWs, March 31, 2003.

24. Report of the International Committee of the Red Cross (ICRC) on the Treatment by the Coalition Forces of Prisoners of War and Other Protected Persons by the Geneva Conventions in Iraq during Arrest, Internment, and Interrogation, February 2004. http://www.globalsecurity.org/military/library/report/2004/icrc_report_iraq_feb2004.htm

25. *Meet the Press*, Tim Russert, Transcript for December 4, 2005, NBC News, p. 9.

26. Sullivan, *The New York Times*, January 23, 2005, op. cit.

27. Karpinski, op. cit., 207–208.

28. Sullivan, *New York Times*, January 23, 2005, op. cit.

29. Report of the International Committee of the Red Cross (ICRC) on the Treatment by the Coalition Forces of Prisoners of War and Other Protected Persons by the Geneva Conventions in Iraq during Arrest, Internment, and Interrogation, op. cit.

30. Sullivan, op. cit., January 23, 2005, op. cit.

31. Amnesty International (London), "Close Guantanamo: Torture and Other ill-treatment," December 8, 2006. AMR 51/189/2006.

32. "Still at Risk: Diplomatic Assurances No Safeguard Against Torture," *Human Rights Watch*, 17(4), (April 2005) (D), 7, 36. For a discussion about the legality of prisoner rendition, see "Reported Removal of Prisoners from Iraq," *The American Journal of International Law*, ed. Sean D. Murphy, 99(1) (January 2005), 265.

33. James Gebhardt, "Road to Abu Ghraib," *Military Review*, 85(1) (2005), 44–50.

34. On April 14, 2003, a group of executive branch attorneys completed a report for Secretary Rumsfeld to consider the legal restraints on the interrogation of detainees held by the United States and despite America's signatory of the Convention Against Torture, concluded that since "'the President enjoys complete discretion in the exercise of his Commander-in-Chief authority including in conducting operations against hostile forces,' any relevant U.S. criminal statutes 'must be construed as inapplicable to interrogations undertaken pursuant to his Commander-in-Chief authority.'" "U.S. Abuse of Iraqi Detainees at Abu Ghraib Prison," *The American Journal of International Law*, 98(3) (July 2004), 593.

Ordinarily, U.S. citizens and foreigners being held inside the country normally have the right to contest their detention before a judge. On February 20, 2007, however, it was announced that the U.S. Court of Appeals for the District of Columbia Circuit ruled 2 v. 1 that civilian courts no longer have the authority to consider whether the military is illegally holding foreigners and ruled that detainees at the U.S. military prison at Guantánamo Bay, Cuba, have no right to challenge their detention in U.S. courts.

The Justice Department said foreign enemy combatants are not protected by the Constitution.

35. Dana Priest, "Secrets and Shame," *Washington Post*, November 3, 2005, A-02.

36. Remarks of historian Sally Marks, German Studies Association Conference, September 2007, Pittsburgh, PA.

37. Donald L. Miller, "POW Hell in Switzerland," *World War II Magazine*, April 2007, 44–51.

38. In the words of former National Security Advisor Zbigniew Brzezinski: "The "war on terror" has created a culture of fear in America. The Bush administration's elevation of these three words into a national mantra since the horrific events of 9/11 has had a pernicious impact on American democracy, on America's psyche and on United States standing in the world. Using this phrase has actually undermined our ability to effectively confront the real challenges we face from fanatics who may use terrorism against us." "By 'War on Terror': How a Three-Word Mantra Has Undermined America," *The Washington Post*, March 25, 2007, B01.

Photo 1. Thousands of French POWs captured by the Germans at the Battle of Champaign in the autumn of 1915. (Private collection of the author)

Photo 2. German appeal for donations to aid its war prisoners on the back of a post card. (Private collection of the author)

Photo 3. Funeral of a German prisoner at Camp Swift, Bastrop, Texas. (U.S. Army photo)

Photo 4. Sunday afternoon soccer championship game, the most popular camp past-time. (UPI)

Photo 5. Newly arrived German POWs await processing in New York even as the guard reads about Germany's surrender.
(World Wide photo)

Photo 6. Calls for donations in Britain and Australia to aid prisoners during World War I. (Private collection of the author)

Photo 7. Although probably posed, the facts are real enough. Many prisoners utilized their time behind barbed wire to learn and study. (Wide World photo)

Photo 8. Map of the major POW camps across the United States as of June 1944. (U.S. Army photo)

Photo 9. The brutal treatment which prisoners could expect during the English Civil War 1642–1660. (Vincent, Lamentations of Germany, 5. Courtesy of the Huntington Library, San Marino, CA)

Photo 10. A German postage stamp issued in 1953 to "Remember Our Prisoners" since hundreds of thousands continued to languish in Soviet prison camps until the mid-1950s. The last 9,626 German POWs did not return home until 1956, more than ten years after the end of the war. (Private collection of the author)

Photo 11. An early, temporary prisoner of war camp at Fort Sam Houston, Texas. (U.S. Army photo)

Photo 12. The prisoners are thoroughly searched again for contraband, military information, and the American soldiers' voracious appetite for souvenirs. (U.S. Army photo)

Photo 13. Immediately after the war, in 1946, Monaco added a postal "surcharge" to raise money for "War Dead and Deported Workers." (Private collection of the author)

Photo 14. At long last, on November 8, 1985, this medal was awarded to all American prisoners dating back to 1917. Prisoners of war were now to be acknowledged and lauded. (Private collection of the author)

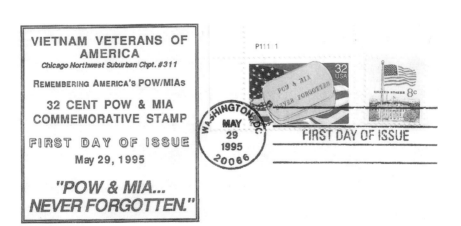

Photo 15. Remembering America's POWs. (Private collection of the author)

Primary Documents

De Jure Belli Ac Pacis (On the Law of War and Peace) by Hugo Grotius, 1625

Published in 1625, *De Jure Belli ac Pacis*, or "On the Law of War and Peace," was one the earliest theses on international law. Its author, Hugo Grotius (1583–1645) was a Dutch lawyer turned politician, widely renowned as a sage in his contemporary society. Grotius began his collegiate studies when he was eleven years old at the University of Leyden and began his law career at The Hague barely five years later. In an essay entitled *De Jure Pradae*, or "On Prize Law," Grotius demonstrated uncommon appreciation for the foundation of moral thought.

Well-trained in classical philosophy, Grotius was an outspoken early theorist of *natural rights*, who sought to support the idea of *just war* by drawing on the principles of *natural law*. His political beliefs led to his arrest and imprisonment from 1618 until 1621. With the help of his wife he escaped from prison and fled to France, where he penned his best-known work, "On the Law of War and Peace." His treatise examined the relationship between natural law and the competing rights of humans, arguing the notion of a just war, and expanding upon the rights and responsibilities of belligerent states once at war.

Taking these theses a step further, Grotius further argued that war is an inevitable consequence of the imposition of human institutions on natural law. He drew upon his own experiences as a political prisoner to set forth a foundation for modern laws governing prisoners of war. Although he likened the Roman tradition of detaining captured enemy soldiers as slaves. Grotius conceded that the common alternative practice was to kill the prisoners of war. Grotius proposed a new alternative which required that nations treat prisoners with decency and allow for repatriation as quickly as possible once a peace agreement could be negotiated.

Supplemental Reading

Haakonssen. Knud. 1985. "Hugo Grotius and the History of Political Thought." *Political Theory*. 12(2): 239–265.

Geyl, Pieter. 1926. "Grotius." *Transactions of the Grotius Society*. Problems of Peace and War, Papers read before the Society in the Year 1926 (1926) 12, pp. 81–97.

On the Law of War and Peace
De Jure Belli ac Pacis
by Hugo Grotius

Translated by A. C. Campbell
London, 1814

CHAPTER 2: In What Manner the Law of Nations Renders the Property of Subjects Answerable for the Debts of Sovereigns. The Nature of Reprisals.
CHAPTER 3: On Just or Solemn War According to the Law of Nations on Declarations of War.
CHAPTER 4: On the Right of Killing an Enemy in Lawful War, and Committing Other Acts of Hostility.
CHAPTER 5: On the Right to Lay Waste an Enemy's Country and Carry off his Effects.
CHAPTER 6: On the Acquisition of Territory and Property by Right of Conquest.
CHAPTER 7: On the Right Over Prisoners of War.
CHAPTER 8: On Empire Over the Conquered.
CHAPTER 9: Of the Right of Postliminium.
CHAPTER 10: [Omitted]
CHAPTER 11: The Right of Killing Enemies, in Just War, To Be Tempered With Moderation and Humanity.
CHAPTER 12: On Moderation in Despoiling an Enemy's Country.
CHAPTER 13: On Moderation in Making Captures in War.
CHAPTER 14: [Omitted]
CHAPTER 15: On Moderation in Acquiring Dominion.
CHAPTER 16: On Moderation with Respect to Things Excluded From the Right of Postliminium by the Law of Nations.
CHAPTER 17: Respecting Those Who Are Neutral in War.
CHAPTER 18: [Omitted]
CHAPTER 19: On Good Faith Between Enemies.
CHAPTER 20: On the Public Faith, by Which War Is Concluded; Comprising Treaties of Peace, and the Nature of Arbitration, Surrender Hostages, Pledges.
CHAPTER 21: On Faith During the Continuance of War, on Truces, Safe-Conducts, and the Redemption of Prisoners.
CHAPTER 22: On the Faith on Those Invested With Subordinate Powers in War.
CHAPTER 23: [Omitted]
CHAPTER 24: On Tacit Faith.
CHAPTER 25: Conclusion.

BOOK III—CHAPTER 7: On the Rights Over Prisoners of War.

I. BY THE law of nature, in its primeval state, apart from human institutions and customs, no men can be slaves: and it is in this sense that legal writers maintain the opinion that slavery is repugnant to nature. Yet, in a former part of this treatise, it was shown that there is nothing repugnant to natural justice, in deriving the origin of servitude from human actions, whether founded upon compact or crime.

II. and III. In ancient times, while slavery was permitted to exist, the offspring, born during captivity or servitude, continued in the same condition as the parents. The consequences of such rules were of wide extent; there was no cruelty, which masters might not inflict upon their slaves;—there was no service, the performance of which they might not compel;—the power even of life and death was in their hands. However the Roman laws at length set bounds to such wanton power, at least to the exercise of it within the Roman territories.

Every thing too, found upon the prisoner's person, became a lawful prize to the captor. For as Justinian observes, one who was entirely in the power of another could have no property of his own.

IV. and V. Incorporeal rights, gained by the enemy, along with the person so captured, cannot be considered in the light of primary and original acquisitions. And there are some rights so purely personal in their nature, that they cannot be lost even by captivity, nor the duties attached thereto ever be relinquished. Of such a nature was the paternal right among the Romans. For rights of this kind cannot exist but immediately with the person to whom they originally belonged.

All these rights to prizes, which were introduced by the law of nations, were intended as an inducement to captors to refrain from the cruel rigour of putting prisoners to death; as they might hope to derive some advantage from sparing and saving them. From hence Pomponius deduces the origin of the word, SERVUS, or SLAVE, being one, who might have been put to death, but from motives of interest or humanity had been saved.

VI. (being the IX. of the original.) It has long been a maxim, universally received among the powers of Christendom, that prisoners of war cannot be made slaves, so as to be sold, or compelled to the hardships and labour attached to slavery. And they have with good reason embraced the latter principle. As it would be inconsistent with every precept of the law of charity, for men to refuse abandoning a cruel right, unless they might be allowed to substitute another, of great, though somewhat inferior rigour, in its place.

And this, as Gregoras informs us, became a traditionary principle among all who professed one common religion; nor was it confined to those, who lived under the authority of the Roman empire, but prevailed among the Thesalians the Illyrians, the Triballians, and Bulgarians. Though such an abolition of slavery, and mitigation of captivity may be considered as of trivial import, yet they were effects produced by the introduction of the Christian religion, especially upon recollection that Socrates tried, but without effect, to prevail upon the Greeks to forbear making slaves of each other.

In this respect the Mahometans act towards each other in the same manner as Christians do. Though it is still the practice among Christian powers to detain prisoners of war, till their ransom be paid, the amount of which depends upon the will of the Conqueror, unless it has been settled by express treaty. The right of detaining such prisoners has sometimes been allowed to the individuals, who took them, except where the prisoners were personages of extraordinary rank, who were always considered as prisoners of war to the state.

BOOK III—CHAPTER 21: On Faith During the Continuance of War, on Truces, Safe-Conducts, and the Redemption of Prisoners.

XXIII. The redemption of prisoners is much favored, particularly among Christian states, to whom the divine law peculiarly recommends it as a kind of mercy. Lactantius calls the redemption of prisoners a great and splendid office of justice.

Source: Constitution Society

Grotius, Hugo. "On the Law of War and Peace." trans. A. C. Campbell. Made available by The Constitution Society. Accessed: 5 May 2007.

http://www.constitution.org/gro/djbp.htm

Lieber's Code (General Orders No. 100), 1863

Dating back to Augustine, philosophers and theorists had long considered the obligations of states engaged in warfare. Until the American Civil War, however, no sovereign nation had codified the formal rights or responsibilities of its army toward the enemy army and the civilian population. Francis Lieber, a German immigrant and law professor at Columbia College in New York, recognized the gap between theory and policy and delivered a series of lectures addressing the "Law and Usages of War." Lieber soon persuaded the General-in-Chief of the Union Army that field officers, many of whom were political appointees and not well-trained, needed a practical guide for engaging with belligerent troops.

On April 24, 1863, President Abraham Lincoln promulgated General Orders No. 100 (Instructions for the Government of Armies of the United States in the Field), also known as Lieber's Code. Many of the basic rights of prisoners of war already considered standard—including the humane treatment of prisoners through reasonable provision of medical care, food, and shelter—were now organized and codified. Under these rules, prisoners could not be punished simply because they were enemy combatants. Although prisoners were honor-bound to state their rank truthfully, they could not be tortured in order to extract military information and could not be punished for providing false information. Lieber's Code also acknowledged private property rights for prisoners and set forth penalties for soldiers who violated these rights. These huge advances were established a century and a half ago.

Although neither Union nor Confederate commanders readily embraced the doctrine, Lieber's Code soon became a basic tool of international law. Later conflicts strengthened Lieber's Code. Less than a decade later, the Prussian Army relied on the code during the Franco-Prussian War of 1870, as did the U.S. Army in the Spanish-American War of 1898. In fact, Lieber's Code inspired future attempts to codify international law, including the Brussels Conference of 1874 and The Hague Conventions of 1899 and 1907.

Suggested Reading

Hartigan, Richard Shelly. 1983. *Lieber's Code and the Law of War*. Chicago: Precedent.

The Lieber Code of 1863

GENERAL ORDERS No. 100.

EXCERPTS FROM INSTRUCTIONS FOR THE GOVERNMENT OF ARMIES OF THE UNITED
STATES IN THE FIELD (THE "LIEBER CODE" 24 APRIL 1863)

24. The almost universal rule in remote times was, and continues to be with barbarous armies, that the private individual of the hostile country is destined to suffer every privation of liberty and protection and every disruption of family ties.... Unjust or inconsiderate retaliation removes the belligerents farther and farther from the mitigating rules of regular war, and by rapid steps leads them nearer to the internecine wars of savages. Peace is their normal condition; war is the exception. The ultimate object of all modern war is a renewed state of peace. The more vigorously wars are pursued the better it is for humanity. Sharp wars are brief.

44. All wanton violence committed against persons in the invaded country, all destruction of property not commanded by the authorized officer, all robbery, all pillage or sacking, even after taking a place by main force, all rape, wounding, maiming, or killing of such inhabitants, are prohibited under the penalty of death, or such other severe punishment as may seem adequate for the gravity of the offense. A soldier, officer, or private, in the act of committing such violence, and disobeying a superior ordering him to abstain from it, may be lawfully killed on the spot by such superior.

SECTION III.—Deserters—Prisoners of war—Hostages—Booty on the battle-field.

48. Deserters from the American Army, having entered the service of the enemy, suffer death if they fall again into the hands of the United States, whether by capture or being delivered up to the American Army; and if a deserter from the enemy, having taken service in the Army of the United States, is captured by the enemy, and punished by them with death or otherwise, it is not a breach against the law and usages of war, requiring redress or retaliation.

49. A prisoner of war is a public enemy armed or attached to the hostile army for active aid, who has fallen into the hands of the captor, either fighting or wounded, on the field or in the hospital, by individual surrender or by capitulation. All soldiers, of whatever species of arms; all men who belong to the rising *en masse* of the hostile country; all those who are attached to the Army for its efficiency and promote directly the object of the war, except such as are hereinafter provided for; all disabled men or officers on the field or elsewhere, if captured; all enemies

who have thrown away their arms and ask for quarter, are prisoners of war, and as such exposed to the inconveniences as well as entitled to the privileges of a prisoner of war.

50. Moreover, citizens who accompany an army for whatever purpose, such as sutlers, editors, or reporters of journals, or contractors, if captured, may be made prisoners of war and be detained as such. The monarch and members of the hostile reigning family, male or female, the chief, and chief officers of the hostile government, its diplomatic agents, and all persons who are of particular and singular use and benefit to the hostile army or its government, are, if captured on belligerent ground, and if unprovided with a safe-conduct granted by the captor's government, prisoners of war.

51. If the people of that portion of an invaded country which is not yet occupied by the enemy, or of the whole country, at the approach of a hostile army, rise, under a duly authorized levy, *en masse* to resist the invader, they are now treated as public enemies, and, if captured, are prisoners of war.

52. No belligerent has the right to declare that he will treat every captured man in arms of a levy *en masse* as a brigand or bandit. If, however, the people of a country, or any portion of the same, already occupied by an army, rise against it, they are violators of the laws of war and are not entitled to their protection.

53. The enemy's chaplains, officers of the medical staff, apothecaries, hospital nurses, and servants, if they fall into the hands of the American Army, are not prisoners of war, unless the commander has reasons to retain them. In this latter case, or if, at their own desire, they are allowed to remain with their captured companions, they are treated as prisoners of war, and may be exchanged if the commander sees fit.

54. A hostage is a person accepted as a pledge for the fulfillment of an agreement concluded between belligerents during the war, or in consequence of a war. Hostages are rare in the present age.

55. If a hostage is accepted, he is treated like a prisoner of war, according to rank and condition, as circumstances may admit.

56. A prisoner of war is subject to no punishment for being a public enemy, nor is any revenge wreaked upon him by the intentional infliction of any suffering, or disgrace, by cruel imprisonment, want of food, by mutilation, death, or any other barbarity.

57. So soon as a man is armed by a sovereign government and takes the soldier's oath of fidelity he is a belligerent; his killing, wounding, or other warlike acts are no individual crimes or offenses. No belligerent has a right to declare that enemies of a certain class, color, or condition, when properly organized as soldiers, will not be treated by him as public enemies.

58. The law of nations knows of no distinction of color, and if an enemy of the United States should enslave and sell any captured persons of their Army, it would be a case for the severest retaliation, if not redressed upon complaint. The United States cannot retaliate by enslavement; therefore death must be the retaliation for this crime against the law of nations.

59. A prisoner of war remains answerable for his crimes committed against the captor's army or people, committed before he was captured, and for which he has not been punished by his own authorities. All prisoners of war are liable to the infliction of retaliatory measures.

60. It is against the usage of modern war to resolve, in hatred and revenge, to give no quarter. No body of troops has the right to declare that it will not give, and therefore will not expect, quarter; but a commander is permitted to direct his troops to give no quarter, in great straits, when his own salvation makes it impossible to cumber himself with prisoners.

61. Troops that give no quarter have no right to kill enemies already disabled on the ground, or prisoners captured by other troops.

62. All troops of the enemy known or discovered to give no quarter in general, or to any portion of the Army, receive none.

63. Troops who fight in the uniform of their enemies, without any plain, striking, and uniform mark of distinction of their own, can expect no quarter.

64. If American troops capture a train containing uniforms of the enemy, and the commander considers it advisable to distribute them for use among his men, some striking mark or sign must be adopted to distinguish the American soldier from the enemy.

65. The use of the enemy's national standard, flag, or other emblem of nationality, for the purpose of deceiving the enemy in battle, is an act of perfidy by which they lose all claim to the protection of the laws of war.

66. Quarter having been given to an enemy by American troops, under a misapprehension of his true character, he may, nevertheless, be ordered to suffer death if, within three days after the battle, it be discovered that he belongs to a corps which gives no quarter.

67. The law of nations allows every sovereign government to make war upon another sovereign State, and, therefore, admits of no rules or laws different from those of regular warfare, regarding the treatment of prisoners of war, although they may belong to the army of a government which the captor may consider as a wanton and unjust assailant.

68. Modern wars are not internecine wars, in which the killing of the enemy is the object. The destruction of the enemy in modern war, and, indeed, modern war itself, are means to obtain that object of the belligerent

which lies beyond the war. Unnecessary or revengeful destruction of life is not lawful.

71. Whoever intentionally inflicts additional wounds on an enemy already wholly disabled, or kills such an enemy, or who orders or encourages soldiers to do so, shall suffer death, if duly convicted, whether he belongs to the Army of the United States, or is an enemy captured after having committed his misdeed.

72. Money and other valuables on the person of a prisoner, such as watches or jewelry, as well as extra clothing, are regarded by the American Army as the private property of the prisoner, and the appropriation of such valuables or money is considered dishonorable, and is prohibited. Nevertheless, if large sums are found upon the persons of prisoners, or in their possession, they shall be taken from them, and the surplus, after providing for their own support, appropriated for the use of the Army, under the direction of the commander, unless otherwise ordered by the Government. Nor can prisoners claim, as private property, large sums found and captured in their train, although they have been placed in the private luggage of the prisoners.

73. All officers, when captured, must surrender their side arms to the captor. They may be restored to the prisoner in marked cases, by the commander, to signalize admiration of his distinguished bravery, or approbation of his humane treatment of prisoners before his capture. The captured officer to whom they may be restored cannot wear them during captivity.

74. A prisoner of war, being a public enemy, is the prisoner of the Government and not of the captor. No ransom can be paid by a prisoner of war to his individual captor, or to any officer in command. The Government alone releases captives, according to rules prescribed by itself.

75. Prisoners of war are subject to confinement or imprisonment such as may be deemed necessary on account of safety, but they are to be subjected to no other intentional suffering or indignity. The confinement and mode of treating a prisoner may be varied during his captivity according to the demands of safety.

76. Prisoners of war shall be fed upon plain and wholesome food, whenever practicable, and treated with humanity. They may be required to work for the benefit of the captor's government, according to their rank and condition.

77. A prisoner of war who escapes may be shot, or otherwise killed, in his flight; but neither death nor any other punishment shall be inflicted upon him simply for his attempt to escape, which the law of war does not consider a crime. Stricter means of security shall be used after an unsuccessful attempt at escape. If, however, a conspiracy is discovered, the purpose of which is a united or general escape, the conspirators may be rigorously punished, even with death; and capital punishment may also be inflicted upon prisoners of war discovered to have

plotted rebellion against the authorities of the captors, whether in union with fellow-prisoners or other persons.

78. If prisoners of war, having given no pledge nor made any promise on their honor, forcibly or otherwise escape, and are captured again in battle, after having rejoined their own army, they shall not be punished for their escape, but shall be treated as simple prisoners of war, although they will be subjected to stricter confinement.

79. Every captured wounded enemy shall be medically treated, according to the ability of the medical staff.

80. Honorable men, when captured, will abstain from giving to the enemy information concerning their own army, and the modern law of war permits no longer the use of any violence against prisoners in order to extort the desired information, or to punish them for having given false information.

81. Partisans are soldiers armed and wearing the uniform of their army, but belonging to a corps which acts detached from the main body for the purpose of making inroads into the territory occupied by the enemy. If captured they are entitled to all the privileges of the prisoner of war.

82. Men, or squads of men, who commit hostilities, whether by fighting, or inroads for destruction or plunder, or by raids of any kind, without commission, without being part and portion of the organized hostile army, and without sharing continuously in the war, but who do so with intermitting returns to their homes and avocations, or with the occasional assumption of the semblance of peaceful pursuits, divesting themselves of the character or appearance of soldiers—such men, or squads of men, are not public enemies, and therefore, if captured, are not entitled to the privileges of prisoners of war, but shall be treated summarily as highway robbers or pirates.

83. Scouts or single soldiers, if disguised in the dress of the country, or in the uniform of the army hostile to their own, employed in obtaining information, if found within or lurking about the lines of the captor, are treated as spies, and suffer death.

84. Armed prowlers, by whatever names they may be called, or persons of the enemy's territory, who steal within the lines of the hostile army for the purpose of robbing, killing, or of destroying bridges, roads, or canals, or of robbing or destroying the mail, or of cutting the telegraph wires, are not entitled to the privileges of the prisoner of war.

85. War-rebels are persons within an occupied territory who rise in arms against the occupying or conquering army, or against the authorities established by the same. If captured, they may suffer death, whether they rise singly, in small or large bands, and whether called upon to do so by their own, but expelled,

government or not. They are not prisoners of war; nor are they if discovered and secured before their conspiracy has matured to an actual rising or to armed violence.

105. Exchanges of prisoners take place—number for number—rank for rank—wounded for wounded—with added condition for added condition—such, for instance, as not to serve for a certain period.

106. In exchanging prisoners of war, such numbers of persons of inferior rank may be substituted as an equivalent for one of superior rank as may be agreed upon by cartel, which requires the sanction of the Government, or of the commander of the army in the field.

107. A prisoner of war is in honor bound truly to state to the captor his rank; and he is not to assume a lower rank than belongs to him, in order to cause a more advantageous exchange, nor a higher rank, for the purpose of obtaining better treatment. Offenses to the contrary have been justly punished by the commanders of released prisoners, and may be good cause for refusing to release such prisoners.

108. The surplus number of prisoners of war remaining after an exchange has taken place is sometimes released either for the payment of a stipulated sum of money, or, in urgent cases, of provision, clothing, or other necessaries. Such arrangement, however, requires the sanction of the highest authority.

109. The exchange of prisoners of war is an act of convenience to both belligerents. If no general cartel has been concluded, it cannot be demanded by either of them. No belligerent is obliged to exchange prisoners of war. A cartel is voidable as soon as either party has violated it.

110. No exchange of prisoners shall be made except after complete capture, and after an accurate account of them, and a list of the captured officers, has been taken.

119. Prisoners of war may be released from captivity by exchange, and, under certain circumstances, also by parole.

120. The term parole designates the pledge of individual good faith and honor to do, or to omit doing, certain acts after he who gives his parole shall have been dismissed, wholly or partially, from the power of the captor.

121. The pledge of the parole is always an individual, but not a private act.

122. The parole applies chiefly to prisoners of war whom the captor allows to return to their country, or to live in greater freedom within the captor's country or territory, on conditions stated in the parole.

123. Release of prisoners of war by exchange is the general rule; release by parole is the exception.

124. Breaking the parole is punished with death when the person breaking the parole is captured again. Accurate lists, therefore, of the paroled persons must be kept by the belligerents.

125. When paroles are given and received there must be an exchange of two written documents, in which the name and rank of the paroled individuals are accurately and truthfully stated.

126. Commissioned officers only are allowed to give their parole, and they can give it only with the permission of their superior, as long as a superior in rank is within reach.

127. No noncommissioned officer or private can give his parole except through an officer. Individual paroles not given through an officer are not only void, but subject the individuals giving them to the punishment of death as deserters. The only admissible exception is where individuals, properly separated from their commands, have suffered long confinement without the possibility of being paroled through an officer.

128. No paroling on the battle-field; no paroling of entire bodies of troops after a battle; and no dismissal of large numbers of prisoners, with a general declaration that they are paroled, is permitted, or of any value.

129. In capitulations for the surrender of strong places or fortified camps the commanding officer, in cases of urgent necessity, may agree that the troops under his command shall not fight again during the war unless exchanged.

130. The usual pledge given in the parole is not to serve during the existing war unless exchanged. This pledge refers only to the active service in the field against the paroling belligerent or his allies actively engaged in the same war. These cases of breaking the parole are patent acts, and can be visited with the punishment of death; but the pledge does not refer to internal service, such as recruiting or drilling the recruits, fortifying places not besieged, quelling civil commotions, fighting against belligerents unconnected with the paroling belligerents, or to civil or diplomatic service for which the paroled officer may be employed.

131. If the government does not approve of the parole, the paroled officer must return into captivity, and should the enemy refuse to receive him he is free of his parole.

132. A belligerent government may declare, by a general order, whether it will allow paroling and on what conditions it will allow it. Such order is communicated to the enemy.

133. No prisoner of war can be forced by the hostile government to parole himself, and no government is obliged to parole prisoners of war or to parole all captured officers, if it paroles any. As the pledging of the parole is an individual act, so is paroling, on the other hand, an act of choice on the part of the belligerent.

145. When an armistice is clearly broken by one of the parties the other party is released from all obligation to observe it.

146. Prisoners taken in the act of breaking an armistice must be treated as prisoners of war, the officer alone being responsible who gives the order for such a violation of an armistice. The highest authority of the belligerent aggrieved may demand redress for the infraction of an armistice.

The Lieber Code of 1863, general Orders No. 100. Made available by Air University at Maxwell AFB. Accessed:[29] September 2007.

http://www.au.af.mil/au/awc/awcgate/law/liebercode.htm

Brussels Declaration of 1874

In the summer of 1874, delegates of fifteen European powers met in Brussels, Belgium, as participants in the Project of an International Declaration Concerning the Laws and Customs of War. Czar Alexander II of Russia submitted to the delegates a draft of proposed laws of war, which further clarified the protections expected for nonbelligerents and the treatment of prisoners of war.

The Brussels Declaration incorporated a number of the provisions of the Lieber Code. The declaration placed prisoners of war in the custody of the captive government rather than individual guards or captors. Consequently, prisoners were subject to the laws of the captive army. The declaration also required the humane treatment of all prisoners, stating that "as a general principle, prisoners of war shall be treated as regards food and clothing, on the same footing as the troops of the Government which captured them," regardless of whether a reciprocal agreement existed between belligerent governments.

Although not all participating governments agreed to be bound by Alexander's proposal, the draft adopted as the Brussels Declaration of 1874 played an important role in shaping future efforts to establish international laws of war. The Brussels Declaration led to a study which resulted in the Oxford Manual of Laws & Customs of War in 1880. These two documents were building blocks for The Hague Conventions.

EXCERPTS FROM THE INTERNATIONAL DECLARATION CONCERNING THE LAWS AND CUSTOMS OF WAR, BRUSSELS (27 August 1874), "Brussels Convention."

Article 9. The laws, rights, and duties of war apply not only to armies, but also to militia and volunteer corps fulfilling the following conditions:

(1) That they be commanded by a person responsible for his subordinates;
(2) That they have a fixed distinctive emblem recognizable at a distance;
(3) That they carry arms openly; and

(4) That they conduct their operations in accordance with the laws and customs of war. In countries where militia constitute the army, or form part of it, they are included under the denomination 'army.'

Article 11. The armed forces of the belligerent parties may consist of combatants and noncombatants. In case of capture by the enemy, both shall enjoy the rights of prisoners of war.

Means of Injuring the Enemy

Article 12. The laws of war do not recognize in belligerents an unlimited power in the adoption of means of injuring the enemy.

Article 13. According to this principle are especially 'forbidden':

(a) Employment of poison or poisoned weapons;
(b) Murder by treachery of individuals belonging to the hostile nation or army;
(c) Murder of an enemy who, having laid down his arms or having no longer means of defense, has surrendered at discretion;
(d) The declaration that no quarter will be given;
(e) The employment of arms, projectiles or material calculated to cause unnecessary suffering, as well as the use of projectiles prohibited by the Declaration of St. Petersburg of 1868;
(f) Making improper use of a flag of truce, of the national flag or of the military insignia and uniform of the enemy, as well as the distinctive badges of the Geneva Convention;
(g) Any destruction or seizure of the enemy's property that is not imperatively demanded by the necessity of war.

Article 14. Ruses of war and the employment of measures necessary for obtaining information about the enemy and the country (excepting the provisions of Article 36) are considered permissible.

Spies

Article 19. A person can only be considered a spy when acting clandestinely or on false pretenses he obtains or endeavors to obtain information in the districts occupied by the enemy, with the intention of communicating it to the hostile party.

Article 20. A spy taken in the act shall be tried and treated according to the laws in force in the army which captures him.

Article 21. A spy who rejoins the army to which he belongs and who is subsequently captured by the enemy is treated as a prisoner of war and incurs no responsibility for his previous acts.

Article 22. Soldiers not wearing a disguise who have penetrated into the zone of operations of the hostile army, for the purpose of obtaining information, are not considered spies.

Similarly, the following should not be considered spies, if they are captured by the enemy: soldiers (and also civilians, carrying out their mission openly) entrusted with the delivery of dispatches intended either for their own army or for the enemy's army.

To this class belong likewise, if they are captured, persons sent in balloons for the purpose of carrying dispatches and, generally, of maintaining communications between the different parts of an army or a territory.

Prisoners of War

Article 23. Prisoners of war are lawful and disarmed enemies.

They are in the power of the hostile Government, but not in that of the individuals or corps who captured them. They must be humanely treated.

Any act of insubordination justifies the adoption of such measures of severity as may be necessary. All their personal belongings except arms shall remain their property.

Article 24. Prisoners of war may be interned in a town, fortress, camp, or other place, under obligation not to go beyond certain fixed limits; but they can only be placed in confinement as an indispensable measure of safety.

Article 25. Prisoners of war may be employed on certain public works which have no direct connection with the operations in the theatre of war and which are not excessive or humiliating to their military rank, if they belong to the army, or to their official or social position, if they do not belong to it.

They may also, subject to such regulations as may be drawn up by the military authorities, undertake private work.

Their wages shall go towards improving their position or shall be paid to them on their release. In this case the cost of maintenance may be deducted from said wages.

Article 26. Prisoners of war cannot be compelled in any way to take any part whatever in carrying on the operations of the war.

Article 27. The Government into whose hands prisoners of war have fallen charges itself with their maintenance. The conditions of such maintenance may be settled by a reciprocal agreement between the belligerent parties. In the absence of this agreement, and as a general principle, prisoners of war shall be treated as regards food and clothing, on the same footing as the troops of the Government which captured them.

Article 28. Prisoners of war are subject to the laws and regulations in force in the army in whose power they are. Arms may be used, after summoning, against a prisoner of war attempting to escape. If recaptured he is liable to disciplinary punishment or subject to a stricter surveillance.

If, after succeeding in escaping, he is again taken prisoner, he is not liable to punishment for his previous acts.

Article 29. Every prisoner of war is bound to give, if questioned on the subject, his true name and rank, and if he infringes this rule, he is liable to a curtailment of the advantages accorded to the prisoners of war of his class.

Article 30. The exchange of prisoners of war is regulated by a mutual understanding between the belligerent parties.

Article 31. Prisoners of war may be set at liberty on parole if the laws of their country allow it, and, in such cases, they are bound, on their personal honour, scrupulously to fulfill, both towards their own Government and the Government by which they were made prisoners, the engagements they have contracted.

In such cases their own Government ought neither to require of nor accept from them any service incompatible with the parole given.

Article 32. A prisoner of war cannot be compelled to accept his liberty on parole; similarly the hostile Government is not obliged to accede to the request of the prisoner to be set at liberty on parole.

Article 33. Any prisoner of war liberated on parole and recaptured bearing arms against the Government to which he had pledged his honour may be deprived of the rights accorded to prisoners of war and brought before the courts.

Article 34. Individuals in the vicinity of armies but not directly forming part of them, such as correspondents, newspaper reporters, sutlers, contractors, etc., can also be made prisoners. These prisoners should however be in possession of a permit issued by the competent authority and of a certificate of identity.

The Sick and Wounded

Article 35. The obligations of belligerents with respect to the service of the sick and wounded are governed by the Geneva Convention of 22 August 1864, save such modifications as the latter may undergo.

On the Military Power with Respect to Private Persons

Article 36. The population of occupied territory cannot be forced to take part in military operations against its own country.

Article 37. The population of occupied territory cannot be compelled to swear allegiance to the hostile Power.

Article 38. Family honor and rights, and the lives and property of persons, as well as their religious convictions and their practice, must be respected. Private property cannot be confiscated.

Article 39. Pillage is formally forbidden.

Text taken from:

Text made available by the University of Minnesota Human Rights Library. Accessed: 29 September 2007.

http://www1.umn.edu/humanrts/instree/1874a.htm

The Laws of War on Land, Oxford Manual, 1880

In 1873, an international group of legal scholars and jurists formed the Institute of International Law. The group was founded as a private, scientific association free from the influence of any single government. Accordingly, the Institute sought to promote the progress of international law through the formulation and codification of policies and by seeking official acceptance of these policies by governments.

Inspired by the Brussels Declaration of 1874, the Institute published its own manual of war. Known as *The Laws of War on Land*, or the Oxford Manual of 1880, this document was neither original nor innovative. It borrowed heavily upon the declaration put forth in Brussels, recognizing the existence of "certain principles of justice which guide the public conscience, which are manifested even by general customs, but which it would be well to fix and make obligatory." Rather than encouraging international treaty, the Institute attempted to clarify and codify commonly accepted notions of decency. The authors of the Oxford Manual hoped their work would be adopted as legislation by various nations.

The Oxford Manual clearly defined prisoners of war and the status of captured civilians, stated the rights and privileges of prisoners, and addressed the procedures for releasing prisoners. The manual stressed, "that the confinement of prisoners of war is not in the nature of a penalty for crime: neither is it an act of vengeance. It is a temporary detention only, entirely without penal character." Accordingly, prisoners were to be treated humanely and were not to be abused, tortured, or humiliated in any way. The manual below was drafted by Gustave Moynier and unanimously adopted by the Institute. Its purpose is stated in the preface.

EXCERPTS FROM THE LAWS OF WAR ON LAND, OXFORD
(Oxford, 9 September 1880) "The Oxford Manual"

Preface

War holds a great place in history, and it is not to be supposed that men will soon give it up—in spite of the protests which it arouses and the horror which it inspires—because it appears to be the only possible issue of disputes which threaten the existence of States, their liberty, their vital interests. But the gradual improvement in customs should be reflected in the method of conducting war. It is worthy of civilized nations to seek, as has been well said (Baron Jomini), "to restrain the destructive force of war, while recognizing its inexorable necessities."

This problem is not easy of solution; however, some points have already been solved, and very recently the draft of Declaration of Brussels has been a solemn pronouncement of the good intentions of governments in this connection. It may be said that independently of the international laws existing on this subject, there are to-day certain principles of justice which guide the public conscience, which are manifested even by general customs, but which it would be well to fix and make obligatory. That is what the Conference of Brussels attempted, at the suggestion of His Majesty the Emperor of Russia, and it is what the Institute of International Law, in its turn, is trying to-day to contribute. The Institute attempts this although the governments have not ratified the draft issued by the Conference at Brussels, because since 1874 ideas, aided by reflection and experience, have had time to mature, and because it seems less difficult than it did then to trace rules which would be acceptable to all peoples.

The Institute, too, does not propose an international treaty, which might perhaps be premature or at least very difficult to obtain; but, being bound by its by-laws to work, among other things, for the observation of the laws of war, it believes it is fulfilling a duty in offering to the governments a 'Manual' suitable as the basis for national legislation in each State, and in accord with both the progress of juridical science and the needs of civilized armies.

Rash and extreme rules will not, furthermore, be found therein. The Institute has not sought innovations in drawing up the 'Manual'; it has contented itself with stating clearly and codifying the accepted ideas of our age so far as this has appeared allowable and practicable.

By so doing, it believes it is rendering a service to military men themselves. In fact so long as the demands of opinion remain indeterminate, belligerents are exposed to painful uncertainty and to endless accusations. A positive set of rules, on the contrary, if they are judicious, serves the interests of belligerents and is far from hindering them, since by preventing the unchaining of passion and savage instincts—which battle always awakens, as much as it awakens courage and manly virtues—it strengthens the discipline which is the strength of armies; it also ennobles their patriotic mission in the eyes of the soldiers by keeping them within the limits of respect due to the rights of humanity.

But in order to attain this end it is not sufficient for sovereigns to promulgate new laws. It is essential, too, that they make these laws known among all people, so that when a war is declared, the men called upon to take up arms to defend the causes of the belligerent States, may be thoroughly impregnated with the special rights and duties attached to the execution of such a command.

The Institute, with a view to assisting the authorities in accomplishing this part of their task, has given its work a popular form, attaching thereto statements of the reasons therefore, from which the text of a law may be easily secured when desired.

PART I: GENERAL PRINCIPLES

Article 1. The state of war does not admit of acts of violence, save between the armed forces of belligerent States.

Persons not forming part of a belligerent armed force should abstain from such acts.

'This rule implies a distinction between the individuals who compose the "armed force" of a State and its other 'ressortissants.' A definition of the term "armed force" is, therefore, necessary.'

Article 2. The armed force of a State includes:

(1) The army properly so called, including the militia;
(2) The national guards, landsturm, free corps, and other bodies which fulfil the three following conditions:
    (a) That they are under the direction of a responsible chief;
    (b) That they must have a uniform, or a fixed distinctive emblem recognizable at a distance, and worn by individuals composing such corps;
    (c) That they carry arms openly;
(3) The crews of men-of-war and other military boats;
(4) The inhabitants of non-occupied territory, who, on the approach of the enemy, take up arms spontaneously and openly to resist the invading troops, even if they have not had time to organize themselves.

Article 3. Every belligerent armed force is bound to conform to the laws of war.

'The only legitimate end that States may have in war being to weaken the military strength of the enemy' (Declaration of St. Petersburg, 1868),

Article 4. The laws of war do not recognize in belligerents an unlimited liberty as to the means of injuring the enemy.

They are to abstain especially from all needless severity, as well as from all perfidious, unjust, or tyrannical acts.

Article 5. Military conventions made between belligerents during the continuance of war, such as armistices and capitulations, must be scrupulously observed and respected.

Article 6. No invaded territory is regarded as conquered until the end of the war; until that time the occupant exercises, in such territory, only a 'de facto' power, essentially provisional in character.

PART II : APPLICATION OF GENERAL PRINCIPLES

I. HOSTILITIES

A. Rules of conduct with regard to individuals

(a) Inoffensive populations

'The contest being carried on by "armed forces" only (Article 1),'

Article 7. It is forbidden to maltreat inoffensive populations.

(b) Means of injuring the enemy

'As the struggle must be honourable (Article 4),'

Article 8. It is forbidden:

(a) To make use of poison, in any form whatever;
(b) To make treacherous attempts upon the life of an enemy; as, for example, by keeping assassins in pay or by feigning to surrender;
(c) To attack an enemy while concealing the distinctive signs of an armed force;
(d) To make improper use of the national flag, military insignia or uniform of the enemy, of the flag of truce and of the protective signs prescribed by the 'Geneva Convention' (Articles 17 and 40).

'As needless severity should be avoided (Article 4),'

Article 9. It is forbidden:

(a) To employ arms, projectiles, or materials of any kind calculated to cause superfluous suffering, or to aggravate wounds—notably projectiles of less weight than four hundred grams which are explosive or are charged with fulminating or inflammable substances (Declaration of St. Petersburg);
(b) To injure or kill an enemy who has surrendered at discretion or is disabled, and to declare in advance that quarter will not be given, even by those who do not ask it for themselves.
(c) The sick and wounded, and the sanitary service:

'The following provisions (Articles 10 to 18), drawn from the 'Geneva Convention,' exempt the sick and wounded, and the personnel of the sanitary service, from many of the needless hardships to which they were formerly exposed':

Article 10. Wounded or sick soldiers should be brought in and cared for, to whatever nation they belong.

Article 11. Commanders in chief have power to deliver immediately to the enemy outposts hostile soldiers who have been wounded in an engagement, when circumstances permit and with the consent of both parties.

Article 12. Evacuations, together with the persons under whose direction they take place, shall be protected by neutrality.

Article 13. Persons employed in hospitals and ambulances—including the staff for superintendence, medical service, administration and transport of wounded, as well as the chaplains, and the members and agents of relief associations which are duly authorized to assist the regular sanitary staff—are considered as neutral while so employed, and so long as there remain any wounded to bring in or to succour.

Article 14. The personnel designated in the preceding article should continue, after occupation by the enemy, to tend, according to their needs, the sick and wounded in the ambulance or hospital which it serves.

Article 15. When such personnel requests to withdraw, the commander of the occupying troops sets the time of departure, which however he can only delay for a short time in case of military necessity.

Article 16. Measures should be taken to assure, if possible, to neutralized persons who have fallen into the hands of the enemy, the enjoyment of fitting maintenance.

Article 17. The neutralized sanitary staff should wear a white arm-badge with a red cross, but the delivery thereof belongs exclusively to the military authority.

Article 18. The generals of the belligerent Powers should appeal to the humanity of the inhabitants, and should endeavour to induce them to assist the wounded by pointing out to them the advantages that will result to themselves from so doing (Articles 36 and 59). They should regard as inviolable those who respond to this appeal.

(d) The dead

Article 19. It is forbidden to rob or mutilate the dead lying on the field of battle.

Article 20. The dead should never be buried until all articles on them which may serve to fix their identity, such as pocket-books, numbers, etc., shall have been collected.

The articles thus collected from the dead of the enemy are transmitted to its army or government.

(e) Who may be made prisoners of war

Article 21. Individuals who form a part of the belligerent armed force, if they fall into the hands of the enemy, are to be treated as prisoners of war, in conformity with Articles 61 *et seq.*

The same rule applies to messengers openly carrying official dispatches, and to civil aeronauts charged with observing the enemy, or with the maintenance of communications between the various parts of the army or territory.

Article 22. Individuals who accompany an army, but who are not a part of the regular armed force of the State, such as correspondents, traders, sutlers, etc., and who fall into the hands of the enemy, may be detained for such length of time only as is warranted by strict military necessity.

(f) Spies

Article 23. Individuals captured as spies cannot demand to be treated as prisoners of war.

'But'

Article 24. Individuals may not be regarded as spies, who, belonging to the armed force of either belligerent, have penetrated, without disguise, into the zone of operations of the enemy, nor bearers of official dispatches, carrying out their mission openly, nor aeronauts (Article 21).

'In order to avoid the abuses to which accusations of espionage too often give rise in war it is important to assert emphatically that'

Article 25. No person charged with espionage shall be punished until the judicial authority shall have pronounced judgment.

'Moreover, it is admitted that'

Article 26. A spy who succeeds in quitting the territory occupied by the enemy incurs no responsibility for his previous acts, should he afterwards fall into the hands of that enemy.

(g) Parlementaires

Article 27. A person is regarded as a parlementaire and has a right to inviolability who has been authorized by one of the belligerents to enter into communication with the other, and who advances bearing a white flag.

Article 28. He may be accompanied by a bugler or a drummer, by a colour-bearer, and, if need be, by a guide and interpreter, who also are entitled to inviolability.

'The necessity of this prerogative is evident. It is moreover, frequently exercised in the interest of humanity. But it must not be injurious to the adverse party. This is why'

Article 29. The commander to whom a parlementaire is sent is not in all cases obliged to receive him.

'Besides,'

Article 30. The commander who receives a parlementaire has a right to take all the necessary steps to prevent the presence of the enemy within his lines from being prejudicial to him.

'The parlementaire and those who accompany him should behave fairly towards the enemy receiving them (Article 4).'

Article 31. If a parlementaire abuse the trust reposed in him he may be temporarily detained, and, if it be proved that he has taken advantage of his privileged position to abet a treasonable act, he forfeits his right to inviolability.

III. Prisoners of War

A. Rules for captivity

'The confinement of prisoners of war is not in the nature of a penalty for crime (Article 21): neither is it an act of vengeance. It is a temporary detention only, entirely without penal character.

In the following provisions, therefore, regard has been had to the consideration due them as prisoners, and to the necessity of their secure detention.'

Article 61. Prisoners of war are in the power of the hostile government, but not in that of the individuals or corps who captured them.

Article 62. They are subject to the laws and regulations in force in the army of the enemy.

Article 63. They must be humanely treated.

Article 64. All their personal belongings, except arms, remain their property.

Article 65. Every prisoner is bound to give, if questioned on the subject, his true name and rank. Should he fail to do so, he may be deprived of all, or a part, of the advantages accorded to prisoners of his class.

Article 66. Prisoners may be interned in a town, a fortress, a camp, or other place, under obligation not to go beyond certain fixed limits; but they may only be placed in confinement as an indispensable measure of safety.

Article 67. Any act of insubordination justifies the adoption towards them of such measure of severity as may be necessary.

Article 68. Arms may be used, after summoning, against a prisoner attempting to escape.

If he is recaptured before being able to rejoin his own army or to quit the territory of his captor, he is only liable to disciplinary punishment, or subject to a stricter surveillance.

But if, after succeeding in escaping, he is again captured, he is not liable to punishment for his previous flight.

If, however, the fugitive so recaptured or retaken has given his parole not to escape, he may be deprived of the rights of a prisoner of war.

Article 69. The government into whose hands prisoners have fallen is charged with their maintenance.

In the absence of an agreement on this point between the belligerent parties, prisoners are treated, as regards food and clothing, on the same peace footing as the troops of the government which captured them.

Article 70. Prisoners cannot be compelled in any manner to take any part whatever in the operations of war, nor compelled to give information about their country or their army.

Article 71. They may be employed on public works which have no direct connection with the operations in the theatre of war, which are not excessive and are not humiliating either to their military rank, if they belong to the army, or to their official or social position, if they do not form part thereof.

Article 72. In case of their being authorized to engage in private industries, their pay for such services may be collected by the authority in charge of them. The sums so received may be employed in bettering their condition, or may be paid to them on their release, subject to deduction, if that course be deemed expedient, of the expense of their maintenance.

B. Termination of captivity

'The reasons justifying detention of the captured enemy exist only during the continuance of the war.'

Article 73. The captivity of prisoners of war ceases, as a matter of right, at the conclusion of peace; but their liberation is then regulated by agreement between the belligerents.

Before that time, and by virtue of the "Geneva Convention,"

Article 74. It also ceases as of right for wounded or sick prisoners who, after being cured, are found to be unfit for further military service. The captor should then send them back to their country.

'During the war'

Article 75. Prisoners of war may be released in accordance with a cartel of exchange, agreed upon by the belligerent parties.

'Even without exchange'

Article 76. Prisoners may be set at liberty on parole, if the laws of their country do not forbid it.

In this case they are bound, on their personal honour, scrupulously to fulfil the engagements which they have freely contracted, and which should be clearly specified. On its part, their own government should not demand or accept from them any service incompatible with the parole given.

Article 77. A prisoner cannot be compelled to accept his liberty on parole. Similarly, the hostile government is not obliged to accede to the request of a prisoner to be set at liberty on parole.

Article 78. Any prisoner liberated on parole and recaptured bearing arms against the government to which he had given such parole may be deprived of his rights as a prisoner of war, unless since his liberation he has been included in an unconditional exchange of prisoners.

IV. PERSONS INTERNED IN NEUTRAL TERRITORY

'It is universally admitted that a neutral State cannot, without compromising its neutrality, lend aid to either belligerent, or permit them to make use of its territory. On the other hand, considerations of humanity dictate that asylum should not be refused to individuals who take refuge in neutral territory to escape death or captivity. Hence the following provisions, calculated to reconcile the opposing interests involved.'

Article 79. A neutral State on whose territory troops or individuals belonging to the armed forces of the belligerents take refuge should intern them, as far as possible, at a distance from the theatre of war.

It should do the same towards those who make use of its territory for military operations or services.

Article 80. The interned may be kept in camps or even confined in fortresses or other places.

The neutral State decides whether officers can be left at liberty on parole by taking an engagement not to leave the neutral territory without permission.

Article 81. In the absence of a special convention concerning the maintenance of the interned, the neutral State supplies them with the food, clothing, and relief required by humanity.

It also takes care of the 'matériel' brought in by the interned.

When peace has been concluded, or sooner if possible, the expenses caused by the internment are repaid to the neutral State by the belligerent State to which the interned belong.

Article 82. The provisions of the 'Geneva Convention' of 22 August 1864 (Articles 10–18, 35–40, 59 and 74 above given), are applicable to the sanitary staff, as well as to the sick and wounded, who take refuge in, or are conveyed to, neutral territory.

'In particular,'

Article 83. Evacuations of wounded and sick not prisoners may pass through neutral territory, provided the personnel and material accompanying them are exclusively sanitary. The neutral State through whose territory these evacuations are made is bound to take whatever measures of safety and control are necessary to secure the strict observance of the above conditions.

Text taken from: http://www.icrc.org/ihl.nsf/Full/140?OpenDocument Accessed: 29 September 2007

Final Act of the International Peace Conference, The Hague, 29 July 1899

Although the European powers had made strides in codifying the conduct of war through the Brussels Declaration of 1874 and the subsequent Oxford Manual published in 1880, the great powers had yet to come to an agreement on armament levels. Increasingly concerned about the sheer cost of maintaining armed peace, the First International Peace Conference was convened in The Hague on 18 May 1899 at the invitation of Queen Wilhelmina of the Netherlands and Czar Nicholas II of Russia. Czar Nicholas II of Russia called for the great powers to convene for the purpose of limiting the size of militaries and the introduction of new weaponry. The location was chosen to avoid the political trappings often attributed to the great capitals.

The twenty-six governments represented at the conference were successful in reaffirming the traditional rules governing combat on land and sea yet made little progress in limiting armament levels. Concerning the innovation of new forms of weaponry, the Conference agreed upon restrictions concerning the use of manned balloons, poisonous gas, and hollow point bullets. One of the most significant accomplishments in The Hague was the adoption of the Pacific Settlement of International Disputes, an agreement which called for nations on the brink of war to exhaust all possible means of peaceful resolution.

Additionally, the Hague Convention of 1899 reaffirmed many of the provisions afforded to war prisoners by the Lieber Code of 1863 and the Brussels Declaration. Among these early provisions, prisoners were to be held under the power of the hostile government rather than individual captors, prisoners were to be treated on the same footing as the soldiers of the hostile government, and paroled prisoners who took up arms against the pardoning country forfeited their rights to prisoner of war status if captured again.

Building upon earlier treaties concerning prisoners of war, the Hague Convention of 1899 required that belligerent states institute an information bureau to keep records on prisoners, including internments and hospitalizations. All correspondence or parcels concerning prisoners were to receive free postage from any country of transit. Belligerent countries were required to afford all necessary resources to relief societies and allow such charities reasonable access to the captives. Prisoners were given the right to observe non-disruptive religious practices, and belligerent countries were directed to expeditiously repatriate prisoners once a peace agreement was negotiated. The First Hague Peace Conference concluded on 29 July 1899.

Supplemental Reading

Tryon, James L. 1911. "The Hague Conferences." *The Yale Law Journal*. 20(6): 470–485;

Geoffrey Best. "Peace Conferences and the Century of Total War: The 1899 Hague Conference and What Came After." *International Affairs*. 75(3), (1999): 619–634.

EXCERPTS FROM THE CONVENTION WITH RESPECT TO THE LAWS AND CUSTOMS OF WAR ON LAND AND ITS ANNEX. THE HAGUE (29 JULY, 1899)

CHAPTER I [. . .]

Article 3. The armed forces of the belligerent parties may consist of combatants and noncombatants. In case of capture by the enemy both have a right to be treated as prisoners of war.

CHAPTER II
On prisoners of war [. . .]

Article 4. Prisoners of war are in the power of the hostile Government, but not in that of the individuals or corps who captured them.

They must be humanely treated.

All their personal belongings, except arms, horses, and military papers remain their property.

Article 5. Prisoners of war may be interned in a town, fortress, camp, or any other locality, and bound not to go beyond certain fixed limits; but they can only be confined as an indispensable measure of safety.

Article 6. The State may utilize the labour of prisoners of war according to their rank and aptitude. Their tasks shall not be excessive, and shall have nothing to do with the military operations.

Prisoners may be authorized to work for the public service, for private persons, or on their own account.

Work done for the State shall be paid for according to the tariffs in force for soldiers of the national army employed on similar tasks.

When the work is for other branches of the public service or for private persons, the conditions shall be settled in agreement with the military authorities.

The wages of the prisoners shall go towards improving their position, and the balance shall be paid them at the time of their release, after deducting the cost of their maintenance.

Article 7. The Government into whose hands prisoners of war have fallen is bound to maintain them.

Failing a special agreement between the belligerents, prisoners of war shall be treated as regards food, quarters, and clothing, on the same footing as the troops of the Government which has captured them.

Article 8. Prisoners of war shall be subject to the laws, regulations, and orders in force in the army of the State into whose hands they have fallen. Any act of insubordination warrants the adoption, as regards them, of such measures of severity as may be necessary. Escaped prisoners, recaptured before they have succeeded in rejoining their army, or before quitting the territory occupied by the army that captured them, are liable to disciplinary punishment.

Prisoners who, after succeeding in escaping are again taken prisoners, are not liable to any punishment for the previous flight.

Article 9. Every prisoner of war, if questioned, is bound to declare his true name and rank, and if he disregards this rule, he is liable to a curtailment of the advantages accorded to the prisoners of war of his class.

Article 10. Prisoners of war may be set at liberty on parole if the laws of their country authorize it, and, in such a case, they are bound, on their personal honour, scrupulously to fulfil, both as regards their own Government and the Government by whom they were made prisoners, the engagements they have contracted.

In such cases, their own Government shall not require of nor accept from them any service incompatible with the parole given.

Article 11. A prisoner of war cannot be forced to accept his liberty on parole; similarly the hostile Government is not obliged to assent to the prisoner's request to be set at liberty on parole.

Article 12. Any prisoner of war, who is liberated on parole and recaptured, bearing arms against the Government to whom he had pledged his honor, or against the allies of that Government, forfeits his right to be treated as a prisoner of war, and can be brought before the courts.

Article 13. Individuals who follow an army without directly belonging to it, such as newspaper correspondents and reporters, sutlers, contractors, who fall into the enemy's hands, and whom the latter think fit to detain, have a right to be treated as prisoners of war, provided they can produce a certificate from the military authorities of the army they were accompanying.

Article 14. A bureau for information relative to prisoners of war is instituted, on the commencement of hostilities, in each of the belligerent States, and, when necessary, in the neutral countries on whose territory belligerents have been received.

This bureau is intended to answer all inquiries about prisoners of war, and is furnished by the various services concerned with all the necessary information to enable it to keep an individual return for each prisoner of war. It is kept informed of internments and changes, as well as of admissions into hospital and deaths.

It is also the duty of the information bureau to receive and collect all objects of personal use, valuables, letters, etc., found on the battlefields or left by prisoners who have died in hospital or ambulance, and to transmit them to those interested.

Article 15. Relief societies for prisoners of war, which are regularly constituted in accordance with the law of the country with the object of serving as the intermediary for charity, shall receive from the belligerents for themselves and their duly accredited agents every facility, within the bounds of military requirements and administrative regulations, for the effective accomplishment of their humane task. Delegates of these societies may be admitted to the places of internment for the distribution of relief, as also to the halting places of repatriated prisoners, if furnished with a personal permit by the military authorities, and on giving an engagement in writing to comply with all their regulations for order and police.

Article 16. The information bureau shall have the privilege of free postage. Letters, money orders, and valuables, as well as postal parcels destined for the prisoners of war or dispatched by them, shall be free of all postal duties both in the countries of origin and destination, as well as in those they pass through.

Gifts and relief in kind for prisoners of war shall be admitted free of all duties of entry and others, as well as of payments for carriage by the Government railways.

Article 17. Officers taken prisoners may receive, if necessary, the full pay allowed them in this position by their country's regulations, the amount to be repaid by their Government.

Article 18. Prisoners of war shall enjoy every latitude in the exercise of their religion, including attendance at their own church services, provided only they comply with the regulations for order and police issued by the military authorities.

Article 19. The wills of prisoners of war are received or drawn up on the same conditions as for soldiers of the national army.

The same rules shall be observed regarding death certificates, as well as for the burial of prisoners of war, due regard being paid to their grade and rank.

Article 20. After the conclusion of peace, the repatriation of prisoners of war shall take place as speedily as possible.

CHAPTER III
On the sick and wounded

Article 21. The obligations of belligerents with regard to the sick and wounded are governed by the Geneva Convention of 22 August 1864, subject to any modifications which may be introduced into it.

SECTION II
ON HOSTILITIES

CHAPTER I [. . .]

Article 23. Besides the prohibitions provided by special Conventions, it is especially prohibited

(a) To employ poison or poisoned arms;
(b) To kill or wound treacherously individuals belonging to the hostile nation or army;
(c) To kill or wound an enemy who, having laid down arms, or having no longer means of defence, has surrendered at discretion;
(d) To declare that no quarter will be given;
(e) To employ arms, projectiles, or material of a nature to cause superfluous injury;
(f) To make improper use of a flag of truce, the national flag or military ensigns and uniform of the enemy, as well as the distinctive badges of the Geneva Convention;
(g) To destroy or seize the enemy's property, unless such destruction or seizure be imperatively demanded by the necessities of war.

Article 24. Ruses of war and the employment of methods necessary to obtain information about the enemy and the country, are considered allowable.

Text made available by the International Committee of the Red Cross. Accessed: 29 September 2007. http://www.icrc.org/ihl.nsf/Full/140?OpenDocument

Final Act of the Second Peace Conference, The Hague, 18 October 1907

The nations of the world entered the twentieth century with a working framework for peace. Although negotiations at The Hague in 1899 had produced the most comprehensive code of war attempted by modern Europe and the Americas thus far, the great powers recognized room for further clarification. Czar Nicholas II of Russia called for a second conference, which convened at The Hague on 15 June 1907 and concluded 18 October 1907.

The process of codifying the international rules of war would be ongoing. Participants at the 1907 peace conference intended for their framework "to serve as a general rule of conduct," for belligerent states, urging military commanders to appeal to the higher laws of humanity for guidance in unforeseen circumstances. As this would be the last major peace conference prior to the outbreak of the First World War, it is notable that forty-four of the nearly fifty nations considered part of the modern world system sent delegations to The Netherlands.

There were no major revisions to the conference of 1899 concerning prisoners of war (POWs). Participants at the 1907 conference expanded upon the mandate for belligerent nations to establish bureaus of inquiry, clarifying that these offices were responsible for maintaining detailed records of prisoners to include everything from internments and transfers to escape attempts and hospitalizations. These offices would also be required to keep detailed records of prisoners' vital statistics. All records would be transferred to the prisoners' home governments once a peace settlement could be negotiated.

Supplemental Reading

Tryon, James L. "The Hague Conferences." *The Yale Law Journal*. 20(6): 1911. 470–485.

EXCERPTS FROM THE 1907 HAGUE CONVENTION WITH RESPECT TO THE LAWS AND CUSTOMS OF WAR ON LAND, THE HAGUE (18 OCTOBER 1907).

CHAPTER I
The Qualifications of Belligerents

Article 1. The laws, rights, and duties of war apply not only to armies, but also to militia and volunteer corps fulfilling the following conditions:

(1) To be commanded by a person responsible for his subordinates;
(2) To have a fixed distinctive emblem recognizable at a distance;
(3) To carry arms openly; and
(4) To conduct their operations in accordance with the laws and customs of war.
(5) In countries where militia or volunteer corps constitute the army, or form part of it, they are included under the denomination "army."

Article 2. The inhabitants of a territory which has not been occupied, who, on the approach of the enemy, spontaneously take up arms to resist the invading troops without having had time to organize themselves in accordance with Article 1, shall be regarded as belligerents if they carry arms openly and if they respect the laws and customs of war.

Article 3. The armed forces of the belligerent parties may consist of combatants and noncombatants. In the case of capture by the enemy, both have a right to be treated as prisoners of war.

CHAPTER II
Prisoners of War

Article 4. Prisoners of war are in the power of the hostile Government, but not of the individuals or corps who capture them. They must be humanely treated.

All their personal belongings, except arms, horses, and military papers, remain their property.

Article 5. Prisoners of war may be interned in a town, fortress, camp, or other place, and bound not to go beyond certain fixed limits; but they cannot be confined except as in indispensable measure of safety and only while the circumstances which necessitate the measure continue to exist.

Article 6. The State may utilize the labour of prisoners of war according to their rank and aptitude, officers excepted. The tasks shall not be excessive and shall have no connection with the operations of the war.

Prisoners may be authorized to work for the public service, for private persons, or on their own account.

Work done for the State is paid for at the rates in force for work of a similar kind done by soldiers of the national army, or, if there are none in force, at a rate according to the work executed.

When the work is for other branches of the public service or for private persons the conditions are settled in agreement with the military authorities.

The wages of the prisoners shall go towards improving their position, and the balance shall be paid them on their release, after deducting the cost of their maintenance.

Article 7. The Government into whose hands prisoners of war have fallen is charged with their maintenance.

In the absence of a special agreement between the belligerents, prisoners of war shall be treated as regards board, lodging, and clothing on the same footing as the troops of the Government who captured them.

Article 8. Prisoners of war shall be subject to the laws, regulations, and orders in force in the army of the State in whose power they are. Any act of insubordination justifies the adoption towards them of such measures of severity as may be considered necessary. Escaped prisoners who are retaken before being able to rejoin their own army or before leaving the territory occupied by the army which captured them are liable to disciplinary punishment.

Prisoners who, after succeeding in escaping, are again taken prisoners, are not liable to any punishment on account of the previous flight.

Article 9. Every prisoner of war is bound to give, if he is questioned on the subject, his true name and rank, and if he infringes this rule, he is liable to have the advantages given to prisoners of his class curtailed.

Article 10. Prisoners of war may be set at liberty on parole if the laws of their country allow, and, in such cases, they are bound, on their personal honour, scrupulously to fulfil, both towards their own Government and the Government by whom they were made prisoners, the engagements they have contracted.

In such cases their own Government is bound neither to require of nor accept from them any service incompatible with the parole given.

Article 11. A prisoner of war cannot be compelled to accept his liberty on parole; similarly the hostile Government is not obliged to accede to the request of the prisoner to be set at liberty on parole.

Article 12. Prisoners of war liberated on parole and recaptured bearing arms against the Government to whom they had pledged their honour, or against the allies of that Government, forfeit their right to be treated as prisoners of war, and can be brought before the courts.

Article 13. Individuals who follow an army without directly belonging to it, such as newspaper correspondents and reporters, sutlers and contractors, who fall into the enemy's hands and whom the latter thinks expedient to detain, are entitled to be treated as prisoners of war, provided they are in possession of a certificate from the military authorities of the army which they were accompanying.

Article 14. An inquiry office for prisoners of war is instituted on the commencement of hostilities in each of the belligerent States, and, when necessary, in neutral countries which have received belligerents in their territory. It is the function of this office to reply to all inquiries about the prisoners. It receives from the various services concerned full information respecting internments arid transfers, releases on parole, exchanges, escapes, admissions into hospital, deaths, as well as other information necessary to enable it to make out and keep up to date an individual return for each prisoner of war. The office must state in this return the regimental number, name and surname, age, place of origin, rank, unit, wounds, date and place of capture, internment, wounding, and death, as well as any observations of a special character. The individual return shall be sent to the Government of the other belligerent after the conclusion of peace.

It is likewise the function of the inquiry office to receive and collect all objects of personal use, valuables, letters, etc., found on the field of battle or left by prisoners who have been released on parole, or exchanged, or who have escaped, or died in hospitals or ambulances, and to forward them to those concerned.

Article 15. Relief societies for prisoners of war, which are properly constituted in accordance with the laws of their country and with the object of serving as the channel for charitable effort shall receive from the belligerents, for themselves and their duly accredited agents every facility for the efficient performance of their humane task within the bounds imposed by military necessities and administrative regulations. Agents of these societies may be admitted to the places of internment for the purpose of distributing relief, as also to the halting places of repatriated prisoners, if furnished with a personal permit by the military authorities, and on giving an undertaking in writing to comply with all measures of order and police which the latter may issue.

Article 16. Inquiry offices enjoy the privilege of free postage. Letters, money orders, and valuables, as well as parcels by post, intended for prisoners of war, or dispatched by them, shall be exempt from all postal duties in the countries of origin and destination, as well as in the countries they pass through.

Presents and relief in kind for prisoners of war shall be admitted free of all import or other duties, as well as of payments for carriage by the State railways.

Article 17. Officers taken prisoners shall receive the same rate of pay as officers of corresponding rank in the country where they are detained, the amount to be ultimately refunded by their own Government.

Article 18. Prisoners of war shall enjoy complete liberty in the exercise of their religion, including attendance at the services of whatever church they may belong to, on the sole condition that they comply with the measures of order and police issued by the military authorities.

Article 19. The wills of prisoners of war are received or drawn up in the same way as for soldiers of the national army.

The same rules shall be observed regarding death certificates as well as for the burial of prisoners of war, due regard being paid to their grade and rank.

Article 20. After the conclusion of peace, the repatriation of prisoners of war shall be carried out as quickly as possible.

Artcle 23. In addition to the prohibitions provided by special Conventions, it is especially forbidden

(a) To employ poison or poisoned weapons;
(b) To kill or wound treacherously individuals belonging to the hostile nation or army;
(c) To kill or wound an enemy who, having laid down his arms, or having no longer means of defense, has surrendered at discretion;
(d) To declare that no quarter will be given.

Above text taken from: http://www.icrc.org/ihl.nsf/FULL/195?OpenDocument

Text available from International Relations and Security Network. Accessed: 29 September 2007. http://net.lib.bgu.edu/~rdh7/wwi/hague/hague5.html

Convention Relative to the Treatment of Prisoners of War, Geneva, 27 July 1929

Although the signatories of The Hague Conventions of 1899 and 1907 had attempted to clarify regulations and protections for prisoners of war, the First World War rendered many of these provisions incomplete or even wholly inadequate. In February 1918, almost nine months prior to the signing of the Armistice, the International Committee of the Red Cross began calling for the assembly of an international delegation to address the inadequacies of international law concerning POWs. Almost eleven years passed before diplomats convened in Geneva, Switzerland, on 1 July 1929 to address this matter.

The Geneva Convention Relative to the Treatment of POWs was signed 27 July 1929 by forty-seven nations. Designed to supplement the strides made at The Hague in 1907, the Geneva Convention further clarified the obligation of captive governments to treat prisoners humanely with provisions on equal footing with national soldiers. Prisoners were only required to provide their captive government with basic identification information and could not be punished for attempting to escape. Those prisoners who could not provide basic identification information due to physical or psychological trauma were to be turned over to medics. Additionally, captive governments were required to provide prisoners with adequate access to healthcare, including a camp infirmary.

The labor required of POWs was a particularly important area of reform. Although previous regulations allowed prisoners to work for wages comparable to that of national soldiers, the Geneva Convention alleviated ambiguity concerning the fitness of any prisoner to work. Prisoners were protected from overly harsh labor, and the captive government assumed responsibility for any injuries. Furthermore, belligerent governments were prohibited from forcing prisoners into services directly supporting the war effort. The convention also strengthened private property rights of prisoners, further clarified the process for transferring POWs in a timely manner, and allowed prisoners to appoint someone to represent them before the belligerent government.

Notably, neither Japan nor the Soviet Union had endorsed the Geneva Convention Relative to the Treatment of POWs of 1929 when the Second World War erupted in 1939. (Japan, however, gave a qualified promise in 1942 to abide by the Geneva rules, and the USSR announced in1941 that it would only observe the terms of The Hague Convention of 1907, which did not provide [as does the Geneva Convention] for neutral inspection of prison camps, for the exchange of prisoners' names, and for correspondence with prisoners). Consequently, neither the Soviets nor the Japanese felt constrained to treat their enemy POWs with any particular care—indeed, both countries tormented their captives, starved, and beat them, and millions died at their hands.

The remaining forty-seven nations which endorsed the Geneva Accord in 1929 allowed its captives the food, shelter, medical help, and protection which the Accords required. Even the Nazis, arguably among history's greatest villains, generally thought twice before straying too far from the demands of the Accords. Any dramatic violation could—and often did—bring an immediate response from the other side. The future treatment of POWs became a delicate balancing act, where camp inspection reports carried back and forth by diplomats and representatives of neutral countries, were of interest to each side. The Geneva Accord of 1929 stood as the gold standard for the civilized world for generations.

EXTRACTS FROM THE GENEVA CONVENTION RELATIVE TO THE TREATMENT OF PRISONERS OF WAR (GENEVA, 27 JULY 1929)

PART I
GENERAL PROVISIONS

Article 1. The present Convention shall apply without prejudice to the stipulations of Part VII:

(1) To all persons referred to in Articles 1, 2 and 3 of the Regulations annexed to the Hague Convention (IV) of 18 October 1907, concerning the Laws and Customs of War on Land, who are captured by the enemy.
(2) To all persons belonging to the armed forces of belligerents who are captured by the enemy in the course of operations of maritime or aerial war, subject to such exceptions (derogations) as the conditions of such capture render inevitable. Nevertheless these exceptions shall not infringe the fundamental principles of the present Convention; they shall cease from the moment when the captured persons shall have reached a prisoners of war camp.

Article 2. Prisoners of war are in the power of the hostile Government, but not of the individuals or formation which captured them. They shall at all times be humanely treated and protected, particularly against acts of violence, from insults and from public curiosity. Measures of reprisal against them are forbidden.

Article 3. Prisoners of war are entitled to respect for their persons and honor. Women shall be treated with all consideration due to their sex. Prisoners retain their full civil capacity.

Article 4. The detaining Power is required to provide for the maintenance of prisoners of war in its charge. Differences of treatment between prisoners are permissible only if such differences are based on the military rank, the state of physical or mental health, the professional abilities, or the sex of those who benefit from them.

PART II
CAPTURE

Article 5. Every prisoner of war is required to declare, if he is interrogated on the subject, his true names and rank, or his regimental number.

If he infringes this rule, he exposes himself to a restriction of the privileges accorded to prisoners of his category.

No pressure shall be exercised on prisoners to obtain information regarding the situation in their armed forces or their country. Prisoners who refuse to reply may not be threatened, insulted, or exposed to unpleasantness or disadvantages of any kind whatsoever.

If, by reason of his physical or mental condition, a prisoner is incapable of stating his identity, he shall be handed over to the Medical Service.

Article 6. All personal effects and articles in personal use—except arms, horses, military equipment and military papers—shall remain in the possession of prisoners of war, as well as their metal helmets and gas-masks.

Sums of money carried by prisoners may only be taken from them on the order of an officer and after the amount has been recorded. A receipt shall be given for them. Sums thus impounded shall be placed to the account of each prisoner.

Their identity tokens, badges of rank, decorations and articles of value may not be taken from prisoners.

PART III
CAPTIVITY

SECTION I
EVACUATION OF PRISONERS OF WAR

Article 7. As soon as possible after their capture, prisoners of war shall be evacuated to depots sufficiently removed from the fighting zone for them to be out of danger.

Only prisoners who, by reason of their wounds or maladies, would run greater risks by being evacuated than by remaining may be kept temporarily in a dangerous zone.

Prisoners shall not be unnecessarily exposed to danger while awaiting evacuation from a fighting zone.

The evacuation of prisoners on foot shall in normal circumstances be effected by stages of not more than 20 kilometres per day, unless the necessity for reaching water and food depôts requires longer stages.

Article 8. Belligerents are required to notify each other of all captures of prisoners as soon as possible, through the intermediary of the Information Bureaux organised in accordance with Article 77. They are likewise required to inform each other of the official addresses to which letter from the prisoners' families may be addressed to the prisoners of war.

As soon as possible, every prisoner shall be enabled to correspond personally with his family, in accordance with the conditions prescribed in Article 36 and the following Articles. As regards prisoners captured at sea, the provisions of the present article shall be observed as soon as possible after arrival in port.

SECTION II
PRISONERS OF WAR CAMPS

Article 9. Prisoners of war may be interned in a town, fortress or other place, and may be required not to go beyond certain fixed limits. They may also be interned in fenced camps; they shall not be confined or imprisoned except as a measure indispensable for safety or health, and only so long as circumstances exist which necessitate such a measure.

Prisoners captured in districts which are unhealthy or whose climate is deleterious to persons coming from temperate climates shall be removed as soon as possible to a more favorable climate.

Belligerents shall as far as possible avoid bringing together in the same camp prisoners of different races or nationalities.

No prisoner may at any time be sent to an area where he would be exposed to the fire of the fighting zone, or be employed to render by his presence certain points or areas immune from bombardment.

CHAPTER 1
Installation of camps

Article 10. Prisoners of war shall be lodged in buildings or huts which afford all possible safeguards as regards hygiene and salubrity.

The premises must be entirely free from damp, and adequately heated and lighted. All precautions shall be taken against the danger of fire.

As regards dormitories, their total area, minimum cubic air space, fittings and bedding material, the conditions shall be the same as for the depot troops of the detaining Power.

CHAPTER 2
Food and clothing of prisoners of war

Article 11. The food ration of prisoners of war shall be equivalent in quantity and quality to that of the depot troops.

Prisoners shall also be afforded the means of preparing for themselves such additional articles of food as they may possess.

Sufficient drinking water shall be supplied to them. The use of tobacco shall be authorized. Prisoners may be employed in the kitchens.

All collective disciplinary measures affecting food are prohibited.

Article 12. Clothing, underwear and footwear shall be supplied to prisoners of war by the detaining Power. The regular replacement and repair of such articles shall be assured. Workers shall also receive working kit wherever the nature of the work requires it.

In all camps, canteens shall be installed at which prisoners shall be able to procure, at the local market price, food commodities and ordinary articles.

The profits accruing to the administrations of the camps from the canteens shall be utilized for the benefit of the prisoners.

CHAPTER 3
Hygiene in camps

Article 13. Belligerents shall be required to take all necessary hygienic measures to ensure the cleanliness and salubrity of camps and to prevent epidemics.

Prisoners of war shall have for their use, day and night, conveniences which conform to the rules of hygiene and are maintained in a constant state of cleanliness.

In addition and without prejudice to the provision as far as possible of baths and shower-baths in the camps, the prisoners shall be provided with a sufficient quantity of water for their bodily cleanliness.

They shall have facilities for engaging in physical exercises and obtaining the benefit of being out of doors.

Article 14. Each camp shall possess an infirmary, where prisoners of war shall receive attention of any kind of which they may be in need. If necessary, isolation establishments shall be reserved for patients suffering from infectious and contagious diseases.

The expenses of treatment, including those of temporary remedial apparatus, shall be borne by the detaining Power.

Belligerents shall be required to issue, on demand, to any prisoner treated, an official statement indicating the nature and duration of his illness and of the treatment received.

It shall be permissible for belligerents mutually to authorize each other, by means of special agreements, to retain in the camps doctors and medical orderlies for the purpose of caring for their prisoner compatriots.

Prisoners who have contracted a serious malady, or whose condition necessitates important surgical treatment, shall be admitted, at the expense of the detaining Power, to any military or civil institution qualified to treat them.

Article 15. Medical inspections of prisoners of war shall be arranged at least once a month. Their object shall be the supervision of the general state of health and cleanliness, and the detection of infectious and contagious diseases, particularly tuberculosis and venereal complaints.

CHAPTER 4
Intellectual and moral needs of prisoners of war

Article 16. Prisoners of war shall be permitted complete freedom in the performance of their religious duties, including attendance at the services of their faith, on the sole condition that they comply with the routine and police regulations prescribed by the military authorities.

Ministers of religion, who are prisoners of war, whatever may be their denomination, shall be allowed freely to minister to their co-religionists.

Article 17. Belligerents shall encourage as much as possible the organization of intellectual and sporting pursuits by the prisoners of war.

CHAPTER 5
Internal discipline of camps

Article 18. Each prisoners of war camp shall be placed under the authority of a responsible officer.

In addition to external marks of respect required by the regulations in force in their own armed forces with regard to their nationals, prisoners of war shall be required to salute all officers of the detaining Power.

Officer prisoners of war shall be required to salute only officers of that Power who are their superiors or equals in rank.

Article 19. The wearing of badges of rank and decorations shall be permitted.

Article 20. Regulations, orders, announcements and publications of any kind shall be communicated to prisoners of war in a language which they understand. The same principle shall be applied to questions.

CHAPTER 6
Special provisions concerning officers and persons of equivalent status

Article 21. At the commencement of hostilities, belligerents shall be required reciprocally to inform each other of the titles and ranks in use in their respective armed forces, with the view of ensuring equality of treatment between the corresponding ranks of officers and persons of equivalent status.

Officers and persons of equivalent status who are prisoners of war shall be treated with due regard to their rank and age.

Article 22. In order to ensure the service of officers' camps, soldier prisoners of war of the same armed forces, and as far as possible speaking the same language, shall be detached for service therein in sufficient number, having regard to the rank of the officers and persons of equivalent status.

Officers and persons of equivalent status shall procure their food and clothing from the pay to be paid to them by the detaining Power. The management of a mess by officers themselves shall be facilitated in every way.

CHAPTER 7

Pecuniary resources of prisoners of war

Article 23. Subject to any special arrangements made between the belligerent Powers, and particularly those contemplated in Article 24, officers and persons of equivalent status who are prisoners of war shall receive from the detaining Power the same pay as officers of corresponding rank in the armed forces of that Power, provided, however, that such pay does not exceed that to which they are entitled in the armed forces of the country in whose service they have been. This pay shall be paid to them in full, once a month if possible, and no deduction therefrom shall be made for expenditure devolving upon the detaining Power, even if such expenditure is incurred on their behalf.

An agreement between the belligerents shall prescribe the rate of exchange applicable to this payment; in default of such agreement, the rate of exchange adopted shall be that in force at the moment of the commencement of hostilities.

All advances made to prisoners of war by way of pay shall be reimbursed, at the end of hostilities, by the Power in whose service they were.

Article 24. At the commencement of hostilities, belligerents shall determine by common accord the maximum amount of cash which prisoners of war of various ranks and categories shall be permitted to retain in their possession. Any excess withdrawn or withheld from a prisoner, and any deposit of money effected by him, shall be carried to his account, and may not be converted into another currency without his consent.

The credit balances of their accounts shall be paid to the prisoners of war at the end of their captivity.

During the continuance of the latter, facilities shall be accorded to them for the transfer of these amounts, wholly or in part, to banks or private individuals in their country of origin.

CHAPTER 8

Transfer of prisoners of war

Article 25. Unless the course of military operations demands it, sick and wounded prisoners of war shall not be transferred if their recovery might be prejudiced by the journey.

Article 26. In the event of transfer, prisoners of war shall be officially informed in advance of their new destination; they shall be authorized to take with them their personal effects, their correspondence and parcels which have arrived for them.

All necessary arrangements shall be made so that correspondence and parcels addressed to their former camp shall be sent on to them without delay.

The sums credited to the account of transferred prisoners shall be transmitted to the competent authority of their new place of residence.

Expenses incurred by the transfers shall be borne by the detaining Power.

SECTION III
WORK OF PRISONERS OF WAR

CHAPTER 1
General

Article 27. Belligerents may employ as workmen prisoners of war who are physically fit, other than officers and persons of equivalent statue, according to their rink and their ability.

Nevertheless, if officers or persons of equivalent status ask for suitable work, this shall be found for them as far as possible.

Non-commissioned officers who are prisoners of war may be compelled to undertake only supervisory work, unless they expressly request remunerative occupation.

During the whole period of captivity, belligerents are required to admit prisoners of war who are victims of accidents at work to the benefit of provisions applicable to workmen of the same category under the legislation of the detaining Power. As regards prisoners of war to whom these legal provisions could not be applied by reason of the legislation of that Power, the latter undertakes to recommend to its legislative body all proper measures for the equitable compensation of the victims.

CHAPTER 2
Organization of work

Article 28. The detaining Power shall assume entire responsibility for the maintenance, care, treatment and the payment of the wages of prisoners of war working for private individuals.

Article 29. No prisoner of war may be employed on work for which he is physically unsuited.

Article 30. The duration of the daily work of prisoners of war, including the time of the journey to and from work, shall not be excessive and shall in no case exceed that permitted for civil workers of the locality employed on the same work. Each prisoner shall be allowed a rest of twenty-four consecutive hours each week, preferably on Sunday.

CHAPTER 3
Prohibited work

Article 31. Work done by prisoners of war shall have no direct connection with the operations of the war. In particular, it is forbidden to employ prisoners in the manufacture or transport of arms or munitions of any kind, or on the transport of material destined for combatant units.

In the event of violation of the provisions of the preceding paragraph, prisoners are at liberty, after performing or commencing to perform the order, to have their complaints presented through the intermediary of the prisoners' representatives whose functions are described in Articles 43 and 44, or, in the absence of a prisoners' representative, through the intermediary of the representatives of the protecting Power.

Article 32. It is forbidden to employ prisoners of war on unhealthy or dangerous work. Conditions of work shall not be rendered more arduous by disciplinary measures.

CHAPTER 4
Labour detachments

Article 33. Conditions governing labour detachments shall be similar to those of prisoners-of-war camps, particularly as concerns hygienic conditions, food, care in case of accidents or sickness, correspondence, and the reception of parcels.

Every labour detachment shall be attached to a prisoners' camp. The commander of this camp shall be responsible for the observance in the labour detachment of the provisions of the present Convention.

CHAPTER 5
Pay

Article 34. Prisoners of war shall not receive pay for work in connection with the administration, internal arrangement and maintenance of camps.

Prisoners employed on other work shall be entitled to a rate of pay, to be fixed by agreements between the belligerents.

These agreements shall also specify the portion which may be retained by the camp administration, the amount which shall belong to the prisoner of war and the manner in which this amount shall be placed at his disposal during the period of his captivity.

Pending the conclusion of the said agreements, remuneration of the work of prisoners shall be fixed according to the following standards:

(a) Work done for the State shall be paid for according to the rates in force for soldiers of the national forces doing the same work, or, if no such rates exist, according to a tariff corresponding to the work executed.
(b) When the work is done for other public administrations or for private individuals, the conditions shall be settled in agreement with the military authorities.

The pay which remains to the credit of a prisoner shall be remitted to him on the termination of his captivity. In case of death, it shall be remitted through the diplomatic channel to the heirs of the deceased.

SECTION IV
RELATIONS OF PRISONERS OF WAR WITH THE EXTERIOR

Article 35. On the commencement of hostilities, belligerents shall publish the measures prescribed for the execution of the provisions of the present section.

Article 36. Each of the belligerents shall fix periodically the number of letters and postcards which prisoners of war of different categories shall be permitted to send per month, and shall notify that number to the other belligerent. These letters and cards shall be sent by post by the shortest route. They may not be delayed or withheld for disciplinary motives.

Not later than one week after his arrival in camp, and similarly in case of sickness, each prisoner shall be enabled to send a postcard to his family informing them of his capture and the state of his health. The said postcards shall be forwarded as quickly as possible and shall not be delayed in any manner.

As a general rule, the correspondence of prisoners shall be written in their native language. Belligerents may authorize correspondence in other languages.

Article 37. Prisoners of war shall be authorized to receive individually postal parcels containing foodstuffs and other articles intended for consumption or clothing. The parcels shall be delivered to the addressees and a receipt given.

Article 38. Letters and remittances of money or valuables, as well as postal parcels addressed to prisoners of war, or despatched by them, either directly or through the intermediary of the information bureaux mentioned in Article 77, shall be exempt from all postal charges in the countries of origin and destination and in the countries through which they pass.

Presents and relief in kind intended for prisoners of war shall also be exempt from all import or other duties, as well as any charges for carriage on railways operated by the State.

Prisoners may, in cases of recognized urgency, be authorized to send telegrams on payment of the usual charges.

Article 39. Prisoners of war shall be permitted to receive individually consignments of books which may be subject to censorship.

Representatives of the protecting Powers and of duly recognized and authorized relief societies may send works and collections of books to the libraries of prisoners, camps. The transmission of such consignments to libraries may not be delayed under pretext of difficulties of censorship.

Article 40. The censoring of correspondence shall be accomplished as quickly as possible. The examination of postal parcels shall, moreover, be effected under such conditions as will ensure the preservation of any foodstuffs which they may contain, and, if possible, be done in the presence of the addressee or of a representative duly recognized by him.

Any prohibition of correspondence ordered by the belligerents, for military or political reasons, shall only be of a temporary character and shall also be for as brief a time as possible.

Article 41. Belligerents shall accord all facilities for the transmission of documents destined for prisoners of war or signed by them, in particular powers of attorney and wills.

They shall take the necessary measures to secure, in case of need, the legalisation of signatures of prisoners.

SECTION V
RELATIONS BETWEEN PRISONERS OF WAR AND THE AUTHORITIES

CHAPTER 1
Complaints of prisoners of war respecting the conditions of captivity

Article 42. Prisoners of war shall have the right to bring to the notice of the military authorities, in whose hands they are, their petitions concerning the conditions of captivity to which they are subjected.

They shall also have the right to communicate with the representatives of the protecting Powers in order to draw their attention to the points on which they have complaints to make with regard to the conditions of captivity.

Such petitions and complaints shall be transmitted immediately.

Even though they are found to be groundless, they shall not give rise to any punishment.

CHAPTER 2
Representatives of prisoners of war

Article 43. In any locality where there may be prisoners of war, they shall be authorized to appoint representatives to represent them before the military authorities and the protecting Powers.

Such appointments shall be subject to the approval of the military authorities.

The prisoners' representatives shall be charged with the reception and distribution of collective consignments. Similarly, in the event of the prisoners deciding to organize amongst themselves a system of mutual aid, such organization shall be one of the functions of the prisoners, representatives. On the other hand, the latter may offer their services to prisoners to facilitate their relations with the relief societies mentioned in Article 78.

In camps of officers and persons of equivalent status the senior officer prisoner of the highest rank shall be recognized as intermediary between the camp authorities and the officers and similar persons who are prisoners. For this purpose he shall have the power to appoint an officer prisoner to assist him as interpreter in the course of conferences with the authorities of the camp.

Article 44. When the prisoners, representatives are employed as workmen, their work as representatives of the prisoners of war shall be reckoned in the compulsory period of labor.

All facilities shall be accorded to the prisoners' representatives for their correspondence with the military authorities and the protecting Power. Such correspondence shall not be subject to any limitation.

No prisoners' representative may be transferred without his having been allowed the time necessary to acquaint his successors with the current business.

CHAPTER 3
Penal sanctions with regard to prisoners of war

I. General provisions

Article 45. Prisoners of war shall be subject to the laws, regulations and orders in force in the armed forces of the detaining Power.

Any act of insubordination shall render them liable to the measures prescribed by such laws, regulations, and orders, except as otherwise provided in this Chapter.

Article 46. Prisoners of war shall not be subjected by the military authorities or the tribunals of the detaining Power to penalties other than those which are prescribed for similar acts by members of the national forces.

Officers, non-commissioned officers or private soldiers, prisoners of war, undergoing disciplinary punishment shall not be subjected to treatment less favorable than that prescribed, as regards the same punishment, for similar ranks in the armed forces of the detaining Power.

All forms of corporal punishment, confinement in premises not lighted by daylight and, in general, all forms of cruelty whatsoever are prohibited.

Collective penalties for individual acts are also prohibited.

Article 47. A statement of the facts in cases of acts constituting a breach of discipline, and particularly an attempt to escape, shall be drawn up in writing without delay. The period during which prisoners of war of whatever rank are detained in custody (pending the investigation of such offences) shall be reduced to a strict minimum.

The judicial proceedings against a prisoner of war shall be conducted as quickly as circumstances will allow. The period during which prisoners shall be detained in custody shall be as short as possible.

In all cases the period during which a prisoner is under arrest (awaiting punishment or trial) shall be deducted from the sentence, whether disciplinary or judicial, provided such deduction is permitted in the case of members of the national forces.

Article 48. After undergoing the judicial or disciplinary punishment which has been inflicted on them, prisoners of war shall not be treated differently from other prisoners.

Nevertheless, prisoners who have been punished as the result of an attempt to escape may be subjected to a special régime of surveillance, but this shall not involve the suppression of any of the safeguards accorded to prisoners by the present Convention.

Article 49. No prisoner of war may be deprived of his rank by the detaining Power.

Prisoners on whom disciplinary punishment is inflicted shall not be deprived of the privileges attaching to their rank. In particular, officers and persons of equivalent status who suffer penalties entailing deprivation of liberty shall not be placed in the same premises as non-commissioned officers or private soldiers undergoing punishment.

Article 50. Escaped prisoners of war who are re-captured before they have been able to rejoin their own armed forces or to leave the territory occupied by the armed forces which captured them shall be liable only to disciplinary punishment.

Prisoners who, after succeeding in rejoining their armed forces or in leaving the territory occupied by the armed forces which captured them, are again taken prisoner shall not be liable to any punishment for their previous escape.

Article 51. Attempted escape, even if it is not a first offence, shall not be considered as an aggravation of the offence in the event of the prisoner of war being brought before the courts for crimes or offences against persons or property committed in the course of such attempt.

After an attempted or successful escape, the comrades of the escaped person who aided the escape shall incur only disciplinary punishment therefore.

Article 52. Belligerents shall ensure that the competent authorities exercise the greatest leniency in considering the question whether an offence committed by a prisoner of war should be punished by disciplinary or by judicial measures.

This provision shall be observed in particular in appraising facts in connection with escape or attempted escape.

A prisoner shall not be punished more than once for the same act or on the same charge.

Article 53. No prisoner who has been awarded any disciplinary punishment for an offence and who fulfils the conditions laid down for repatriation shall be retained on the ground that he has not undergone his punishment.

Prisoners qualified for repatriation against whom any prosecution for a criminal offence has been brought may be excluded from repatriation until the termination of the proceedings and until fulfillment of their sentence, if any; prisoners already serving a sentence of imprisonment may be retained until the expiry of the sentence.

Belligerents shall communicate to each other lists of those who cannot be repatriated for the reasons indicated in the preceding paragraph.

II. Disciplinary punishments

Article 54. Imprisonment is the most severe disciplinary punishment which may be inflicted on a prisoner of war.

The duration of any single punishment shall not exceed thirty days.

This maximum of thirty days shall, moreover, not be exceeded in the event of there being several acts for which the prisoner is answerable to discipline at the time when his case is disposed of, whether such acts are connected or not.

Where, during the course or after the termination of a period of imprisonment, a prisoner is sentenced to a fresh disciplinary penalty, a period of at least three days shall intervene between each of the periods of imprisonment, if one of such periods is of ten days or over.

Article 55. Subject to the provisions of the last paragraph of Article 11, the restrictions in regard to food permitted in the armed forces of the detaining Power may be applied, as an additional penalty, to prisoners of war undergoing disciplinary punishment.

Such restrictions shall, however, only be ordered if the state of the prisoner's health permits.

Article 56. In no case shall prisoners of war be transferred to penitentiary establishments (prisoners, penitentiaries, convict establishments, etc.) in order to undergo disciplinary sentence there.

Establishments in which disciplinary sentences are undergone shall conform to the requirements of hygiene.

Facilities shall be afforded to prisoners undergoing sentence to keep themselves in a state of cleanliness.

Every day, such prisoners shall have facilities for taking exercise or for remaining out of doors for at least two hours.

Article 57. Prisoners of war undergoing disciplinary punishment shall be permitted to read and write and to send and receive letters.

On the other hand, it shall be permissible not to deliver parcels and remittances of money to the addressees until the expiration of the sentence. If the undelivered parcels contain perishable foodstuffs, these shall be handed over to the infirmary or to the camp kitchen.

Article 58. Prisoners of war undergoing disciplinary punishment shall be permitted, on their request, to present themselves for daily medical inspection. They shall receive such attention as the medical officers may consider necessary, and, if need be, shall be evacuated to the camp infirmary or to hospital.

Article 59. Without prejudice to the competency of the courts and the superior military authorities, disciplinary sentences may only be awarded by an officer vested with disciplinary powers in his capacity as commander of the camp or detachment, or by the responsible officer acting as his substitute.

III. Judicial proceedings

Article 60. At the commencement of a judicial hearing against a prisoner of war, the detaining Power shall notify the representative of the protecting Power as soon as possible, and in any case before the date fixed for the opening of the hearing.

The said notification shall contain the following particulars:

(a) Civil status and rank of the prisoner.
(b) Place of residence or detention.
(c) Statement of the charge or charges, and of the legal provisions applicable.

If it is not possible in this notification to indicate particulars of the court which will try the case, the date of the opening of the hearing and the place where it will take place, these particulars shall be furnished to the representative of the protecting Power at a later date, but as soon as possible and in any case at least three weeks before the opening of the hearing.

Article 61. No prisoner of war shall be sentenced without being given the opportunity to defend himself.

No prisoner shall be compelled to admit that he is guilty of the offence of which he is accused.

Article 62. The prisoner of war shall have the right to be assisted by a qualified advocate of his own choice and, if necessary, to have recourse to the offices of a competent interpreter. He shall be informed of his right by the detaining Power in good time before the hearing.

Failing a choice on the part of the prisoner, the protecting Power may procure an advocate for him. The detaining Power shall, on the request of the protecting Power, furnish to the latter a list of persons qualified to conduct the defense.

The representatives of the protecting Power shall have the right to attend the hearing of the case.

The only exception to this rule is where the hearing has to be kept secret in the interests of the safety of the State. The detaining Power would then notify the protecting Power accordingly.

Article 63. A sentence shall only be pronounced on a prisoner of war by the same tribunals and in accordance with the same procedure as in the case of persons belonging to the armed forces of the detaining Power.

Article 64. Every prisoner of war shall have the right of appeal against any sentence against him in the same manner as persons belonging to the armed forces of the detaining Power.

Article 65. Sentences pronounced against prisoners of war shall be communicated immediately to the protecting Power.

Article 66. If sentence of death is passed on a prisoner of war, a communication setting forth in detail the nature and the circumstances of the offence shall be addressed as soon as possible to the representative of the protecting Power for transmission to the Power in whose armed forces the prisoner served.

The sentence shall not be carried out before the expiration of a period of at least three months from the date of the receipt of this communication by the protecting Power.

Article 67. No prisoner of war may be deprived of the benefit of the provisions of Article 42 of the present Convention as the result of a judgment or otherwise.

PART IV
END OF CAPTIVITY

SECTION I
DIRECT REPATRIATION AND ACCOMMODATION IN A NEUTRAL
COUNTRY

Article 68. Belligerents shall be required to send back to their own country, without regard to rank or numbers, after rendering them in a fit condition for transport, prisoners of war who are seriously ill or seriously wounded.

Agreements between the belligerents shall therefore determine, as soon as possible, the forms of disablement or sickness requiring direct repatriation and cases which may necessitate accommodation in a neutral country. Pending the conclusion of such agreements, the belligerents may refer to the model draft agreement annexed to the present Convention.

Article 69. On the opening of hostilities, belligerents shall come to an understanding as to the appointment of mixed medical commissions. These commissions shall consist of three members, two of whom shall belong to a neutral country and one appointed by the detaining Power; one of the medical officers of the neutral country shall preside. These mixed medical commissions shall proceed to the examination of sick or wounded prisoners and shall make all appropriate decisions with regard to them.

The decisions of these commissions shall be decided by majority and shall be carried into effect as soon as possible.

Article 70. In addition to those prisoners of war selected by the medical officer of the camp, the following shall be inspected by the mixed medical Commission mentioned in Article 69, with a view to their direct repatriation or accommodation in a neutral country:

(a) Prisoners who make a direct request to that effect to the medical officer of the camp;

(b) Prisoners presented by the prisoners' representatives mentioned in Article 43, the latter acting on their own initiative or on the request of the prisoners themselves;

(c) Prisoners nominated by the Power in whose armed forces they served or by a relief society duly recognized and authorized by that Power.

Article 71. Prisoners of war who meet with accidents at work, unless the injury is self-inflicted, shall have the benefit of the same provisions as regards repatriation or accommodation in a neutral country.

Article 72. During the continuance of hostilities, and for humanitarian reasons, belligerents may conclude agreements with a view to the direct repatriation or accommodation in a neutral country of prisoners of war in good health who have been in captivity for a long time.

Article 73. The expenses of repatriation or transport to a neutral country of prisoners of war shall be borne, as from the frontier of the detaining Power, by the Power in whose armed forces such prisoners served.

Article 74. No repatriated person shall be employed on active military service.

SECTION II
LIBERATION AND REPATRIATION AT THE END OF HOSTILITIES

Article 75. When belligerents conclude an armistice convention, they shall normally cause to be included therein provisions concerning the repatriation of prisoners of war. If it has not been possible to insert in that convention such stipulations, the belligerents shall, nevertheless, enter into communication with each other on the question as soon as possible. In any case, the repatriation of prisoners shall be effected as soon as possible after the conclusion of peace.

Prisoners of war who are subject to criminal proceedings for a crime or offence at common law may, however, be detained until the end of the proceedings, and, if need be, until the expiration of the sentence. The same applies to prisoners convicted for a crime or offence at common law.

By agreement between the belligerents, commissions may be instituted for the purpose of searching for scattered prisoners and ensuring their repatriation.

PART V
DEATHS OF PRISONERS OF WAR

Article 76. The wills of prisoners of war shall be received and drawn up under the same conditions as for soldiers of the national armed forces.

The same rules shall be followed as regards the documents relative to the certification of the death.

The belligerents shall ensure that prisoners of war who have died in captivity are honorably buried, and that the graves bear the necessary indications and are treated with respect and suitably maintained.

PART VI
BUREAU OF RELIEF AND INFORMATION CONCERNING PRISONERS OF
WAR

Article 77. At the commencement of hostilities, each of the belligerent Powers and the neutral Powers who have belligerents in their care, shall institute an official bureau to give information about the prisoners of war in their territory.

Each of the belligerent Powers shall inform its Information Bureau as soon as possible of all captures of prisoners affected by its armed forces, furnishing them with all particulars of identity at its disposal to enable the families concerned to be quickly notified, and stating the official addresses to which families may write to the prisoners.

The Information Bureau shall transmit all such information immediately to the Powers concerned, on the one hand through the intermediary of the protecting Powers, and on the other through the Central Agency contemplated in Article 79.

The Information Bureau, being charged with replying to all enquiries relative to prisoners of war, shall receive from the various services concerned all particulars respecting internments and transfers, releases on parole, repatriations, escapes, stays in hospitals, and deaths, together with all other particulars necessary for establishing and keeping up to date an individual record for each prisoner of war.

The Bureau shall note in this record, as far as possible, and subject to the provisions of Article 5, the regimental number, names and surnames, date and place of birth, rank and unit of the prisoner, the surname of the father and name of the mother, the address of the person to be notified in case of accident, wounds, dates and places of capture, of internment, of wounds, of death, together with all other important particulars.

Weekly lists containing all additional particulars capable of facilitating the identification of each prisoner shall be transmitted to the interested Powers.

The individual record of a prisoner of war shall be sent after the conclusion of peace to the Power in whose service he was.

The Information Bureau shall also be required to collect all personal effects, valuables, correspondence, pay-books, identity tokens, etc., which have been left by prisoners of war who have been repatriated or released on parole, or who have escaped or died, and to transmit them to the countries concerned.

Article 78. Societies for the relief of prisoners of war, regularly constituted in accordance with the laws of their country, and having for their object to serve as intermediaries for charitable purposes, shall receive from the belligerents, for themselves and their duly accredited agents, all facilities for the efficacious performance of their humane task within the limits imposed by military exigencies. Representatives of these societies shall be permitted to distribute relief in the camps and at the halting places of repatriated prisoners under a personal permit issued by the military authority, and on giving an undertaking in writing to comply with all routine and police orders which the said authority shall prescribe.

Article 79. A Central Agency of information regarding prisoners of war shall be established in a neutral country. The International Red Cross Committee shall, if they consider it necessary, propose to the Powers concerned with the organization of such an agency.

This agency shall be charged with the duty of collecting all information regarding prisoners which they may be able to obtain through official or private channels, and the agency shall transmit the information as rapidly as possible to the prisoners' own country or the Power in whose service they have been.

These provisions shall not be interpreted as restricting the humanitarian work of the International Red Cross Committee.

Article 80. Information Bureaux shall enjoy exemption from fees on postal matter as well as all the exemptions prescribed in Article 38.

PART VII
APPLICATION OF THE CONVENTION TO CERTAIN CATEGORIES
OF CIVILIANS

Article 81. Persons who follow the armed forces without directly belonging thereto, such as correspondents, newspaper reporters, sutlers, or contractors, who fall into the hands of the enemy, and whom the latter think fit to detain, shall be entitled to be treated as prisoners of war, provided they are in possession of an authorization from the military authorities of the armed forces which they were following.

PART VIII
EXECUTION OF THE CONVENTION

SECTION I
GENERAL PROVISIONS

Article 82. The provisions of the present Convention shall be respected by the High Contracting Parties in all circumstances.

In time of war if one of the belligerents is not a party to the Convention, its provisions shall, nevertheless, remain binding as between the belligerents who are parties thereto.

Article 83. The High Contracting Parties reserve to themselves the right to conclude special conventions on all questions relating to prisoners of war concerning which they may consider it desirable to make special provisions.

Prisoners of war shall continue to enjoy the benefits of these agreements until their repatriation has been effected, subject to any provisions expressly to the contrary contained in the above-mentioned agreements or in subsequent agreements, and subject to any more favorable measures by one or the other of the belligerent Powers concerning the prisoners detained by that Power.

In order to ensure the application, on both sides, of the provisions of the present Convention, and to facilitate the conclusion of the special conventions mentioned above, the belligerents may, at the commencement of hostilities, authorize meetings of representatives of the respective authorities charged with the administration of prisoners of war.

Article 84. The text of the present Convention and of the special conventions mentioned in the preceding Article shall be posted, whenever possible, in the native language of the prisoners of war, in places where it may be consulted by all the prisoners.

The text of these conventions shall be communicated, on their request, to prisoners who are unable to inform themselves of the text posted.

Article 85. The High Contracting Parties shall communicate to each other, through the intermediary of the Swiss Federal Council, the official translations of the present Convention, together with such laws and regulations as they may adopt to ensure the application of the present Convention.

SECTION II
ORGANIZATION OF CONTROL

Article 86. The High Contracting Parties recognize that a guarantee of the regular application of the present Convention will be found in the possibility of collaboration between the protecting Powers charged with the protection of the interests of the belligerents; in this connection, the protecting Powers may, apart from their diplomatic personnel, appoint delegates from among their own nationals or the nationals of other neutral Powers. The appointment of these delegates shall be subject to the approval of the belligerent with whom they are to carry out their mission.

The representatives of the protecting Power or their recognized delegates shall be authorized to proceed to any place, without exception, where prisoners of war are interned. They shall have access to all premises occupied by prisoners and may hold conversation with prisoners, as a general rule without witnesses, either personally or through the intermediary of interpreters.

Belligerents shall facilitate as much as possible the task of the representatives or recognized delegates of the protecting Power. The military authorities shall be informed of their visits.

Belligerents may mutually agree to allow persons of the prisoners own nationality to participate in the tours of inspection.

Article 87. In the event of dispute between the belligerents regarding the application of the provisions of the present Convention, the protecting Powers shall, as far as possible, lend their good offices with the object of settling the dispute.

To this end, each of the protecting Powers may, for instance, propose to the belligerents concerned that a conference of representatives of the latter should be held, on suitably chosen neutral territory. The belligerents shall be required to give effect to proposals made to them with this object. The protecting Power may, if necessary, submit for the approval of the Powers in dispute the name of a person belonging to a neutral Power or nominated by the International Red Cross Committee, who shall be invited to take part in this conference.

Article 88. The foregoing provisions do not constitute any obstacle to the humanitarian work which the International Red Cross Committee may perform for the protection of prisoners of war with the consent of the belligerents concerned.

SECTION III
FINAL PROVISIONS

Article 89. In the relations between the Powers who are bound either by The Hague Convention concerning the Laws and Customs of War on Land of 29 July 1899, or that of 18 October 1907, and are parties to the present Convention, the latter shall be complementary to Chapter 2 of the Regulations annexed to the above-mentioned Conventions of The Hague.

Article 90. The present Convention, which shall bear this day's date, may be signed up to 1 February 1930, on behalf of any of the countries represented at the Conference which opened at Geneva on 1 July 1929.

Article 91. The present Convention shall be ratified as soon as possible.
   The ratifications shall be deposited at Berne.
   In respect of the deposit of each instrument of ratification, a 'procès-verbal' shall be drawn up, and copy thereof, certified correct, shall be sent by the Swiss Federal Council to the Governments of all the countries on whose behalf the Convention has been signed or whose accession has been notified.

Article 92. The present Convention shall enter into force six months after at least two instruments of ratification have been deposited.
   Thereafter it shall enter into force for each High Contracting Party six months after the deposit of its instrument of ratification.

Article 93. As from the date of its entry into force, the present Convention shall be open to accession notified in respect of any country on whose behalf this Convention has not been signed.

Article 94. Accessions shall be notified in writing to the Swiss Federal Council and shall take effect six months after the date on which they have been received.
   The Swiss Federal Council shall notify the accessions to the Governments of all the countries on whose behalf the Convention has been signed or whose accession has been notified.

Article 95. A state of war shall give immediate effect to ratifications deposited, and to accessions notified by the belligerent Powers before or after the commencement of hostilities. The communication of ratifications or accessions received from

Powers in a state of war shall be effected by the Swiss Federal Council by the quickest method.

Article 96. Each of the High Contracting Parties shall have the right to denounce the present Convention. The denunciation shall only take effect one year after notification thereof has been made in writing to the Swiss Federal Council. The latter shall communicate this notification to the Governments of all the High Contracting Parties.

The denunciation shall only be valid in respect of the High Contracting Party which has made notification thereof.

Such denunciation shall, moreover, not take effect during a war in which the denouncing Power is involved. In this case, the present Convention shall continue binding, beyond the period of one year, until the conclusion of peace and, in any case, until operations of repatriation shall have terminated.

Article 97. A copy of the present Convention, certified to be correct, shall be deposited by the Swiss Federal Council in the archives of the League of Nations. Similarly, ratifications, accessions and denunciations notified to the Swiss Federal Council shall be communicated by them to the League of Nations.

In faith whereof the above-mentioned Plenipotentiaries have signed the present Convention.

Done at Geneva the twenty-seventh of July, one thousand nine hundred and twenty-nine, in a single copy, which shall remain deposited in the archives of the Swiss Confederation, and of which copies, certified correct, shall be transmitted to the Governments of all the countries invited to the Conference.

ANNEX TO THE CONVENTION OF 27 JULY 1929, RELATIVE TO THE TREATMENT OF PRISONERS OF WAR

Model draft agreement concerning the direct repatriation or accommodation in a neutral country of prisoners of war for reasons of health

I. Guiding Principles for Direct Repatriation or Accommodation in a Neutral Country

A. 'Guiding Principles for Direct Repatriation'
The following shall be repatriated directly:

(1) Sick and wounded whose recovery within one year is not probable according to medical prognosis, whose condition requires treatment, and whose intellectual or bodily powers appear to have undergone a considerable diminution.
(2) Incurable sick and wounded whose intellectual or bodily powers appear to have undergone a considerable diminution.
(3) Convalescent sick and wounded, whose intellectual or bodily powers appear to have undergone a considerable diminution.

B. 'Guiding Principles for Accommodation in a Neutral Country.'
The following shall be accommodated in a neutral country:

(1) Sick and wounded whose recovery is presumable within the period of one year, which it appears that such recovery would be more certain and more rapid if the sick and wounded were given the benefit of the resources offered by the neutral country than if their captivity, properly so called, were prolonged.
(2) Prisoners of war whose intellectual or physical health appears, according to medical opinion, to be seriously threatened by continuance in captivity, while accommodation in a neutral country would probably diminish that risk.

C. 'Guiding Principles for the Repatriation of Prisoners in a Neutral Country.'
Prisoners of war who have been accommodated in a neutral country, and belong to the following categories, shall be repatriated:

(1) Those whose state of health appears to be, or likely to become such that they would fall into the categories of those to be repatriated for reasons of health.
(2) Those who are convalescent, whose intellectual or physical powers appear to have undergone a considerable diminution.

Above text provided by the International Committee of the Red Cross. Accessed: 29 September 2007.

http://www.icrc.org/IHL.nsf/52d68d14de6160e0c12563da005fdb1b/eb1571b00 daec90ec125641e00402aa6?OpenDocument

Convention Relative to the Treatment of Prisoners of War, Geneva, 12 August 1949

Just as the inadequacies of The Hague Conventions of 1899 and 1907 were made evident by the atrocities of the First World War, German and Japanese atrocities of the Second World War revealed the dismal inadequacies of the Geneva Convention of 1929. National Red Cross organizations worldwide began lobbying their respective countries for revisions to the existing laws of war. Finally, in 1949, the Diplomatic Conference for the Establishment of International Conventions for the Protection of War Victims convened in Geneva, Switzerland, with sixty-three governments represented—making the Fourth Geneva Conference: 1899, 1907, 1929, and 1949.

Four sections (or conventions) came out of the 1949 conference: First Convention—wounded and sick members of the armed forces in the field; Second Convention—wounded, sick, and shipwrecked members of the armed forces at sea as well as shipwreck victims; Third Convention—prisoners of the war (POWs); Fourth Convention—civilians in times of war. Of particular interest was the Third Convention (III) which revised the earlier directive from 1929 to clarify those persons entitled to prisoner of war protection status. Importantly, the new document dramatically extended the humane treatment of POWs, to now include civilian members of military aircraft crews who fell into enemy hands, as well as the crews of merchant marine ships or civil aircraft. Additionally, the 1949 Geneva Convention extended the protection of prisoner of war status to those partisan forces which met the conditions required of militia forces by the document, combatants of governments not recognized by the Detaining Power (i.e. governments in exile), and belligerents participating in a *levy en masse*.

Under the new doctrine, medical personnel and chaplains who fell under the power of the enemy could be detained in order to provide further care for prisoners. The protections of the Geneva Convention of 1949 applied to all prisoners for the duration of their detention, and the document was to be posted in every camp in the native language of prisoners. Although prisoners could work, Detaining Powers were expressly prohibited from requiring prisoners to remove or disarm mines. The 1949 doctrine also addressed starvation of prisoners in the Pacific Theater by requiring daily rations "sufficient in quantity, quality, and variety to keep POWs in good health, and to prevent loss of weight or the development of nutritional deficiencies."

While the Geneva Convention of 1949 clarified and expanded upon a number of points, it did not resolve every discrepancy. The Soviet Union and other countries in Eastern Europe agreed to the convention with specific reservations against the continued protection under the Geneva Convention of prisoners tried and convicted of war crimes. Additionally, the International Committee of the Red Cross strongly lobbied against a clause allowing Detaining Powers to repatriate prisoners against their will. Although the signatory nations resisted the Red Cross on this point, forced repatriation became an issue during the Korean War.

The current controversy about POWs in the War on Terror revolves around the treatment of prisoners who fall into the Bush Administration's interpretation of "unlawful combatants" as described in Article 4. The phrase "unlawful combatants," although it does not appear in the Convention itself, has been used since at least the 1940s to describe prisoners not subject to the protections of the Convention.

Supplemental Reading

Yingling, Raymund T. and Robert W. Ginnane. 1952. "The Geneva Conventions of 1949."
    The American Journal of International Law. 46(3): 393–427.
See: http://law.suite101.com/article.cfm/the_geneva_convention
See: http://www.infoplease.com/ce6/society/A0860529.html
See: http://www.defenddemocracy.org/publications/publications_show.htm?doc_id=
    155712

EXCERPTS FROM THE GENEVA CONVENTION RELATIVE TO THE
TREATMENT OF PRISONERS OF WAR (12 AUGUST 1949)

Article 4.

A. Prisoners of war, in the sense of the present Convention, are persons belonging to one of the following categories, who have fallen into the power of the enemy:

(1) Members of the armed forces of a Party to the conflict, as well as members of militias or volunteer corps forming part of such armed forces.
(2) Members of other militias and members of other volunteer corps, including those of organized resistance movements, belonging to a Party to the conflict and operating in or outside their own territory, even if this territory is occupied, provided that such militias or volunteer corps, including such organized resistance movements, fulfill the following conditions:
    (a) that of being commanded by a person responsible for his subordinates;
    (b) that of having a fixed distinctive sign recognizable at a distance;

    (c) that of carrying arms openly;

    (d) that of conducting their operations in accordance with the laws and customs of war.

(3) Members of regular armed forces who profess allegiance to a government or an authority not recognized by the Detaining Power.

(4) Persons who accompany the armed forces without actually being members thereof, such as civilian members of military aircraft crews, war correspondents, supply contractors, members of labor units or of services responsible for the welfare of the armed forces, provided that they have received authorization from the armed forces which they accompany, who shall provide them for that purpose with an identity card similar to the annexed model.

(5) Members of crews, including masters, pilots and apprentices, of the merchant marine and the crews of civil aircraft of the Parties to the conflict, who do not benefit by more favorable treatment under any other provisions of international law.

(6) Inhabitants of a non-occupied territory, who on the approach of the enemy spontaneously take up arms to resist the invading forces, without having had time to form themselves into regular armed units, provided they carry arms openly and respect the laws and customs of war.

B. The following shall likewise be treated as prisoners of war under the present Convention:

(1) Persons belonging, or having belonged, to the armed forces of the occupied country, if the occupying Power consider it necessary by reason of such allegiance to intern them, even though it has originally liberated them while hostilities were going on outside the territory it occupies, in particular where such persons have made an unsuccessful attempt to rejoin the armed forces to which they belong and which are engaged in combat, or where they fail to comply with a summons made to them with a view to internment.

(2) The persons belonging to one of the categories enumerated in the present Article, who have been received by neutral or non-belligerent Powers on their territory and whom these Powers are required to intern under international law, without prejudice to any more favorable treatment which these Powers may choose to give and with the exception of Articles 8, 10, 15, 30, fifth paragraph, 58–67, 92, 126 and, where diplomatic relations exist between the Parties to the conflict and the neutral or non-belligerent Power concerned, those Articles concerning the Protecting Power. Where such diplomatic relations exist, the Parties to a conflict on whom these persons depend shall be allowed to perform towards them the functions of a Protecting Power as provided in the present Convention, without prejudice to the functions which these Parties normally exercise in conformity with diplomatic and consular usage and treaties.

C. This Article shall in no way affect the status of medical personnel and chaplains as provided for in Article 33 of the present Convention.

Article 5. The present Convention shall apply to the persons referred to in Article 4 from the time they fall into the power of the enemy and until their final release and repatriation.

Should any doubt arise as to whether persons, having committed a belligerent act and having fallen into the hands of the enemy, belong to any of the categories enumerated in Article 4, such persons shall enjoy the protection of the present Convention until such time as their status has been determined by a competent tribunal.

Part II. General Protection of Prisoners of War

Article 12. Prisoners of war are in the hands of the enemy Power, but not of the individuals or military units who have captured them. Irrespective of the individual responsibilities that may exist, the Detaining Power is responsible for the treatment given them.

Prisoners of war may only be transferred by the Detaining Power to a Power which is a party to the Convention and after the Detaining Power has satisfied itself of the willingness and ability of such transferee Power to apply the Convention. When prisoners of war are transferred under such circumstances, responsibility for the application of the Convention rests on the Power accepting them while they are in its custody.

Nevertheless, if that Power fails to carry out the provisions of the Convention in any important respect, the Power by whom the prisoners of war were transferred shall, upon being notified by the Protecting Power, take effective measures to correct the situation or shall request the return of the prisoners of war. Such requests must be complied with.

Article 13. Prisoners of war must at all times be humanely treated. Any unlawful act or omission by the Detaining Power causing death or seriously endangering the health of a prisoner of war in its custody is prohibited, and will be regarded as a serious breach of the present Convention. In particular, no prisoner of war may be subjected to physical mutilation or to medical or scientific experiments of any kind which are not justified by the medical, dental or hospital treatment of the prisoner concerned and carried out in his interest.

Likewise, prisoners of war must at all times be protected, particularly against acts of violence or intimidation and against insults and public curiosity.

Measures of reprisal against prisoners of war are prohibited.

Article 14. Prisoners of war are entitled in all circumstances to respect for their persons and their honor.

Women shall be treated with all the regard due to their sex and shall in all cases benefit by treatment as favorable as that granted to men.

Prisoners of war shall retain the full civil capacity which they enjoyed at the time of their capture. The Detaining Power may not restrict the exercise, either within or without its own territory, of the rights such capacity confers except in so far as the captivity requires.

Article 15. The Power detaining prisoners of war shall be bound to provide free of charge for their maintenance and for the medical attention required by their state of health.

Article 16. Taking into consideration the provisions of the present Convention relating to rank and sex, and subject to any privileged treatment which may be accorded to them by reason of their state of health, age or professional qualifications, all prisoners of war shall be treated alike by the Detaining Power, without any adverse distinction based on race, nationality, religious belief or political opinions, or any other distinction founded on similar criteria.

Part III. Captivity
Section 1. Beginning of Captivity

Article 17. Every prisoner of war, when questioned on the subject, is bound to give only his surname, first names and rank, date of birth, and army, regimental, personal or serial number, or failing this, equivalent information.

If he willfully infringes this rule, he may render himself liable to a restriction of the privileges accorded to his rank or status.

Each Party to a conflict is required to furnish the persons under its jurisdiction who are liable to become prisoners of war, with an identity card showing the owner's surname, first names, rank, army, regimental, personal or serial number or equivalent information, and date of birth. The identity card may, furthermore, bear the signature or the fingerprints, or both, of the owner, and may bear, as well, any other information the Party to the conflict may wish to add concerning persons belonging to its armed forces. As far as possible the card shall measure 6.5 x 10 cm. and shall be issued in duplicate. The identity card shall be shown by the prisoner of war upon demand, but may in no case be taken away from him.

No physical or mental torture, nor any other form of coercion, may be inflicted on prisoners of war to secure from them information of any kind whatever. Prisoners of war who refuse to answer may not be threatened, insulted, or exposed to unpleasant or disadvantageous treatment of any kind.

Prisoners of war who, owing to their physical or mental condition, are unable to state their identity, shall be handed over to the medical service. The identity of such prisoners shall be established by all possible means, subject to the provisions of the preceding paragraph.

The questioning of prisoners of war shall be carried out in a language which they understand.

Article 18. All effects and articles of personal use, except arms, horses, military equipment and military documents, shall remain in the possession of prisoners of war, likewise their metal helmets and gas masks and like articles issued for personal protection. Effects and articles used for their clothing or feeding shall likewise remain in their possession, even if such effects and articles belong to their regulation military equipment.

At no time should prisoners of war be without identity documents. The Detaining Power shall supply such documents to prisoners of war who possess none.

Badges of rank and nationality, decorations and articles having above all a personal or sentimental value may not be taken from prisoners of war.

Sums of money carried by prisoners of war may not be taken away from them except by order of an officer, and after the amount and particulars of the owner have been recorded in a special register and an itemized receipt has been given, legibly inscribed with the name, rank and unit of the person issuing the said receipt. Sums in the currency of the Detaining Power, or which are changed into such currency at the prisoner's request, shall be placed to the credit of the prisoner's account as provided in Article 64.

The Detaining Power may withdraw articles of value from prisoners of war only for reasons of security; when such articles are withdrawn, the procedure laid down for sums of money impounded shall apply.

Such objects, likewise sums taken away in any currency other than that of the Detaining Power and the conversion of which has not been asked for by the owners, shall be kept in the custody of the Detaining Power and shall be returned in their initial shape to prisoners of war at the end of their captivity.

Article 19. Prisoners of war shall be evacuated, as soon as possible after their capture, to camps situated in an area far enough from the combat zone for them to be out of danger. Only those prisoners of war who, owing to wounds or sickness, would run greater risks by being evacuated than by remaining where they are, may be temporarily kept back in a danger zone.

Prisoners of war shall not be unnecessarily exposed to danger while awaiting evacuation from a fighting zone.

Article 20. The evacuation of prisoners of war shall always be effected humanely and in conditions similar to those for the forces of the Detaining Power in their changes of station.

The Detaining Power shall supply prisoners of war who are being evacuated with sufficient food and potable water, and with the necessary clothing and medical attention. The Detaining Power shall take all suitable precautions to ensure their safety during evacuation, and shall establish as soon as possible a list of the prisoners of war who are evacuated.

If prisoners of war must, during evacuation, pass through transit camps, their stay in such camps shall be as brief as possible.

Section II. Internment of Prisoners of War
Chapter I. General Observations

Article 21. The Detaining Power may subject prisoners of war to internment. It may impose on them the obligation of not leaving, beyond certain limits, the camp where they are interned, or if the said camp is fenced in, of not going outside its perimeter. Subject to the provisions of the present Convention relative to penal and disciplinary sanctions, prisoners of war may not be held in close confinement except where necessary to safeguard their health and then only during the continuation of the circumstances which make such confinement necessary.

Prisoners of war may be partially or wholly released on parole or promise, in so far as is allowed by the laws of the Power on which they depend. Such measures shall be taken particularly in cases where this may contribute to the improvement of their state of health. No prisoner of war shall be compelled to accept liberty on parole or promise.

Upon the outbreak of hostilities, each Party to the conflict shall notify the adverse Party of the laws and regulations allowing or forbidding its own nationals to accept liberty on parole or promise. Prisoners of war who are paroled or who have given their promise in conformity with the laws and regulations so notified, are bound on their personal honour scrupulously to fulfill, both towards the Power on which they depend and towards the Power which has captured them, the engagements of their paroles or promises. In such cases, the Power on which they depend is bound neither to require nor to accept from them any service incompatible with the parole or promise given.

Article 22. Prisoners of war may be interned only in premises located on land and affording every guarantee of hygiene and healthfulness. Except in particular cases which are justified by the interest of the prisoners themselves, they shall not be interned in penitentiaries.

Prisoners of war interned in unhealthy areas, or where the climate is injurious for them, shall be removed as soon as possible to a more favorable climate.

The Detaining Power shall assemble prisoners of war in camps or camp compounds according to their nationality, language and customs, provided that such prisoners shall not be separated from prisoners of war belonging to the armed forces with which they were serving at the time of their capture, except with their consent.

Article 23. No prisoner of war may at any time be sent to, or detained in, areas where he may be exposed to the fire of the combat zone, nor may his presence be used to render certain points or areas immune from military operations.

Prisoners of war shall have shelters against air bombardment and other hazards of war, to the same extent as the local civilian population. With the exception of those engaged in the protection of their quarters against the aforesaid hazards, they may enter such shelters as soon as possible after the giving of the alarm. Any other protective measure taken in favor of the population shall also apply to them.

Detaining Powers shall give the Powers concerned, through the intermediary of the Protecting Powers, all useful information regarding the geographical location of prisoner of war camps.

Whenever military considerations permit, prisoner of war camps shall be indicated in the day-time by the letters PW or PG, placed so as to be clearly visible from the air. The Powers concerned may, however, agree upon any other system of marking. Only prisoner of war camps shall be marked as such.

Article 24. Transit or screening camps of a permanent kind shall be fitted out under conditions similar to those described in the present Section, and the prisoners therein shall have the same treatment as in other camps.

Chapter II. Quarters, Food and Clothing of Prisoners of War

Article 25. Prisoners of war shall be quartered under conditions as favorable as those for the forces of the Detaining Power who are billeted in the same area. The said conditions shall make allowance for the habits and customs of the prisoners and shall in no case be prejudicial to their health.

The foregoing provisions shall apply in particular to the dormitories of prisoners of war as regards both total surface and minimum cubic space, and the general installations, bedding and blankets.

The premises provided for the use of prisoners of war individually or collectively shall be entirely protected from dampness and adequately heated and lighted, in particular between dusk and lights out. All precautions must be taken against the danger of fire.

In any camps in which women prisoners of war, as well as men, are accommodated, separate dormitories shall be provided for them.

Article 26. The basic daily food rations shall be sufficient in quantity, quality and variety to keep prisoners of war in good health and to prevent loss of weight or the development of nutritional deficiencies. Account shall also be taken of the habitual diet of the prisoners.

The Detaining Power shall supply prisoners of war who work with such additional rations as are necessary for the labor on which they are employed.

Sufficient drinking water shall be supplied to prisoners of war. The use of tobacco shall be permitted.

Prisoners of war shall, as far as possible, be associated with the preparation of their meals; they may be employed for that purpose in the kitchens. Furthermore, they shall be given the means of preparing, themselves, the additional food in their possession.

Adequate premises shall be provided for messing.

Collective disciplinary measures affecting food are prohibited.

Article 27. Clothing, underwear and footwear shall be supplied to prisoners of war in sufficient quantities by the Detaining Power, which shall make allowance for the climate of the region where the prisoners are detained. Uniforms of enemy armed forces captured by the Detaining Power should, if suitable for the climate, be made available to clothe prisoners of war.

The regular replacement and repair of the above articles shall be assured by the Detaining Power. In addition, prisoners of war who work shall receive appropriate clothing, wherever the nature of the work demands.

Article 28. Canteens shall be installed in all camps, where prisoners of war may procure foodstuffs, soap and tobacco and ordinary articles in daily use. The tariff shall never be in excess of local market prices.

The profits made by camp canteens shall be used for the benefit of the prisoners; a special fund shall be created for this purpose. The prisoners' representative shall have the right to collaborate in the management of the canteen and of this fund.

When a camp is closed down, the credit balance of the special fund shall be handed to an international welfare organization, to be employed for the benefit of prisoners of war of the same nationality as those who have contributed to the fund. In case of a general repatriation, such profits shall be kept by the Detaining Power, subject to any agreement to the contrary between the Powers concerned.

Chapter III. Hygiene and Medical Attention

Article 29. The Detaining Power shall be bound to take all sanitary measures necessary to ensure the cleanliness and healthfulness of camps and to prevent epidemics.

Prisoners of war shall have for their use, day and night, conveniences which conform to the rules of hygiene and are maintained in a constant state of cleanliness. In any camps in which women prisoners of war are accommodated, separate conveniences shall be provided for them.

Also, apart from the baths and showers with which the camps shall be furnished prisoners of war shall be provided with sufficient water and soap for their personal toilet and for washing their personal laundry; the necessary installations, facilities and time shall be granted them for that purpose.

Article 30. Every camp shall have an adequate infirmary where prisoners of war may have the attention they require, as well as appropriate diet. Isolation wards shall, if necessary, be set aside for cases of contagious or mental disease.

Prisoners of war suffering from serious disease, or whose condition necessitates special treatment, a surgical operation or hospital care, must be admitted to any military or civilian medical unit where such treatment can be given, even if their repatriation is contemplated in the near future. Special facilities shall be afforded for the care to be given to the disabled, in particular to the blind, and for their rehabilitation, pending repatriation.

Prisoners of war shall have the attention, preferably, of medical personnel of the Power on which they depend and, if possible, of their nationality.

Prisoners of war may not be prevented from presenting themselves to the medical authorities for examination. The Detaining authorities shall, upon request, issue to every prisoner who has undergone treatment, an official certificate indicating the nature of his illness or injury, and the duration and kind of treatment received. A duplicate of this certificate shall be forwarded to the Central Prisoners of War Agency.

The costs of treatment, including those of any apparatus necessary for the maintenance of prisoners of war in good health, particularly dentures and other artificial appliances, and spectacles, shall be borne by the Detaining Power.

Article 31. Medical inspections of prisoners of war shall be held at least once a month. They shall include the checking and the recording of the weight of each prisoner of war. Their purpose shall be, in particular, to supervise the general state of health, nutrition and cleanliness of prisoners and to detect contagious diseases, especially tuberculosis, malaria and venereal disease. For this purpose the most efficient methods available shall be employed, e.g. periodic mass miniature radiography for the early detection of tuberculosis.

Article 32. Prisoners of war who, though not attached to the medical service of their armed forces, are physicians, surgeons, dentists, nurses or medical orderlies, may be required by the Detaining Power to exercise their medical functions in the interests of prisoners of war dependent on the same Power. In that case they shall continue to be prisoners of war, but shall receive the same treatment as corresponding medical personnel retained by the Detaining Power. They shall be exempted from any other work under Article 49.

Chapter IV. Medical Personnel and Chaplains Retained to Assist Prisoners of War

Article 33. Members of the medical personnel and chaplains while retained by the Detaining Power with a view to assisting prisoners of war, shall not be considered as prisoners of war. They shall, however, receive as a minimum the benefits and protection of the present Convention, and shall also be granted all facilities necessary to provide for the medical care of and religious ministration to prisoners of war.

They shall continue to exercise their medical and spiritual functions for the benefit of prisoners of war, preferably those belonging to the armed forces upon which they depend, within the scope of the military laws and regulations of the Detaining Power and under the control of its competent services, in accordance with their professional etiquette. They shall also benefit by the following facilities in the exercise of their medical or spiritual functions:

(a) They shall be authorized to visit periodically prisoners of war situated in working detachments or in hospitals outside the camp. For this purpose, the Detaining Power shall place at their disposal the necessary means of transport.
(b) The senior medical officer in each camp shall be responsible to the camp military authorities for everything connected with the activities of retained medical personnel. For this purpose, Parties to the conflict shall agree at the outbreak of hostilities on the subject of the corresponding ranks of the medical personnel, including that of societies mentioned in Article 26 of the Geneva Convention for the Amelioration of the Condition of the Wounded and Sick in Armed Forces in the Field of August 12, 1949. This senior medical officer, as well as chaplains, shall have the right to deal with the competent authorities of the camp on all questions relating to their duties. Such authorities shall afford them all necessary facilities for correspondence relating to these questions.

(c) Although they shall be subject to the internal discipline of the camp in which they are retained, such personnel may not be compelled to carry out any work other than that concerned with their medical or religious duties.

During hostilities, the Parties to the conflict shall agree concerning the possible relief of retained personnel and shall settle the procedure to be followed.

None of the preceding provisions shall relieve the Detaining Power of its obligations with regard to prisoners of war from the medical or spiritual point of view.

Chapter V. Religious, Intellectual and Physical Activities

Article 34. Prisoners of war shall enjoy complete latitude in the exercise of their religious duties, including attendance at the service of their faith, on condition that they comply with the disciplinary routine prescribed by the military authorities.

Adequate premises shall be provided where religious services may be held.

Article 35. Chaplains who fall into the hands of the enemy Power and who remain or are retained with a view to assisting prisoners of war, shall be allowed to minister to them and to exercise freely their ministry amongst prisoners of war of the same religion, in accordance with their religious conscience. They shall be allocated among the various camps and labor detachments containing prisoners of war belonging to the same forces, speaking the same language or practicing the same religion. They shall enjoy the necessary facilities, including the means of transport provided for in Article 33, for visiting the prisoners of war outside their camp. They shall be free to correspond, subject to censorship, on matters concerning their religious duties with the ecclesiastical authorities in the country of detention and with international religious organizations. Letters and cards which they may send for this purpose shall be in addition to the quota provided for in Article 71.

Article 36. Prisoners of war who are ministers of religion, without having officiated as chaplains to their own forces, shall be at liberty, whatever their denomination, to minister freely to the members of their community. For this purpose, they shall receive the same treatment as the chaplains retained by the Detaining Power. They shall not be obliged to do any other work.

Article 37. When prisoners of war have not the assistance of a retained chaplain or of a prisoner of war minister of their faith, a minister belonging to the prisoners' or a similar denomination, or in his absence a qualified layman, if such a course is feasible from a confessional point of view, shall be appointed, at the request of the prisoners concerned, to fill this office. This appointment, subject to the approval of the Detaining Power, shall take place with the agreement of the community of prisoners concerned and, wherever necessary, with the approval of the local religious authorities of the same faith. The person thus appointed shall comply with all regulations established by the Detaining Power in the interests of discipline and military security.

Article 38. While respecting the individual preferences of every prisoner, the Detaining Power shall encourage the practice of intellectual, educational, and recreational pursuits, sports and games amongst prisoners, and shall take the measures necessary to ensure the exercise thereof by providing them with adequate premises and necessary equipment. Prisoners shall have opportunities for taking physical exercise, including sports and games, and for being out of doors. Sufficient open spaces shall be provided for this purpose in all camps.

Chapter VI. Discipline

Article 39. Every prisoner of war camp shall be put under the immediate authority of a responsible commissioned officer belonging to the regular armed forces of the Detaining Power. Such officer shall have in his possession a copy of the present Convention; he shall ensure that its provisions are known to the camp staff and the guard and shall be responsible, under the direction of his government, for its application.

Prisoners of war, with the exception of officers, must salute and show to all officers of the Detaining Power the external marks of respect provided for by the regulations applying in their own forces.

Officer prisoners of war are bound to salute only officers of a higher rank of the Detaining Power; they must, however, salute the camp commander regardless of his rank.

Article 40. The wearing of badges of rank and nationality, as well as of decorations, shall be permitted.

Article 41. In every camp the text of the present Convention and its Annexes and the contents of any special agreement provided for in Article 6, shall be posted, in the prisoners' own language, in places where all may read them. Copies shall be supplied, on request, to the prisoners who cannot have access to the copy which has been posted. Regulations, orders, notices and publications of every kind relating to the conduct of prisoners of war shall be issued to them in a language which they understand. Such regulations, orders and publications shall be posted in the manner described above and copies shall be handed to the prisoners' representative. Every order and command addressed to prisoners of war individually must likewise be given in a language which they understand.

Article 42. The use of weapons against prisoners of war, especially against those who are escaping or attempting to escape, shall constitute an extreme measure, which shall always be preceded by warnings appropriate to the circumstances.

Chapter VII. Rank of Prisoners of War

Article 43. Upon the outbreak of hostilities, the Parties to the conflict shall communicate to one another the titles and ranks of all the persons mentioned in Article 4 of the present Convention, in order to ensure equality of treatment between prisoners of equivalent rank. Titles and ranks which are subsequently created shall form the subject of similar communications.

The Detaining Power shall recognize promotions in rank which have been accorded to prisoners of war and which have been duly notified by the Power on which these prisoners depend.

Article 44. Officers and prisoners of equivalent status shall be treated with the regard due to their rank and age.

In order to ensure service in officers' camps, other ranks of the same armed forces who, as far as possible, speak the same language, shall be assigned in sufficient numbers, account being taken of the rank of officers and prisoners of equivalent status. Such orderlies shall not be required to perform any other work.

Supervision of the mess by the officers themselves shall be facilitated in every way.

Article 45. Prisoners of war other than officers and prisoners of equivalent status shall be treated with the regard due to their rank and age.

[. . .]

Article 47. Sick or wounded prisoners of war shall not be transferred as long as their recovery may be endangered by the journey, unless their safety imperatively demands it.

If the combat zone draws closer to a camp, the prisoners of war in the said camp shall not be transferred unless their transfer can be carried out in adequate conditions of safety, or unless they are exposed to greater risks by remaining on the spot than by being transferred.

Article 48. In the event of transfer, prisoners of war shall be officially advised of their departure and of their new postal address. Such notifications shall be given in time for them to pack their luggage and inform their next of kin.

They shall be allowed to take with them their personal effects, and the correspondence and parcels which have arrived for them. The weight of such baggage may be limited, if the conditions of transfer so require, to what each prisoner can reasonably carry, which shall in no case be more than twenty-five kilograms per head.

Mail and parcels addressed to their former camp shall be forwarded to them without delay. The camp commander shall take, in agreement with the prisoners' representative, any measures needed to ensure the transport of the prisoners' community property and of the luggage they are unable to take with them in consequence of restrictions imposed by virtue of the second paragraph of this Article.

The costs of transfers shall be borne by the Detaining Power.

Section III. Labor of Prisoners of War

Article 49. The Detaining Power may utilize the labor of prisoners of war who are physically fit, taking into account their age, sex, rank and physical aptitude, and with a view particularly to maintaining them in a good state of physical and mental health.

Non-commissioned officers who are prisoners of war shall only be required to do supervisory work. Those not so required may ask for other suitable work which shall, so far as possible, be found for them.

If officers or persons of equivalent status ask for suitable work, it shall be found for them, so far as possible, but they may in no circumstances be compelled to work.

Article 50. Besides work connected with camp administration, installation or maintenance, prisoners of war may be compelled to do only such work as is included in the following classes:

(a) agriculture;
(b) industries connected with the production or the extraction of raw materials, and manufacturing industries, with the exception of metallurgical, machinery and chemical industries; public works and building operations which have no military character or purpose;
(c) transport and handling of stores which are not military in character or purpose;
(d) commercial business, and arts and crafts;
(e) domestic service;
(f) public utility services having no military character or purpose.

Should the above provisions be infringed, prisoners of war shall be allowed to exercise their right of complaint, in conformity with Article 78.

Article 51. Prisoners of war must be granted suitable working conditions, especially as regards accommodation, food, clothing and equipment; such conditions shall not be inferior to those enjoyed by nationals of the Detaining Power employed in similar work; account shall also be taken of climatic conditions.

The Detaining Power, in utilizing the labor of prisoners of war, shall ensure that in areas in which such prisoners are employed, the national legislation concerning the protection of labor, and, more particularly, the regulations for the safety of workers, are duly applied.

Prisoners of war shall receive training and be provided with the means of protection suitable to the work they will have to do and similar to those accorded to the nationals of the Detaining Power. Subject to the provisions of Article 52, prisoners may be submitted to the normal risks run by these civilian workers.

Conditions of labor shall in no case be rendered more arduous by disciplinary measures.

Article 52. Unless he be a volunteer, no prisoner of war may be employed on labor which is of an unhealthy or dangerous nature.

No prisoner of war shall be assigned to labor which would be looked upon as humiliating for a member of the Detaining Power's own forces.

The removal of mines or similar devices shall be considered as dangerous labor.

Article 53. The duration of the daily labor of prisoners of war, including the time of the journey to and fro, shall not be excessive, and must in no case exceed that permitted for civilian workers in the district, who are nationals of the Detaining Power and employed on the same work.

Prisoners of war must be allowed, in the middle of the day's work, a rest of not less than one hour. This rest will be the same as that to which workers of the Detaining Power are entitled, if the latter is of longer duration. They shall be allowed in addition a rest of twenty-four consecutive hours every week, preferably on Sunday or the day of rest in their country of origin. Furthermore, every prisoner who has worked for one year shall be granted a rest of eight consecutive days, during which his working pay shall be paid him.

If methods of labor such as piece work are employed, the length of the working period shall not be rendered excessive thereby.

Article 55. The fitness of prisoners of war for work shall be periodically verified by medical examinations at least once a month. The examinations shall have particular regard to the nature of the work which prisoners of war are required to do.

If any prisoner of war considers himself incapable of working, he shall be permitted to appear before the medical authorities of his camp. Physicians or surgeons may recommend that the prisoners who are, in their opinion, unfit for work, be exempted therefrom.

Article 56. The organization and administration of labor detachments shall be similar to those of prisoner of war camps.

Every labor detachment shall remain under the control of and administratively part of a prisoner of war camp. The military authorities and the commander of the said camp shall be responsible, under the direction of their government, for the observance of the provisions of the present Convention in labor detachments.

The camp commander shall keep an up-to-date record of the labor detachments dependent on his camp, and shall communicate it to the delegates of the Protecting Power, of the International Committee of the Red Cross, or of other agencies giving relief to prisoners of war, who may visit the camp.

Section IV. Financial Resources of Prisoners of War

Article 60. The Detaining Power shall grant all prisoners of war a monthly advance of pay, the amount of which shall be fixed by conversion, into the currency of the said Power, of the following amounts:

Category I: Prisoners ranking below sergeants: eight Swiss francs.

Category II: Sergeants and other non-commissioned officers, or prisoners of equivalent rank: twelve Swiss francs.

Category III: Warrant officers and commissioned officers below the rank of major or prisoners of equivalent rank: fifty Swiss francs.

Category IV: Majors, lieutenant-colonels, colonels or prisoners of equivalent rank: sixty Swiss francs.

Category V: General officers or prisoners of war of equivalent rank: seventy-five Swiss francs.

Chapter III. Penal and Disciplinary Sanctions

I. General Provisions

Article 82. A prisoner of war shall be subject to the laws, regulations and orders in force in the armed forces of the Detaining Power; the Detaining Power shall be justified in taking judicial or disciplinary measures in respect of any offence committed by a prisoner of war against such laws, regulations or orders. However, no proceedings or punishments contrary to the provisions of this Chapter shall be allowed.

If any law, regulation or order of the Detaining Power shall declare acts committed by a prisoner of war to be punishable, whereas the same acts would not be punishable if committed by a member of the forces of the Detaining Power, such acts shall entail disciplinary punishments only.

Article 83. In deciding whether proceedings in respect of an offence alleged to have been committed by a prisoner of war shall be judicial or disciplinary, the Detaining Power shall ensure that the competent authorities exercise the greatest leniency and adopt, wherever possible, disciplinary rather than judicial measures.

Article 84. A prisoner of war shall be tried only by a military court, unless the existing laws of the Detaining Power expressly permit the civil courts to try a member of the armed forces of the Detaining Power in respect of the particular offence alleged to have been committed by the prisoner of war.

In no circumstances whatever shall a prisoner of war be tried by a court of any kind which does not offer the essential guarantees of independence and impartiality as generally recognized, and, in particular, the procedure of which does not afford the accused the rights and means of defense provided for in Article 105.

Article 85. Prisoners of war prosecuted under the laws of the Detaining Power for acts committed prior to capture shall retain, even if convicted, the benefits of the present Convention.

Article 86. No prisoner of war may be punished more than once for the same act or on the same charge.

Collective punishment for individual acts, corporal punishment, imprisonment in premises without daylight and, in general, any form of torture or cruelty, are forbidden.

No prisoner of war may be deprived of his rank by the Detaining Power, or prevented from wearing his badges.

Article 88. Officers, non-commissioned officers and men who are prisoners of war undergoing a disciplinary or judicial punishment, shall not be subjected to more severe treatment than that applied in respect of the same punishment to members of the armed forces of the Detaining Power of equivalent rank.

A woman prisoner of war shall not be awarded or sentenced to a punishment more severe, or treated whilst undergoing punishment more severely, than a woman member of the armed forces of the Detaining Power dealt with for a similar offence.

In no case may a woman prisoner of war be awarded or sentenced to a punishment more severe, or treated whilst undergoing punishment more severely, than a male member of the armed forces of the Detaining Power dealt with for a similar offence.

II. Disciplinary Sanctions

Article 89. The disciplinary punishments applicable to prisoners of war are the following:

(1) A fine which shall not exceed 50 per cent of the advances of pay and working pay which the prisoner of war would otherwise receive under the provisions of Articles 60 and 62 during a period of not more than thirty days.
(2) Discontinuance of privileges granted over and above the treatment provided for by the present Convention.
(3) Fatigue duties not exceeding two hours daily.
(4) Confinement.

The punishment referred to under (3) shall not be applied to officers.

In no case shall disciplinary punishments be inhuman, brutal or dangerous to the health of prisoners of war.

Article 91. The escape of a prisoner of war shall be deemed to have succeeded when:

(1) he has joined the armed forces of the Power on which he depends, or those of an allied Power;
(2) he has left the territory under the control of the Detaining Power, or of an ally of the said Power;
(3) he has joined a ship flying the flag of the Power on which he depends, or of an allied Power, in the territorial waters of the Detaining Power, the said ship not being under the control of the last named Power.

Prisoners of war who have made good their escape in the sense of this Article and who are recaptured, shall not be liable to any punishment in respect of their previous escape.

Article 94. If an escaped prisoner of war is recaptured, the Power on which he depends shall be notified thereof in the manner defined in Article 122, provided notification of his escape has been made.

Article 95. A prisoner of war accused of an offence against discipline shall not be kept in confinement pending the hearing unless a member of the armed forces of the Detaining Power would be so kept if he were accused of a similar offence, or if it is essential in the interests of camp order and discipline.

Any period spent by a prisoner of war in confinement awaiting the disposal of an offence against discipline shall be reduced to an absolute minimum and shall not exceed fourteen days.

The provisions of Articles 97 and 98 of this Chapter shall apply to prisoners of war who are in confinement awaiting the disposal of offences against discipline.

Article 96. Acts which constitute offences against discipline shall be investigated immediately.

Officers and persons of equivalent status shall not be lodged in the same quarters as non-commissioned officers or men.

Women prisoners of war undergoing disciplinary punishment shall be confined in separate quarters from male prisoners of war and shall be under the immediate supervision of women.

Article 98. A prisoner of war undergoing confinement as a disciplinary punishment, shall continue to enjoy the benefits of the provisions of this Convention except in so far as these are necessarily rendered inapplicable by the mere fact that he is confined. In no case may he be deprived of the benefits of the provisions of Articles 78 and 126.

A prisoner of war awarded disciplinary punishment may not be deprived of the prerogatives attached to his rank.

They shall have permission to read and write, likewise to send and receive letters. Parcels and remittances of money however, may be withheld from them until the completion of the punishment; they shall meanwhile be entrusted to the prisoners' representative, who-will hand over to the infirmary the perishable goods contained in such parcels.

III. Juridicial Proceedings

No moral or physical coercion may be exerted on a prisoner of war in order to induce him to admit himself guilty of the act of which he is accused.

No prisoner of war may be convicted without having had an opportunity to present his defense and the assistance of a qualified advocate or counsel.

Article 100. Prisoners of war and the Protecting Powers shall be informed as soon as possible of the offences which are punishable by the death sentence under the laws of the Detaining Power.

Part IV. Termination of Captivity

Section I. Direct Repatriation and Accommodation in Neutral Countries

Article 109. Subject to the provisions of the third paragraph of this Article, Parties to the conflict are bound to send back to their own country, regardless of number or rank, seriously wounded and seriously sick prisoners of war, after having cared for them until they are fit to travel, in accordance with the first paragraph of the following Article.

Throughout the duration of hostilities, Parties to the conflict shall endeavor, with the cooperation of the neutral Powers concerned, to make arrangements for the accommodation in neutral countries of the sick and wounded prisoners of war referred to in the second paragraph of the following Article. They may, in addition, conclude agreements with a view to the direct repatriation or internment in a neutral country of able-bodied prisoners of war who have undergone a long period of captivity.

No sick or injured prisoner of war who is eligible for repatriation under the first paragraph of this Article, may be repatriated against his will during hostilities.

Article 110. The following shall be repatriated direct:

(1) Incurably wounded and sick whose mental or physical fitness seems to have been gravely diminished.
(2) Wounded and sick who, according to medical opinion, are not likely to recover within one year, whose condition requires treatment and whose mental or physical fitness seems to have been gravely diminished.
(3) Wounded and sick who have recovered, but whose mental or physical fitness seems to have been gravely and permanently diminished.

The following may be accommodated in a neutral country:

(1) Wounded and sick whose recovery may be expected within one year of the date of the wound or the beginning of the illness, if treatment in a neutral country might increase the prospects of a more certain and speedy recovery.
(2) Prisoners of war whose mental or physical health, according to medical opinion, is seriously threatened by continued captivity, but whose accommodation in a neutral country might remove such a threat.

The conditions which prisoners of war accommodated in a neutral country must fulfill in order to permit their repatriation shall be fixed, as shall likewise their status, by agreement between the Powers concerned. In general, prisoners of war who have been accommodated in a neutral country, and who belong to the following categories, should be repatriated:

(1) Those whose state of health has deteriorated so as to fulfill the condition laid down for direct repatriation;

(2) Those whose mental or physical powers remain, even after treatment, considerably impaired.

If no special agreements are concluded between the Parties to the conflict concerned, to determine the cases of disablement or sickness entailing direct repatriation or accommodation in a neutral country, such cases shall be settled in accordance with the principles laid down in the Model Agreement concerning direct repatriation and accommodation in neutral countries of wounded and sick prisoners of war and in the Regulations concerning Mixed Medical Commissions annexed to the present Convention.

Section II. Release and Repatriation of Prisoners of War at the Close of Hostilities

Article 118. Prisoners of war shall be released and repatriated without delay after the cessation of active hostilities.

Above text available from the United Nations, Office of the High Commissioner for Human Rights. Accessed: 29 September 2007. http://www.unhchr.ch/html/menu3/b/91.htm

ESTIMATED POWs (Prisoners of War), MIA (Missing in Action) and KIA (Killed in Action) since 1775

(Sources: Dept. of Defense, Defense POW/Missing Personnel Office; and POW Network. org)

WAR OF THE REVOLUTION 19 April 1775 to 20 September 1783

Participants: 217,000; POWs: 18,152; MIAs: 1,426; Deaths in Service: 4,435

WAR OF 1812 18 June 1812 to 24 December 1814

Participants: 60,000 U.S. Army forces Supported by 470,000 volunteer troops; POWs: 20,000; MIAs: 695; Deaths in Service: 2,260

MEXICAN WAR 24 April 1846 to 2 February 1848

Participants: 78,718; POWs: unknown; MIAs: unknown; Deaths in Service: 13,780

CIVIL WAR 12 April 1861 to 26 May 1865

Union Participants: 2,213,365; Union POWs: 194,743; Union Deaths in Service: 364,511

Confederate Participants: 1,082,119; Confederate POWs: 214,865; Confederate Deaths in Service: 134,563

SPANISH-AMERICAN WAR 21 April 1898 to 12 August 1898

Participants: 306,760; POWs: 8; MIAs: 72; Deaths in Service: 2,446

WORLD WAR I 6 April 1917 to 11 November 1918

Participants: 4,743,826; POWs: 4,120; MIAs: 3,350; Deaths in theater: 116,708

WORLD WAR II 7 December 1941 to 2 September 1945

Participants: 16,353,659; POWs: 124,079; Died in Captivity—Pacific Theater: 12,500 + European Theater: 1,200; MIAs: 30,314; Deaths in Service: Disputed Numbers—References:

- Keegan: 292,000
- Harper Collins: 292,100
- Britannica: 292,131 (not incl. 115,187 non-battle)
- Compton's: 293,986
- Urlanis: 300,000
- Infoplease: 291,557 KIA + 113,842 other causes = 405,399
- DoD: 291,557 KIA + 113,842 other = 405,399
- Ellis: 405,400
- Encarta: 292,131 KIA + 115,187 other causes = 407,318
- Wallechinsky: 292,131 KIA + 115,187 other = 407,318
- Eckhardt: 408,000
- Small & Singer: 408,300

WORLD WAR II (Soviet) It is hard to estimate how many American prisoners died as a result of the former USSR's actions in transporting U.S. POWs to Soviet bloc nations during and immediately after WW II. There is no doubt that some of the unaccounted-for US POW-MIAs ended up in Soviet gulags, psychiatric hospitals, and third-party nations such as Czechoslovakia. We know that at least several hundred men were interrogated by the Soviets; we have the interrogation reports, but the men never returned

U.S. MERCHANT MARINES: 8,300 mariners killed at sea, at least 1,100 died from wounds. Total killed estimated 9,300. [http://www.usmm.org/ww2.html]

COLD WAR 2 September 1945 to 21 August 1991

Participants: Classified; POWs: 165; MIAS: 126; Deaths in Service: unknown

KOREAN WAR 25 June 1950 to 27 July 1953

Participants: 5,764,143; POWs: 7,140; Died in Captivity: 2,471, MIAs: 8,177; Deaths in Theater: 36,914

VIETNAM WAR 08 July 1959 to 27 January 1973

Active Duty: 9,087,000; In-Country: 2,594,000; POWs: 2,583; Died in Captivity: 114; MIAs: 2,338; Deaths in Theater: 58,285.

GRENADA 25 October 1983 to 2 November 1983

Participants: 2,700; POWs: Unknown; MIAs: 4; Deaths in Service: 20

PERSIAN GULF WAR 16 January 1991 to 27 February 1991

Participants: 665,476; POWs — MIAs: 52; Deaths in Service: 255

SOMALIA 02 December 1992 to 15 September 1994

Participants: Classified; POWs: 6; MIAs: 2; Deaths in Service: 44

AFGHANISTAN and IRAQ In progress

(Afghanistan) 1 Confirmed, Neil Roberts, Navy SEAL Captured and Executed; (Iraq) 2 known (Lori Piestewa and Donald Walters), more suspected. At the time of an-Nasiriyah (23 MAR 03) reports and film footage showed that some of the ambushed 507th personnel had been evidently captured and eventually executed. Official USG statements immediately afterwards confirm this. There is an ongoing investigation.

NOTE: These figures do not include civilians. A large number of nurses, doctors, missionaries, journalists, civilian contractors and others were captured, known to be POWs, yet never repatriated. We have some eyewitness reports of these people in captivity, being executed or dying of mistreatment, starvation or disease, but no remains have been returned.

Bibliography

General

Bailey, Ronald H. *Prisoners of War* (Alexandria, VA: Time-Life Books, 1981).

Barker, A. J. *Behind Barbed Wire* (London: B. T. Batsford, 1974).

Beaumont, Joan. "Rank, Privilege and Prisoners of War." *War and Society* 1 (1983): 67–94.

Biess, Frank. *Homecomings: Returning POWs and the Legacies of Defeat in Postwar Germany* (Princeton: Princeton University Press, 2006).

Bird, Tim. *American POWs of World War II: Forgotten Men Tell Their Stories* (Westport, CT: Praeger, 1992).

Bunbury, Bill. *Rabbits and Spaghetti: Captives and Comrades—Australians, Italians and the War* (Fremantle, Australia: Fremantle Arts Centre Press, 1995).

Carlson, Lewis H. *We Were Each Other's Prisoners: An Oral History of World War II American and German Prisoners of War* (New York: Basic Books, 1997).

Chillenden, Edmund. (fl. 1656). *The Inhumanity of the Kings Prison-keeper at Oxford.* (London: Printed by G.D. for John Bull, 1643).

Clarke, Hugh, and Colin Burgess. *Barbed Wire and Bamboo: Australian POW Stories* (St. Leonards, Australia: Allen and Unwin, 1992).

Clarke, Hugh, Colin Burgess, and Russell Braddon. *Prisoners of War* (North Sydney, Australia: Time-Life Books, 1988).

Dancocks, Daniel G. *In Enemy Hands: Canadian Prisoners of War, 1939–45* (Edmonton, Canada: Hurtig, 1983).

Danner, Mark. *Torture and Truth: America, Abu Ghraib, and the War on Terror* (New York: New York Review Books, 2004).

Davis, Vernon E. *The Long Road Home: U.S. Prisoner of War Policy and Planning in Southeast Asia* (Washington, DC: Historical Office, Office of the Secretary of Defense, 2002).

Devenish, Thomas. *To the Supreme Authority of England, the Commons Assembled in Parliament: The Humble Address of Thomas Devenish* (London: 1642).

Doyle, Robert C. *Voices from Captivity: Interpreting the American POW Narrative* (Lawrence: University Press of Kansas, 1994).

Fairfax, Thomas. 1612–1671. *A Humble Remonstrance from His Excellency Sir Thomas Fairfax: Concerning the Great Sufferings and Grievances of Divers, Whose Cases Are Represented to the Parliament* (London: by Robert Ibbitson).

Farrar-Hockley, Anthony H. *The Edge of the Sword* (London: Buchan & Enright, 1985).

Hansen, Kenneth K. *Heroes Behind Barbed Wire* (Princeton: Van Nostrand, 1957).

Fooks, Herbert C. *Prisoners of War* (Federalsburg, MD: J. W. Stowell, 1924).

Garrett, Richard. *POW: The Uncivil Face of War* (Newton Abbot [Devon]: David and Charles, 1981).

Jacobs, Susan. *Fighting with the Enemy: New Zealand POWs and the Italian Resistance* (New York: Penguin Books, 2003).

Laffin, John. *The Anatomy of Captivity* (London: Abelard-Schuman, 1968).

Lech, Raymond B. *Broken Soldiers* (Urbana: University of Illinois Press, 2000).

Lewis, George G., and John Mewha. *History of Prisoner of War Utilization by the United States Army 1776–1945* (Washington, DC: Center of Military History, U.S. Army, 1988).

Lilburne, John. (1614?–1657). *To Every Individual Member of the Honourable House of Commons* (London: 1648).

———. (1614?–1657). *The Just Mans Justification: Or a Letter by Way of Plea in Barre; Written by L. Col. John Lilburne to the Honourble Justice Reeves* (London: 1647).

Maher, William L. *A Shepherd in Combat Boots: Chaplain Emil Kapaun of the 1st Cavalry Division* (Shippensburg, PA: Burd Street Press, 1997).

Moore, Bob, and Kent Fedorowich, eds. *Prisoners of War and Their Captors in World War II* (Washington, DC: Oxford/Berg, 1996).

Newman, George. *The Prisoners of Voronesh: The Diary of Sergeant George Newman, 23rd Regiment of Foot, the Royal Welch Fusiliers, Taken Prisoner at Inkerman* (Old Woking, Eng.: Unwin Brothers Limited and the trustees of the Regimental Museum, The Royal Welch Fusiliers, 1977).

Nichol, John, and Tony Rennell. *The Last Escape: the Untold Story of Allied Prisoners of War in Europe, 1944–1945* (New York: Viking, 2003).

Noble, Anne. *Narrative of the Shipwreck of the "Kite" and of the Imprisonment and Sufferings of the Crew and Passengers: In a Letter from Mrs. Anne Noble to a Friend, Macao, China, March, 1841* (China: 1841, Goldsmiths'-Kress library of economic literature, no. 31962).

Page, William Frank. *The Health of Former Prisoners of War: Results from the Medical Examination Survey of Former POWs of World War II and the Korean Conflict* (Washington, DC: National Academy Press, 1992).

Rajiva, Lila. *The Language of Empire: Abu Ghraib and the American Media* (New York: Monthly Review Press, 2005).

Reid, P. R., and Maurice Michael. *Prisoner of War* (London: Hamlyn Publishing Group, 1984).

Strutton, Richard. *A True Relation of the Cruelties and Barbarities of the French Upon the English Prisoners of War [Electronic Resource]: Being a Journal of Their Travels from Dinan in Britany, to Thoulon in Provence, and Back Again* (London: Printed for Richard Baldwin, 1690).

Swedberg, Claire, ed. *In Enemy Hands: Personal Accounts of Those Taken Prisoner in World War II* (Mechanicsburg, PA: Stackpole Books, 1997).

Thompson, William. (d. 1649). *England's Freedom, Soldiers Rights: Vindicated against All Arbitrary Unjust Invaders of Them, and in Particular against Those New Tyrants at Windsore* (London: 1647).

Vance, Jonathan F. *Objects of Concern: Canadian Prisoners of War through the Twentieth Century* (Vancouver, Canada: UBC Press, 1994).

Vance, Jonathan F., ed. *Encyclopedia of Prisoners of War and Internment* (Santa Barbara: ABC-CLIO, 2000).

Vetter, Hal. *Mutiny on Koje Island* (Rutland, Vt.: C. E. Tuttle Co., 1965).

Voglis, Polymeris. *Becoming a Subject: Political Prisoners during the Greek Civil War* (New York: Berghahn Books, 2002).

Williams, Kristian. *American Methods: Torture and the Logic of Domination* (Cambridge, MA: South End Press, 2006).

Winchester, Simon. *Prison Diary: Argentina* (London: Chatto & Windus, Hogarth Press, 1983).

McCoy, Alfred W. *A Question of Torture: Interrogation, From the Cold War to the War on Terror* (New York: Metropolitan Books, 2006).

Escape

Ackerley, J. R. *Escapers All* (London: John Lane, 1932).

Blair, Clay, Jr. *Beyond Courage* (New York: David Mackay, 1955).

Brickhill, Paul. *Escape—or Die: Authentic Stories of RAF Escaping Society* (London: Evans Brothers, 1952).

Burgess, Colin. *Freedom or Death: Australia's Greatest Escape Stories from Two World Wars* (St. Leonards, Australia: Allen and Unwin Australia, 1994).

Cook, Graeme. *Breakout!: Great Wartime Escape Stories* (London: Hart-Davis, MacGibbon, 1974).

Davenport, Basil, ed. *Great Escapes* (New York: Sloane, 1952).

Doyle, Robert C. *A Prisoner's Duty: Great Escapes in U.S. Military History* (Annapolis, MD: Naval Institute Press, 1997).

Evans, A. J. *Escape and Liberation, 1940–1945* (London: Hodder and Stoughton, 1945).

Fellowes-Gordon, Ian. *The World's Greatest Escapes* (London: Odhams Books, 1966).

Foot, M. R. D., and J. M. Langley. *M19: Escape and Evasion 1939–1945* (London: Bodley Head, 1979).

Graham, Burton. *Escape from the Nazis* (Secaucus, NJ: Castle Books, 1975).

Jackson, Robert. *When Freedom Calls: Great Escapes of the Second World War* (London: Arthur Barker, 1973).

Reid, P. R. *My Favourite Escape Stories* (Guildford: Lutterworth Press, 1975).

Royal Air Force Flying Review, ed., *They Got Back: The Best Escape Stories from the RAF Flying Review* (London: Herbert Jenkins, 1961).

Schutzer, A. I. *Great Civil War Escapes* (New York: G. P. Putnam's Sons, 1967).

Williams, Eric, ed. *The Escapers* (London: Collins, 1953).

———. *Great Escape Stories* (London: Arthur Barker, 1958).

Korean War

Bassett, Richard M. *And the Wind Blew Cold: The Story of an American POW in North Korea* (Kent, Ohio: Kent State University Press, 2002).

Biderman, Albert D. *March to Calumny: The Story of American POWs in the Korean War* (New York: Macmillan, 1963).

Bradbury, William Chapman. *Mass Behavior in Battle and Captivity; the Communist Soldier in the Korean War* (Chicago: University of Chicago Press, 1968).

Brown, Wallace L. *The Endless Hours: My Two and a Half Years as a Prisoner of War of the Chinese Communists* (New York: Norton, 1961).

Chinnery, Philip D. *Korean Atrocity!: Forgotten War Crimes, 1950–1953* (Annapolis: Naval Institute Press, 2000).

Condron, Andrew M. *Thinking Soldiers, By Men Who Fought in Korea* (Peking: New World Press, 1955).

Crosbie, Philip. *March Till They Die* (Dublin: Browne & Nolan, 1955).

Dean, William Frishe. *"General Dean's Story," as Told to William L. Worden* (New York: Viking Press, 1954).

Deane, Philip. *I Was a Captive in Korea* (New York: Norton, 1953).

Deane, Philip. *I Should Have Died* (New York: Atheneum, 1977).

Farrar-Hockley, Anthony. *The Edge of the Sword* (Stroud, England: Alan Sutton, 1993 [1954]).

Goldich, Robert L. *POWs and MIAs in Indochina and Korea* (Washington, DC: Congressional Research Service, Library of Congress, 1988).

Hansen, Kenneth K. *Heroes Behind Barbed Wire* (Princeton, NJ: Van Nostrand, 1957).

Holland, Thomas D. *Problems and Observations Related to the Forensic Identification of Human Remains Repatriated to the United States by North Korea* (Santa Monica, CA: Rand Corporation, 1993).

Jolidon, Laurence. *Last Seen Alive: The Search for Missing POWs from the Korean War* (Austin, TX: Ink-Slinger Press, 1995).

Kinkead, Eugene. *In Every War but One* (New York: Norton, 1959).

Kinnie, Derek G. *The Wooden Boxes* (London: Muller, 1955).

The "Korean War" section should include the following: Mahurin, Walker L. "Bud." *Honest John: The Extraordinary Autobiography of the Famous World War II Ace Who Was Brainwashed By the Communists* (New York: G. P. Putnam's Sons, 1962). Millar, Ward M. *Valley of the Shadow* (New York: David McKay, 1955).

Lankford, Dennis. *I Defy!* (London: Wingate, 1954).

Meyers, Samuel M., and Albert Biderman, eds. *Mass Behavior in Battle and Captivity: The Communist Soldier in the Korean War* (Chicago: University of Chicago Press, 1968).

Ministry of Defence, *Treatment of British Prisoners of War in Korea* (London: HMSO, 1955).

Pasley, Virginia. *21 Stayed: The Story of the American GI's Who Chose Communist China: Who They Were and Why They Stayed* (New York: Farrar, Straus and Cudahy, 1955).

Schein, Edgar, Inge Schneier, and Curtis H. Barker. *Coercive Persuasion: A Sociopsychological Analysis of the "Brainwashing" of American Civilian Prisoners by the Chinese Communists* (New York: W.W. Norton, 1961).

Spiller, Harry, ed. *American POWs in Korea: 16 Personal Accounts* (Jefferson, NC: McFarland & Co., 1998).

Strait, Sandy. *What Happened to American Prisoners of War in Korea* (Unionville, NY: Royal Fireworks Press, 1997).

Thornton, John W., with John W. Thornton, Jr. *Believed to Be Alive* (Middlebury, VT: P.S. Eriksson, 1981).

Weintraub, Stanley. *The War in the Wards: Korea's Unknown Battle in a Prisoner-of-War Hospital Camp* (New York: Doubleday, 1964).

White, William Lindsay. *The Captives of Korea* (New York: Scribner, 1957).

Wills, Morris R. *Turncoat; An American's 12 Years in Communist China; The Story of Morris R. Wills As Told to J. Robert Moskin* (Englewood Cliffs, NJ, Prentice-Hall, 1968).

Zellers, Larry. *In Enemy Hands: A Prisoner in North Korea* (Lexington: University Press of Kentucky, 1991).

U.S. Civil War

Blakey, Arch Fredric. *General John H. Winder, CSA* (Gainesville: University of Florida Press, 1990).

Booth, Benjamin F. *Dark Days of the Rebellion: Life in Southern Military Prisons*, ed. Steve Meyer (Garrison, IA: Meyer Publishing, 1996 [1897]).

Bryant, William O. *Cahaba Prison and the Sultana Disaster* (Tuscaloosa: University of Alabama Press, 1990).

Cimprich, John, and Robert C. Mainfort. "The Fort Pillow Massacre: A Statistical Note." *Journal of American History* 76 (1989): 830–837.

Denney, Robert E. *Civil War Prisons and Escapes: A Day-by-Day Chronicle* (New York: Sterling, 1993).

Hesseltine, William Best. *Civil War Prisons: A Study in War Psychology* (Columbus: Ohio State University Press, 1930).

Joslyn, Muriel Phillips. *Immortal Captives: The Story of 600 Confederate Officers and the United States Prisoner of War Policy* (Shippensburg, PA: White Mane, 1996).

Levy, George. *To Die in Chicago: Confederate Prisoners at Camp Douglas, 1862–1865* (Gretna, LA: Pelican Publishing, 1995).

Lynn, John. *800 Paces to Hell: Andersonville* (Fredericksburg, VA: Sergeant Kirkland's Museum and Historical Society Press, 1998).

Marvel, William. *Andersonville: The Last Depot* (Chapel Hill: University of North Carolina Press, 1994).

Snell, Mark A., and Ezra Hoyt Ripple, eds. *Dancing along the Deadline: The Andersonville Memoir of a Prisoner of the Confederacy* (Novato, CA: Presidio, 1996).

Speer, Lonnie R. *Portals to Hell: Military Prisons of the Civil War* (Mechardcsburg, PA: Stackpole Books, 1997).

The War of the Rebellion: A Compilation of the Official Records of the Union and Confederate Armies, series 2 (Washington, DC: Government Printing Office, 1880–1901).

Watson, Ronald G., ed. *From Ashby to Andersonville: The Civil War Diary and Reminiscences of George A. Hitchcock* (Campbell, CA: Savas Publishing, 1997).

Vietnam War

Alvarez, Everett. Jr., and Anthony S. Pitch. *Chained Eagle* (New York: Donald I. Fine, 1989).

Bailey, Laurence. *Solitary Survivor: The First American POW in Southeast Asia* (Washington, DC: Brassey's, 1995).

Blakely, Richard. *Prisoner at War: The Survival of Commander Richard A. Stratton* (Garden City, NY: Doubleday, 1978).

Cawthorne, Nigel. *Bamboo Cage: The Full Story of the American Servicemen Still Held Hostage in South-East Asia* (London: Leo Cooper, 1991).

Chesley, Larry. *Seven Years in Hanoi: A POW Tells His Story* (Salt Lake City, UT: Book Craft, 1973).

Colvin, Rod. *First Heroes: The POWs Left Behind in Vietnam* (New York: Irvington, 1987).

Dengler, Dieter. *Escape from Laos* (San Rafael, CA: Presidio Press, 1979).

Denton, Jeremiah A., Jr. *When Hell Was in Session* (New York: Readers Digest Press, 1976).

Grant, Zalin. *Survivors: American POWs in Vietnam 1964–1973* (New York: Berkley Books, 1985).

Guarino, Larry. *A POW's Story: 2801 Days in Hanoi* (New York: Ivy Books, 1990).

Hirsh, James S. *Two Souls Indivisible: The Friendship That Saved Two POWs in Vietnam* (Boston: Houghton Mifflin, 2004).

Hubbell, John G. *POW: A Definitive History of the American Prisoner of War Experience in Vietnam, 1964–1973* (New York: Reader's Digest Press, 1976).

Johnson, Sam, and Jan Winebrenner. *Captive Warriors: A Vietnam POW's Story* (College Station: Texas A&M University Press, 1992).

McConnell, Malcolm. *Into the Mouth of the Cat: The Story of Lance Sijan, Hero of Vietnam* (New York: Norton, 1985).

McGrath, John M. *Prisoners of War: Six Years in Hanoi* (Annapolis, MD: Naval Institute Press, 1975).

Moyar, Mark. *Phoenix and the Birds of Prey: The CIA's Secret Campaign to Destroy the Viet Cong* (Annapolis, MD: Naval Institute Press, 1997).

Risner, Robinson. *The Passing of the Night: My Seven Years as a Prisoner of the North Vietnamese* (New York: Random House, 1973).

Robertson, Chimp. *POW/MIA America's Missing Men: The Men We Left Behind* (Lancaster, PA: Starburst, 1995).

Rochester, Stuart I., and Frederick Kiley *Honor Bound: The History of American Prisoners of War in Southeast Asia, 1961–1973* (Washington, DC: Office of the Secretary of Defense, 1998).

Rowe, James N. *Five Years to Freedom* (Boston: Little, Brown and Company, 1971).

Veith, George J. *Code-Name Bright Light: The Untold Story of U.S. POW Rescue Efforts during the Vietnam War* (New York: Free Press, 1998).

War Crimes

Andrews, Allen. *Exemplary Justice* (London: Harrap, 1976).

Brode, Patrick. *Casual Slaughters and Accidental Judgements: Canadian War Crimes Prosecutions, 1944–1948* (Toronto: University of Toronto Press, 1997).

Buscher, Frank. *The U.S. War Crimes Trial Program in Germany, 1946–1955* (Westport, CT: Greenwood Press, 1989).

Conot, Robert E. *Justice at Nuremberg* (New York: Harper and Row, 1983).

Dalner, Szymon. *Crimes against POWs: Responsibility of the Wehrmacht* (Warsaw, Poland: Zachodnia Agencja Prasowa, 1964).

Davidson, Eugene. *The Nuremberg Fallacy: Wars and War Crimes since World War II* (New York: Macmillan, 1973).

de Zayas, Alfred M. *The Wehrmacht War Crimes Bureau, 1939–1945* (Lincoln: University of Nebraska Press, 1989).

Goodwin, Michael J. *Shobun: A Forgotten War Crime in the Pacific* (Mechanicsburg, PA: Stackpole Books, 1995).

Greenberg, Karen J. *The Torture Debate in America* (Cambridge: Cambridge University Press, 2006).

Greenberg, Karen J., and Joshua L. Dratel, eds. *The Torture Papers: The Road to Abu Ghraib* (Cambridge: Cambridge University Press, 2005).

Hamburg Institute. *The German Army and Genocide: Crimes against War Prisoners, Jews and Other Civilians in the East, 1939–1944* (New York: New Press, 1999).

Kogon, Eugen. *The Theory and Practice of Hell: The German Concentration Camps and the System behind Them* (New York: Farrar, Straus and Cudahy, 1950).

Margolian, Howard. *Conduct Unbecoming: The Story of the Murder of Canadian Prisoners of War in Normandy* (Toronto: University of Toronto Press, 1998).

Minear, Richard H. *Victors' Justice: The Tokyo War Crimes Trials* (Princeton, NJ: Princeton University Press, 1971).

Piccigallo, Philip R. *The Japanese on Trial: Allied War Crimes Operations in the East, 1945–1951* (Austin: University of Texas Press, 1979).

Russell, Lord of Liverpool. (Edward Frederick Langley Russell, Baron Russell of Liverpool). *The Scourge of the Swastika: A Short History of Nazi War Crimes* (London: Cassell, 1954).

———. *The Knights of Bushido: A Short History of Japanese War Crimes* (New York: E. P. Dutton, 1958).

Scotland, A. P. *The London Cage* (London: Evans Brothers, 1957)

Smith, Bradley F. *Reaching Judgement at Nuremberg* (New York: Basic Books, 1977).

Taguba, Antonio M. *Article 15–6 Investigation of the 800th Military Police Brigade* (800th Military Police, 2004).

Tanaka, Yuki. *Hidden Horrors: Japanese War Crimes in World War II* (Boulder, CO: Westview Press, 1996).

Women

Abkhazi, Peggy. *A Curious Cage: A Shanghai Journal, 1941–1945* (Victoria, BC: Sono Nis Press, 1981).

Bloom, Lynn Z. "Escaping Voices: Women's South Pacific Internment Diaries and Memoirs." *Mosaic* 23 (1990): 101–112.

Bruhn, Sheila. *Diary of a Girl in Changi, 1941–1945* (Kenthurst, Australia: Kangaroo Press, 1996).

Colijn, Helen. *Song of Survival: Women Interned* (Ashland, OR: White Cloud Press, 1995).

Cornum, Rhonda, and Peter Copeland. *She Went to War: The Rhonda Cornum Story* (Novato, CA: Presidio, 1992).

De Pauw, Linda Grant. *Battle Cries and Lullabies: Women in War from Prehistory to the Present* (Norman: University of Oklahoma Press, 1998).

Herman, Ronny. *In the Shadow of the Sun* (Surrey, BC: Vanderheide Publishing, 1992).

Hyland, Judith S. *In the Shadow of the Rising Sun* (Minneapolis, MN: Augsburg, 1984).

Karpinski, Janis L. *One Woman's Army: The Commanding General of Abu Ghraib Tells Her Story* (New York: Miramax, 2005).

Litoff, Judy Barrett, and David C. Smith. *We're in This War, Too: World War II Letters From American Women in Uniform* (New York: Oxford University Press, 1994).

Lucas, Celia. *Prisoners of Santo Tomas: A True Account of Women POWs under Japanese Control* (London: Leo Cooper, 1997).

Miles, Fern. *Captive Community: Life in a Japanese Internment Camp* (Jefferson City, TN: Mossy Creek, 1987).

Myers, Bessy. *Captured: My Experiences as an Ambulance Driver and as a Prisoner of the Nazis* (London: George G. Harrap, 1941).

Rinser, Luise. *A Woman's Prison Journal: Germany, 1944* (New York: Schocken Books, 1987).

Rose, Darlene Deibler. *Evidence Not Seen: A Woman's Miraculous Faith in the Jungles of World War II* (San Francisco: Harper, 1990).

Sams, Margaret. *Forbidden Family: A Wartime Memoir of the Philippines, 1941–1945*, ed. Lynn Z. Bloom (Madison: University of Wisconsin Press, 1997).

Steinhilper, Ulrich, and Peter Osborne. *Ten Minutes to Buffalo: The Story of Germany's Great Escaper* (Bromley, Great Britain: Independent Books, 1991).

Thompson, Dorothy Davis. *The Road Back: A Pacific POW's Liberation Story* (Lubbock: Texas Tech University Press, 1996).

Vaughan, Elizabeth. *The Ordeal of Elizabeth Vaughan: A Wartime Diary of the Philippines* (Athens: University of Georgia Press, 1985).

Warner, Lavinia, and John Sandilands. *Women Beyond the Wire: A Story of Prisoners of the Japanese* (London: Michael Joseph, 1982).

Williams, Denny. *To the Angels* (San Francisco: Denson Press, 1985).

World War I

Archibald, Norman. *Heaven High, Hell Deep, 1917–18* (New York: A.C. Boni, 1935).

Connes, George. *A POW's Memoir of the First World War*, ed. Lois Davis Vines (Oxford: Berg, 2004).

Dennett, Carl P. *Prisoners of the Great War: Authoritative Statement of Conditions in the Prison Camps of Germany* (Boston: Houghton Mifflin, 1919).

Dwinger, Edwin Erich. *The Army behind Barbed Wire: A Siberian Diary* (London: G. Allen and Unwin, 1930).

Dyboski, Roman. *Seven Years in Russia and Siberia, 1914–1921* (Cheshire, CT: Cherry Hill Books, 1971 [1922]).

Evans, A. J. *The Escaping Club* (London: John Lane, 1934).

Grinnell-Milne, Duncan. *An Escaper's Log* (London: John Lane, 1926).

Hardy, J. L. *I Escape!* (New York: Dodd, Mead, 1928).

Harrison, M. C. C., and H. A. Cartwright. *Within Four Walls* (London: Edward Arnold, 1930).

Jackson, Robert. *The Prisoners, 1914–18* (New York: Routledge, 1989).

Kleinrichert, Denise. *Republican Internment and the Prison Ship Argenta 1922* (Dublin: Irish Academic Press, 2001).

McCarthy, Daniel J. *The Prisoner of War in Germany: The Care and Treatment of the Prisoner of War with a History of the Development of the Principle of Neutral Inspection and Control* (New York: Moffat, Yard, 1918).

Morton, Desmond. *Silent Battle: Canadian Prisoners of War in Germany, 1914–1919* (Toronto: Lester Publishing, 1992).

Moynihan, Michael. *Black Bread and Barbed Wire: Prisoners in the First World War* (London: Leo Cooper, 1978).

Nachtigal, Reinhard. "German Prisoners of War in Tsarist Russia: A Glance at Petrograd/St. Petersburg." *German History* 13 (1995): 198–204.

Pluschow, Gunther. *My Escape from Donington Hall* (London: John Lane, 1922).

Rachamimov, Alon. "Imperial Loyalties and Private Concerns: Nation, Class and State in the Correspondence of Austro-Hungarian POWs in Russia." *Austrian History Yearbook* 31 (2000): 87–105.

Speed, Richard B. *Prisoners, Diplomats and the Great War: A Study in the Diplomacy of Captivity* (New York: Greenwood Press, 1990).

Tucker, W. A. *The Lousier War* (London: New English Library, 1974).

Williamson, Samuel R., and Peter Pastor, eds. *Essays on World War I: Origins and Prisoners of War* (New York: Columbia University Press, 1983).

World War II—European Theater

Arct, B. *Prisoner of War: My Secret Journal* (Oxford: Past Times, 1995).

Barber, Noel. *Prisoner of War: The Story of British Prisoners Held by the Enemy* (London: George G. Harrap, 1944).

Bard, Mitchell G. *Forgotten Victims: The Abandonment of Americans in Hitler's Camps* (Boulder, CO: Westview Press, 1994).

Baybutt, Ron. *Camera in Colditz* (London: Hodder and Stoughton, 1982).

Beltrone, Art, and Lee Beltrone. *A Wartime Log: A Remembrance from Home through the American YMCA* ([S.I.] Spellmount, 1998).

Bischof, Günter, Stephen E. Ambrose, and Eisenhower Center (University of New Orleans), *Eisenhower And The German POWs: Facts against Falsehood* (Baton Rouge: Louisiana State University Press, 1992).

Bunyak, Dawn Trimble. *Our Last Mission: A World War II Prisoner in Germany* (Norman: University of Oklahoma Press, 2003).

Calnan, T. D. *Free As a Running Fox* (New York: Dial Press, 1970).

Carlson, Lewis H. *We Were Each Other's Prisoners: An Oral History of World War II American and German Prisoners of War* (New York: Basic Books, 1997).

Cawthorne, Nigel. *The Iron Cage: Are British Prisoners of War Abandoned in Soviet Hands Still Alive in Siberia?* (London: Fourth Estate, 1993).

Crawley, Aidan. *Escape from Germany* (London: HMSO, 1985).

Derry, Sam. *The Rome Escape Line: The Story of the British Organization in Rome for Assisting Escaped Prisoners of War, 1943–44* (New York: Norton, 1960).

de Wiart, Adrian Carton. *Happy Odyssey* (London: Jonathan Cape, 1950).

Duke, Florimond. *Name, Rank and Serial Number* (New York: Meredith Press, 1969).

The Earl of Cardigan, *I Walked Alone* (London: Routledge and Kegan Paul, 1950).

Edgar, Donald. *The Stalag Men* (London: John Clare, 1982).

Foy, David A. *For You the War Is Over: American Prisoners of War in Nazi Germany* (New York: Stein and Day, 1984).

Gammon, Victor F. *Not All Glory!: True Accounts of RAF Airmen Taken Prisoner in Europe, 1939–1945* (London: Arms and Armour, 1996).

Garioch, Robert. *Two Men and a Blanket: Memoirs of Captivity* (Edinburgh: Southside, 1975).

Halmos, Eugene E., Jr., *The Wrong Side of the Fence: A United States Army Air Corps POW in World War II* (Shippensburg, PA: White Mane, 1996).

Hargest, James. *Farewell Campo 12* (London: Michael Joseph, 1945).

Harsh, George. *Lonesome Road* (London: Longman, 1971).

Hays, Otis. *Home from Siberia: The Secret Odysseys of Interned American Airmen in World War II* (College Station: Texas A&M University Press, 1990).

James, B. A. *Moonless Night: One Man's Struggle for Freedom, 1940–1945* (London: William Kimber, 1983).

James, David. *Escaper's Progress* (London: Corgi, 1954).

Jones, Ewart C. *Germans Under My Bed* (London: Arthur Barker, 1957).

Jordan, Martin. *For You the War Is Over* (London: Peter Davies, 1946).

Langley, J. M. *Fight Another Day* (London: Collins, 1974).

Larive E. H., *The Man Who Came In from Colditz* (London: Robert Hale, 1975).

Leeming, John F. *Always Tomorrow* (London: George G. Harrap, 1951).

Marchione, Margherita. *Crusade of Charity: Pius XII and POWs (1939–1945)* (New York: Paulist Press, 2006).

Morgan, Guy. *POW* (New York: McGraw-Hill, 1945).

Nabarr, Derrick *Wait for the Dawn* (London: Cassel, 1952).

Prittie, T. C. F., and W. Earle Edwards. *South to Freedom* (London: Hutchinson, 1946).

Ramsay, Ian. *P.O.W: A Digger in Hitler's Prison Camps, 1941–45* (Melbourne: Macmillan, 1985).

Reid, Miles. *Last on the List* (London: Leo Cooper, 1974); *Into Colditz* (Wilton: Michael Russell, 1983).

Rieul, Roland. *Escape into Espionage: The True Story of a French Patriot in World War Two* (New York: Walker and Company, 1987).

Rolf, David. *Prisoners of the Reich: Germany's Captives, 1939–1945* (London: Leo Cooper, 1988).

Romilly Giles, and Michael Alexander. *The Privileged Nightmare* (London: Weidenfeld and Nicolson, 1954).

Sage, Jerry. *Sage: The Man They Called "Dagger" of the OSS* (Wayne, PA: Tobey Publishing, 1985).

Smith, Sydney. *Wings Day: The Man Who Led the RAF's Epic Battle in German Captivity* (London: Collins, 1968).

Spiller, Harry. *Prisoners of Nazis: Accounts by American POWs in World War II* (Jefferson, NC: McFarland, 1998).

Spivey, Delmar T. *POW Odyssey: Recollections of Center Compound, Stalag Luft III, and the Secret German Peace Mission in World War II* (Attleboro, MA: Colonial Lithograph, 1984).

Taylor, Geoff. *Return Ticket* (London: Peter Davies, 1972).

Thomas, W. B. *Dare to Be Free* (London: Reader's Union, 1953).

Vance, Jonathan F. *A Gallant Company: The Men of the Great Escape* (Pacifica, CA: Pacifica Military History, 2000).

Vanderstok, Bob. *War Pilot of Orange* (Missoula, MT: Pictorial Histories, 1987).

Vietor, John A. *Time Out: American Airmen in Stalag Luft I* (Falibrook, CA: Aero Publishers, 1951).

Wood, J. E. R, ed. *Detour: The Story of Oflag IVC* (London: Falcon Press, 1946).

Worsley, John, and Kenneth Giggal. *John Worsley's War: An Official War Artist in World War II* (Shrewsbury, England: Airlife, 1993).

World War II—North America

Billinger, Robert D., Jr. *Hitler's Soldiers in the Sunshine State: German POWs in Florida* (Gainesville, FL: University of Florida, 2000).

Bland, John Paul. *Secret War at Home: The Pine Grove Furnace Prisoner of War Interrogation Camp* (Carlisle, PA: Cumberland County Historical Society, 2006).

Buck, Anita. *Behind Barbed Wire: German Prisoners of War in Minnesota* (St. Cloud, MN: North Star Press, 1998).

Carter, David J. *Behind Canadian Barbed Wire: Alien, Refugee and Prisoner of War Camps in Canada, 1914–1946* (Ellwater, Alberta: Eagle Butte Press, 1998).

Cook, Ruth Beaumont. *Guests Behind the Barbed Wire: German POWs in America: A True Story of Hope and Friendship* (Birmingham: Crane Hill, 2007).

Fiedler, David. *The Enemy Among Us: POWs in Missouri during World War II* (St. Louis: Society Press, 2003).

Gansberg, Judith M. *Stalag U.S.A.: The Remarkable Story of German POWs in America* (New York: Thomas Y. Crowell, 1977).

Gärtner, Georg, and Arnold Krammer. *Hitler's Last Soldier in America* (New York: Stein and Day, 1985).

Geiger, Jeffrey E. *German Prisoners of War at Camp Cooke, California: Personal Accounts of 14 Soldiers, 1944–1946* (Jefferson, NC: McFarland, 1996).

Homer, Helmut. *A German Odyssey: The Journal of a German Prisoner of War* (Golden, CO: Fulcrum Publishing, 1991).

Jones, Ted. *Both Sides of the Wire: The Fredericton Internment Camp*, 2 vols. (Fredericton, NB: New Ireland Press, 1989).

Keefer, L. E. *Italian Prisoners of War in America, 1942–1946* (New York: Praeger, 1992).

Koop, Allen V. *Stark Decency: German Prisoners of War in a New England Village* (Hanover, NH: University Press of New England, 1988).

Krammer, Arnold. *Nazi Prisoners of War in America* (New York: Stein and Day, 1979).

———. *Deutsche Kriegsgefangene in Amerika 1942–1946* (Tübingen: Universitas Verlag, 1995).

May, Lowell A. *Camp Concordia: German POWs in the Midwest* (Manhattan, KS: Sunflower University Press, 1995).

McCarver, Norman L., and Norman L. McCarver, Jr. *Hearne on the Brazos* (San Antonio: San Antonio Century Press of Texas, 1958).

Melady, John. *Escape from Canada!: The Untold Story of German POWs in Canada, 1939–1945* (Toronto: Macmillan, 1981).

Moore, John Hammond. *The Faustball Tunnel: German POWs in America and Their Great Escape* (New York: Random House, 1978).

Pabel, Reinhold. *Enemies Are Human* (Philadelphia: John C. Winston, 1955).

Parkinson, James W. *Soldier Slaves: Abandoned by the White House, Courts, and Congress* (Annapolis, Md.: Naval Institute Press, 2006).

Schmid, Walter. *A German POW in New Mexico* (Albuquerque: University of New Mexico Press, 2005).

Valkenburg, Carol Van. *An Alien Place: The Fort Missoula, Montana, Detention Camp, 1941–44* (Missoula, MT: Pictorial Histories, 1995).

Walker, Richard Paul. *The Lone Star and the Swastika: Prisoners of War in Texas* (Austin, TX: Eakin Press, 2000).

Waters, Michael R., Mark Long, William Dickens, Sam Sweitz, Anna Lee Presley, Ian Buvit, Michelle Raisor, Bryan Mason, Hilary Standish and Norbert Dannhaeuser. *Lone Star Stalag: German Prisoners of War at Camp Hearne* (College Station: Texas A&M University Press, 2004).

Williams, Donald Mace. *Italian POWs and a Texas Church: The Murals of St. Mary's* (Lubbock: Texas Tech University Press, 1992).

Wolter, Tim *POW Baseball in W.W.II: The National Pastime Behind Barbed Wire* (Jefferson, NC: McFarland & Co., 2002).

World War II—Pacific Theater

Allister, William. *Where Life and Death Hold Hands* (Toronto: Stoddart, 1989).

Beaumont, Joan. *Gull Force: Survival and Leadership in Captivity* (Sydney: Allen and Unwin, 1988).

Berry, William A. *Prisoner of the Rising Sun* (Norman: University of Oklahoma Press, 1993).

Blain, Geoffrey. *Huryo: The Emperor's Captives* (New York: Vantage, 1995).

Chalker, Jack. *Burma Railway Artist: The Drawings of Jack Walker* (London: Leo Cooper, 1994).

Daws, Gavan. *Prisoners of the Japanese: POWs of World War II in the Pacific* (New York: William Morrow, 1994).

Feuer, A. B., ed. *FDR's Prisoner Spy: The POW Diary of Cdr Thomas Hayes, USN* (Pacifica, CA: Pacifica Military History, 1999 [1987]).

Flanagan, Eugene M. *Angels at Dawn: The Los Baños Raid* (Novato, CA: Presidio Press, 1999).

Fletcher-Cooke, John. *The Emperor's Guest, 1942–45* (London: Leo Cooper, 1972).

Grady, Frank J., and Rebecca Dickson. *Surviving the Day: An American POW in Japan* (Annapolis, MD: Naval Institute Press, 1997).

Home, James. *Their Last Tenko* (Huddersfield, England: Quoin Publishing, 1989).

James, D. Clayton, ed. *South to Bataan, North to Mukden: The Prison Diary of Brigadier General W. E. Brougher* (Athens: University of Georgia Press, 1971).

Kerr, E. Bartlett. *Surrender and Survival: The Experience of American POWs in the Pacific, 1941–1945* (New York: William Morrow, 1985).

Kirby, S. Woodburn. *The War against Japan*, Vol. 5, *The Surrender of Japan* (London: HMSO, 1969).

La Forte, Robert S., and Ronald E. Marcello, eds. *Building the Death Railway: The Ordeal of American POWs in Burma, 1942–1945* (Wilmington, DE: SR Books, 1993).

La Forte, Robert S., Ronald E. Marcello and Richard L. Himmel, eds. *With Only the Will to Live: Accounts of Americans in Japanese Prison Camps, 1941–1945* (Wilmington, DE: SR Books, 1994).

Lomax, Eric. *The Railway Man: A POW's Searing Account of War, Brutality and Forgiveness* (New York: Norton, 1995).

Mason, W. Wynne. *Prisoners of War: Official History of New Zealand in the Second World War 1939–45* (Wellington, New Zealand: War History Branch, Department of Internal Affairs, 1954).

McIntosh, David. *Hell on Earth: Aging Faster, Dying Sooner—Canadian Prisoners of the Japanese during World War II* (Whitby, Ontario: McGraw-Hill Ryerson, 1997).

Meilnik, Steve. *Philippine Diary, 1939–1945* (New York: Van Nostrand Reinhold, 1969).

Nelson, Hank. *Prisoners of War: Australians under Nippon* (Sydney, Australia: ABC Enterprises, 1985).

Nimmo, William F. *Behind a Curtain of Silence: Japanese in Soviet Custody, 1945–1956* (New York: Greenwood Press, 1988).

Roland, Charles G. "Massacre and Rape in Hong Kong: Two Case Studies Involving Medical Personnel and Patients." *Journal of Contemporary History* 32 (1997): 43–61.

———. "Stripping Away the Veneer: P.O.W. Survival in the Far East as an Index of Cultural Atavism." *Journal of Military History* 53 (1989): 79–94.

Sano, Iwao Peter. *One Thousand Days in Siberia: The Odyssey of a Japanese-American POW* (Lincoln: University of Nebraska Press, 1997).

Straus, Ulrich. *The Anguish of Surrender: Japanese POWs of World War II* (Seattle and London: University of Washington Press, 2003).

Tenney, Lester I. *My Hitch in Hell: The Bataan Death March* (New York: Brassey's, 1995).

Waterford, Van. *Prisoners of the Japanese in World War II* (Jefferson, NC: McFarland, 1994).

Weissinger, William Jacob. *Attention Fool! A USS Houston Crewman Survives the Burma Death Camps* (Austin, TX: Eakin Press, 1997).

Wigmore, Lionel. *Australia in the War of 1939–1945*, Vol. 4, *The Japanese Thrust* (Canberra: Australian War Memorial, 1957).

Official Papers with No Single Author

The Abu Ghraib Investigations: The Official Reports of the Independent Panel and Pentagon on the Shocking Prisoner Abuse in Iraq, edited by Steven Strasser with an introduction by Craig R. Whitney (New York: Public Affairs, 2004).

Considerations on the Exchange of Seamen, Prisoners of War microform (London: Printed for J. Noon, 1758).

The Examination of Colonell Lunsford, Colonell Vavasor, Captaine Noes, Lieutenant Colonell Ballard, Sergeant Major Wallis, Cornet Strangewaies, Lieutenant Wh[i]te, Sergeant Iones, and Mr. Bland, Delinquents. [electronic resource]: Who Were Taken in the Fight at Kineton in Warwickshire, and Were Committed to Warwicke Castle, and on the 17. of November Were Examined upon Some Particular Articles. Whereunto Is Annexed a Speech of Colonell Lunsfords, Which He Spoke at His Examination (London: Printed for Tho. Cooke, November 19, 1642).

Facts & documents on the treatment of prisoners of war: Yom Kippur war, Syrian front (Jerusalem: Ministry of Defence, Israel, c1977).

The Handling of Prisoners of War during the Korean War microform, *prepared by Military History Office, Office of the Assistant Chief of Staff, G-3* (San Francisco, CA: Headquarters, U.S. Army, Pacific, 1968).

Independent Panel to Review DoD Detention Operations. *Final report of the Independent Panel to Review DOD Detention Ops.* (Arlington, Va.: Independent Panel to Review DoD Detention Operations, 2004).

Intelligence from the Army, in a Letter, Dated from His Excellencie's Quarters, Near Reading, June 5, 1643. With a Relation of Captain Wingates Escape from Oxford, and the Condition of the Prisoners There, Being about 70 (London: printed for Samuel Gellibrand, 1643).

Investigation of intelligence activities at Abu Ghraib. [electronic resource] (Washington, DC: U.S. Army Public Affairs, 2004). Electronic Resource(s): http://purl.access.gpo.gov/GPO/LPS53415

Keeping the Promise: Benefits and Services for Former Prisoners of War (Washington, DC: Dept. of Veterans Affairs, 2004).

The Manner How the Prisoners Are to be Brought into the City of London, This Present Saturday being the 21th day of Iune, 1645. And Met by the Greene and Yellow Regiments at Islington (London: Printed by T.F. and J. Coe, 1645).

POW/MIA's in Indochina and Korea: Hearing before the Subcommittee on Asian and Pacific Affairs of the Committee on Foreign Affairs, House of Representatives, One Hundred First Congress, second session, June 25, 1990 (Washington, DC: U.S. G.P.O., 1991).

United States Congress Senate Committee on Armed Services. *Review of Department of Defense detention and interrogation operations: hearings before the Committee on Armed Services, United States Senate, One Hundred Eighth Congress, second session, May 7, 11, 19, July 22, September 9, 2004* (Washington, DC: U.S. G.P.O., 2005).

United States Congress House Committee on International Relations, *A worldwide review of the Clinton administration's POW/MIA policies and programs: hearing before the Committee on International Relations, House of Representatives, One Hundred Fifth Congress, second session, June 17, 1998* (Washington, DC: U.S. G.P.O., 1998).

United States Congress House Committee on the Judiciary. *American Ex-prisoners of War: Report (to accompany H.R. 5380) (including the cost estimate of the Congressional Budget Office)* (Washington, DC: U.S. G.P.O., 1982).

United States Congress Senate Committee on the Judiciary. *Granting a Federal Charter to the American Ex-Prisoners of War, Inc.: Report to Accompany S. 1590* (Washington, DC: U.S. Govt. Print Off., 1977).

United States Congress House Committee on National Security, Military Personnel Subcommittee. *Accounting for POW/MIA's from the Korean War and the Vietnam War: Hearing before the Military Personnel Subcommittee of the Committee on National Security, House of Representatives, One Hundred Fourth Congress, second session, hearing held September 17, 1996* (Washington, DC: U.S. G.P.O., 1997).

United States Congress House Committee on National Security, Military Personnel Subcommittee. *POW/MIA Oversight: Hearing before the Military Personnel Subcommittee of the Committee on National Security, House of Representatives, One Hundred Fifth Congress, second session, hearing held October 2, 1998* (Washington, DC: U.S. G.P.O., 1999).

United States Congress House Committee on National Security, Military Personnel Subcommittee. *Status of POW/MIA negotiations with North Korea: Hearing before the Military Personnel Subcommittee of the Committee on National Security, House of Representatives, One Hundred Fourth Congress, second session, hearing held June 20, 1996* (Washington, DC: U.S. G.P.O., 1997).

United States Congress House Committee on Rules. *Providing for Consideration of H. Res. 627, Deploring the Abuse of Persons in United States Custody in Iraq, Regardless of the Circumstances of Their Detention, Urging the Secretary of the Army to Bring to Swift Justice to Any Member of the Armed Forces Who Has Violated the Uniform Code of Military Justice, Expressing the Deep Appreciation of the Nation to the Courageous and Honorable Members of the Armed Forces Who Have Selflessly Served, or Are Currently Serving, in Operation Iraqi Freedom, and for Other Purposes: Report (to accompany H. Res. 628)* (Washington, DC: U.S. G.P.O., 2004). Electronic Resource(s): http://purl.access.gpo.gov/GPO/LPS49562

United States Congress Senate Committee on Veterans' Affairs. *Health-care legisla-tion, oversight of health-facility security matters, and VA prosthetic special-disability programs: hearing before the Committee on Veterans' Affairs, United States Sen-ate, One Hundred Second Congress, first session, on S. 127 (Title II, parts A, B, and C), S. 327, and S. 869, April 23, 1991* (Washington, DC: U.S. G.P.O., 1992).

United States Congress House Committee on Veterans' Affairs, Subcommittee on Com-pensation, Pension, and Insurance. *Implementation of Public Laws Affecting Bene-fits for Former Prisoners of War: Hearing before the Subcommittee on Compensation, Pension, and Insurance of the Committee on Veterans' Affairs, House of Representatives, One Hundred Second Congress, second session, June 4, 1992* (Washington, DC: U.S. G.P.O., 1993).

United States National Archives and Records Administration. *Records relating to Ameri-can prisoners of war and missing-in-action personnel from the Korean War and during the Cold War era* (Washington, DC: National Archives and Records Administration, 1997).

Internet Addresses for Prisoners of War

General Sources for Military History and POWs

Dept. of Defense Database for 78,000 Missing Personnel during and since WW II: http://www.dtic.mil/dpmo

The National Archives and Record Center: In a stupendous project which is a blessing for genealogists and other researchers, the National Archives and Records Adminis-tration has placed more than 50 million historical documents online. Its Access to Archival Databases System allows you to search records by subject, geographic area, time span, and other criteria. http://www.archives.gov/aad/

The Outstanding Bibliography of Websites Related to Military History, By Richard Jensen: http://www.h-net.msu.edu/logs/showlog.cgi?list=h-war&file=h-war.log9902d/ 34& ent=0

U.S. Army Heritage & Educational Center: http://carlisle-www.army.mil/usamhi/

Specific Sites for Various Topics of Interest

American Civil War: The Official Records of the War of the Rebellion: All the original reports and correspondence pertaining to the American Civil War, from both sides. Absolutely the core source for study of this conflict. http://cdl.library.cornell.edu/ moa/browse.monographs/waro.html

British War Memoirs: http://www.warlinks.com/memories/durey/

Digitized versions of the four Geneva Conventions of 1949: http://www.loc.gov/rr/frd/ Military_Law/Geneva_conventions-1949.html

German Prisoners of War: http://www.kriegsgefangen.de/

Guantanamo Bay: http://www.fas.org/sgp/crs/natsec/RS22173.pdf

Human Rights Watch: http://hrw.org/advocacy/index.htm

Mexican War: http://www.elbalero.gob.mx/historia/html/gober/j_salas.html; http://www. dtic.mil/doctrine/jel/jfq_pubs/2310.pdf

POW/MIA Site-Chatroom: http://www.miafacts.org/readbook.htm contains often heated discussions on the possibility that POW were left behind in 1973. The owner of the site, a Col. (ret.) Joe Schlatter, claims that there were none. His references: http://www.miafacts.org

POW Research Network Japan: http://homepage3.nifty.com/pow-j/e/

Soviet Prisoners of War: http://www.gendercide.org/case_soviet.html

Torture in the Algerian War (1954–1962): http://www.wsws.org/articles/2001/apr2001/alg-a09.shtml

USS *PUEBLO* (1968) and SS *MAYAGUEZ* (1973) Incidents: http://members.aol.com/akl44/pueblo.htm; http://www.geocities.com/Pentagon/Bunker/9062/; http://members.home.net/b-carlson/pueblo.html

Vietnam Era POW/MIA Database Of Nearly 150,000 Records: http://lcweb2.loc gov/pow/powhome.html

Vietnam War—General POW Site with close associations to Vietnam POWs: http://www.pownetwork.org/

Women Prisoners of War: http://userpages.aug.com/captbarb/prisoners.html

World War One—British Pows: 3,000 British Prisoners of War: World War One Interviews and Reports (National Archives, UK): http://www.nationalarchives.gov.uk/documentsonline/pow.asp

World War Two—British POWs: http://www.warlinks.com/memories/durey/

World War Two—Pacific Theater: Two hundred interviews with Pacific Theater POWs. Most of the interviewees were members of the 2d Bn, 131st Field Artillery, Texas National Guard, which surrendered en masse on Java, or sailors and Marines from the USS *Houston* sunk in the Battle of Sunda Strait. These POWs became slave laborers on the Thailand-Burma Railway or in the Japanese home islands. The oral history program's website (the annotated catalog found online is outdated), holds many of the POWs' interviews and gives a good sense of its holdings). http://www.library.unt.edu/ohp/default.htm

Index

About the Author

ARNOLD KRAMMER is Professor of History at Texas A&M. A highly praised teacher for more than three decades, Krammer has written a number of books in both English and German about POWs, among them *Nazi Prisoners of War in America, Hitler's Last Soldier in America* (with Georg Gaertner), *Undue Process: The Untold Story of America's German Enemy Aliens*, and more than forty articles ranging from WWI, through the Spanish Civil War, to WWII, and the Holocaust.